Limit Cinema

Thinking Cinema

Series Editors
David Martin-Jones, University of Glasgow, UK
Sarah Cooper, King's College, University of London, UK

Volume 9

Titles in the Series:
Afterlives: Allegories of Film and Mortality in Early Weimar Germany
by Steve Choe
Deleuze, Japanese Cinema, and the Atom Bomb by David Deamer
Ex-centric Cinema by Janet Harbord
The Body and the Screen by Kate Ince
The Grace of Destruction by Elena del Rio
Non-Cinema: Global Digital Filmmaking and the Multitude
by William Brown
Sensuous Cinema: The Body in Contemporary Maghrebi Film
by Kaya Davies Hayon
*Fertile Visions: The Uterus as a Narrative Space in Cinema
from the Americas* by Anne Carruthers

Limit Cinema

*Transgression and the Nonhuman in
Contemporary Global Film*

Chelsea Birks

BLOOMSBURY ACADEMIC
NEW YORK • LONDON • OXFORD • NEW DELHI • SYDNEY

BLOOMSBURY ACADEMIC
Bloomsbury Publishing Inc
1385 Broadway, New York, NY 10018, USA
50 Bedford Square, London, WC1B 3DP, UK
29 Earlsfort Terrace, Dublin 2, Ireland

BLOOMSBURY, BLOOMSBURY ACADEMIC and the Diana logo are
trademarks of Bloomsbury Publishing Plc

First published in the United States of America 2021
Paperback edition published 2023

Copyright © Chelsea Birks, 2021

For legal purposes the Acknowledgements on p. xv constitute an
extension of this copyright page.

Cover design: Eleanor Rose
Cover image: *Tropical Malady*, 2004 © TIFA / DR / Collection Christophel /
ArenaPAL ; www.arenapal.com

All rights reserved. No part of this publication may be reproduced or transmitted in any
form or by any means, electronic or mechanical, including photocopying,
recording, or any information storage or retrieval system, without prior permission
in writing from the publishers.

Bloomsbury Publishing Inc does not have any control over, or responsibility for, any
third-party websites referred to or in this book. All internet addresses given in this
book were correct at the time of going to press. The author and publisher regret any
inconvenience caused if addresses have changed or sites have ceased to exist, but
can accept no responsibility for any such changes.

Library of Congress Cataloging-in-Publication Data
Names: Birks, Chelsea, author.
Title: Limit cinema : transgression and the nonhuman in
contemporary global film / Chelsea Birks.
Description: New York : Bloomsbury Academic, 2021. |
Series: Thinking cinema; book 10 | Includes bibliographical references and index.
Identifiers: LCCN 2021006775 (print) | LCCN 2021006776 (ebook) |
ISBN 9781501352867 (hardback) | ISBN 9781501352874 (ebook) |
ISBN 9781501352881 (pdf)
Subjects: LCSH: Motion pictures–Philosophy. | Motion pictures–Social aspects. |
Nature–Effect of human beings on.
Classification: LCC PN1995 .B47735 2021 (print) |
LCC PN1995 (ebook) | DDC 791.4301–dc23
LC record available at https://lccn.loc.gov/2021006775
LC ebook record available at https://lccn.loc.gov/2021006776

ISBN: HB: 978-1-5013-5286-7
PB: 978-1-5013-8132-4
ePDF: 978-1-5013-5288-1
eBook: 978-1-5013-5287-4

Series: Thinking Cinema

Typeset by Newgen KnowledgeWorks Pvt. Ltd., Chennai, India

To find out more about our authors and books visit www.bloomsbury.com
and sign up for our newsletters.

For my parents

Contents

Preface		ix
Acknowledgements		xv
Introduction: Cinema at the limit		1
The end of the world		1
Film theory, speculative realism and the nonhuman turn		8
Bataille, transgression, ecology		12
The impossible imperative		21

Part 1 Objectivity

1	Sacrifice and the sacred in Apichatpong Weerasethakul and Ben Wheatley	35
	Introduction	35
	Wheatley, post-theology and the sacrifice of sacrifice	37
	Paganism and British folk horror	40
	Irrational violence in *Kill List*	42
	Circularity in *A Field in England*	48
	Ambivalent Apichatpong	53
	Desublimating the sacred	59
	Conclusion	64
2	Objectivity, speculative realism and the cinematic apparatus	69
	Introduction	69
	Speculative realism and film theory	71
	Objectivity and nature	78
	Subjectivity and apparatus	86
	Conclusion	95

Part 2 Subjectivity

3	Eco-consciousness in *Under the Skin* and *Nymphomaniac*	103
	Introduction	103

viii *Contents*

Subjectivity and excess		104
Interiority and inner experience		109
Sex and transgression		116
Death and discontinuity		124
Conclusion		130
4	Limits of love in *Grizzly Man* and *Konelīne: Our Land Beautiful*	137
	Introduction	137
	Love for the real	138
	'Warring simplifications' in *Grizzly Man*	144
	The bears don't love you, Timothy (or do they?)	146
	Herzog's romantic nihilism	150
	Our mind/our land beautiful	157
	Conclusion	166
Conclusion		175
Bibliography		183
Filmography		195
Index		197

Preface

This book explores how contemporary global cinema pushes against the limits of the human in our age of ecological crisis. The threat of impending catastrophe demands that we reconsider what it means to be human, and that we attempt to position ourselves in relation to a reality that exceeds the anthropocentric frameworks of thought and language. I argue that cinema can help us do this, and I identify a group of contemporary films that I call *limit cinema* because they interrogate the boundaries between human and nonhuman realities. I approach these films through a philosophical lens and connect them to current movements such as speculative realism and posthumanism that seek less anthropocentric modes of thought. My method can therefore be described as film-philosophical: more than simply interpreting films through ethical and philosophical concepts, film-philosophy engages with philosophical thought through film and explores what might be gained by bringing the two disciplines into conversation with each other. This work therefore investigates not only what philosophy might be able to tell us about the representation of nature in contemporary film but also what films might contribute to philosophical discussions of humanity's relationship with the natural world. I argue that contemporary cinema can not only reflect on societal concerns regarding issues such as global warming but can also find new ways of representing nonhuman[1] perspectives and their relationships (or lack thereof) to humans. As such, I argue that film is essential to the ethical reconsiderations made necessary by the ecological crisis.

Recent philosophies of the nonhuman turn, including speculative realism, new materialism and posthumanism, argue that we ought to break from the anthropocentrism that has dominated Western thinking since the Enlightenment. I agree with this position, and in the pages that follow I use ideas on how to think about and relate to nonhuman reality from thinkers like Graham Harman, Steven Shaviro, Jane Bennett, Timothy Morton and Cary Wolfe. However, I do not share the view – advocated especially by Harman and other speculative realists – that an outright rejection of idealism (any metaphysics that views reality as mentally constituted or related to human ideas) is the proper antidote to the overly subjective and human-centred philosophies of the twentieth century, from phenomenology to poststructuralism to psychoanalysis. Broadening our world views to include nonhuman agents and ways of thinking is undoubtedly important, but I do not see a reason to abandon important lessons about humanity, ideology and subjectivity taught by the philosophies that Harman and others emphatically reject. I therefore look to Georges Bataille, who wrote about topics as varied as pornography, economics and human sacrifice, to ground a new film-philosophy for the Anthropocene. While there is a group of twentieth-century philosophers commonly referenced in posthumanism and film ecocriticism, including Gilles Deleuze, Martin Heidegger, Alfred North Whitehead and Simone Weil, Bataille is not ordinarily among them; I argue that Bataille should be brought into the canon, and that his notions of transgression, excess and inner experience can provide new ways of understanding how the nonhuman informs and is evoked by cinema. Through this new Bataillean film-philosophy, I see myself as belonging to this new wave of thought that emphasizes the nonhuman; however, I occupy a place somewhere at the margins and only with many reservations. This tentative and peripheral positioning is inherent in my philosophical approach overall, and the book details my reasons for this and provides a new alternative through the idea of limit cinema.

One of the central tenets of this book is that knowledge is situated and particular, and I therefore think it is important to acknowledge my position from the outset. The motivation behind writing this book is as much personal as philosophical: my feelings about climate change and associated problems such as ocean acidification and mass extinction vary daily between anxiety and abject terror (with the occasional glimmer of hope), and the more I learn, the more I am overwhelmed. It is simply too huge and complex a problem for me to ever feel as though I have a handle on it. Moreover, I do not come by environmentalism easily. I grew up in Alberta, Canada, in an economy heavily reliant on the oil and gas production and a culture largely defined through pride in – and defence of – the industry; my father worked for small companies involved in tar sands extraction until he was laid off after the drop in global oil prices in 2014. At the same time as I have become more politically engaged in environmental issues – voting based on climate policy, attending protests, watching Greta Thunberg speak after a climate strike in Vancouver – my parents have become equally politically motivated in the other direction, attending pro-pipeline protests, driven by the threat to their retirement posed by long unemployment and a collapsing industry. This polarization has been difficult, because my own convictions are continually complicated by a desire to find common ground with people who are worried about the social and economic implications of the necessary transition away from fossil fuels. This book is not a political treatise, but its emphasis on the human and human subjectivity (despite recognizing the need to expand our ethics and ontologies) is largely driven by these personal experiences. The ecological crisis poses unprecedented problems; while some are practical or technological, a great number are political and ideological. This is why I return to Bataille – who is interested in human politics and ideology as well as ecology – in addition to film theorists like Jean-Louis Baudry who approach cinema through the lens of ideological critique. My paradoxical experiences in attempting to understand climate change and ecological crisis (the more information I have, the less I feel I know) have driven me to embrace irrationality and nonknowledge as a mode of relationship with nature.

A personal anecdote will help me explain the view of nature at stake in *Limit Cinema*. After I finished the first draft of this book, I visited the *Musée de la chasse et la nature* in Paris. The museum houses expected items such as hunting weapons, taxidermized animals and placards detailing hunting methods throughout history; however, the selection and arrangement of these objects (by chief curator Claude d'Anthenaise) encourage a series of strange encounters that complicate divides between subject and object, nature and culture. The museum is a series of rooms, which are organized thematically through the names of animals (Room of the Boar, Stag and Wolf Room) and that combine archival materials with contemporary art works. There is seldom a fixed separation between visitor and object: stuffed bears, wolves and boars stand in the open next to doorways and ornate furniture; a fox rests curled up in a corner chair; various curiosities line shelves and tables; and there are no signs warning not to touch, except for cleverly placed thistles preventing visitors from sitting on certain objects. There is also no fixed distinction between past and present. In the Room of Diana, two paintings, interpretations of Diana the Huntress from Rubens and Brugel, are arranged under lights on a pitch-black wall, while the ceiling, by contemporary Dutch artist Jon Fabre, is covered in owl feathers and staring faces. The impression is decidedly not one of contemplative distance and feels more like being pulled into the paintings under a pair of dark, enormous wings.

Roland Barthes writes that the tableau, a frequent mode of representation in the museum, as well as in cinema and photography, is 'a pure cut out segment with clearly defined edges …; everything that surrounds it is banished into nothingness, remains unnamed, while everything that it admits within its field is

promoted into essence, into light, into view'.[2] The completeness of the tableau –
for example, of a museum diorama in which animals are positioned in their
natural habitats – makes it seem as though all relevant knowledge is available to
the observer. The *Musée de la chasse et la nature*, on the other hand, embraces
the darkness at the outskirts of knowledge and enfolds the visitor in a space
where nonknowledge is a privileged relation with nature. The museum placards
seldom elucidate things and frequently emphasize mythology and symbolism
over objective fact: the *Cabinet de la Licorne*, for example, displays artefacts
related to unicorns and other mythical creatures without differentiating them
from actual animal specimens. The museum does not place animals 'out there',
othered by an objective, scientific gaze (as in Barthes's tableaux), but instead
recognizes the mutual implication of nature and culture, myth and reality.
Bringing animals into domestic spaces – parlours, hallways, perched on tables
and mantelpieces – curiously does not domesticate them, but instead unsettles
the entire humanist framework that positions humans as knowers and the rest
of nature as something to be known. The *Musée* is not a 'natural' space in the
sense of envisioning a pristine wilderness untouched by human influence, and
indeed the space emphasizes the uncanny and the artificial; the owl eyes in the
Room of Diana, for instance, are glass eyes intended for human use. Culture is
instead articulated as something in communication with, rather than separating
us from, the environment. Crucially, these communications are not framed in
terms of reciprocity or harmony, but instead are frequently expressed through
hunting and other forms of violence. This aligns with a Bataillean view of nature
that embraces the ambivalent, unknowable, and sometimes even terrifying
aspects of the nonhuman.

A Bataillean emphasis on death as a mode of relationship with the nonhuman
often elicits anxieties about extinction, as evidenced by a number of recent
films imagining planetary destruction. Lars von Trier's *Melancholia* (2011) for
instance, has become an oft-repeated example in discourses about finitude,
extinction and our collective anxieties about the Anthropocene.[3] I will return to
these discussions in the introduction with a more complete reading of the film,
but for now, a brief example from the film will help me explain what is at stake
in limit cinema. *Melancholia* is about the end of the world and, crucially, by the
time the narrative begins we already know that this death is inevitable: we see
the Earth collide with the large blue planet Melancholia at both the beginning
and the end of the film. This means that the film occurs entirely within the
span of time in which death is inevitable but not yet actual – a liminal space

between two ends, a state of (to invoke Barthes again) being 'dead and going to die'.[4] Bataille would call this a *limit experience* because it exposes the limits of subjectivity, the unstable place where being slips into nothingness. It is a vision of the experience of death, of the threshold where death is inevitable but sense and consciousness have not yet been extinguished. *Melancholia* therefore links personal, subjective limit experiences with fears about our collective deaths, while also articulating these experiences as non-rational and characterized by paradox and contradiction. This impossibility at the limit of the human is symbolized by the presence of an extra hole on the golf course surrounding the house where the film takes place: while the owner of the house repeats several times throughout the film that there are 18 holes on the course, there is a number 19 on a flagpole in shots both at the beginning and the end of the film. The presence of the extra hole in the moments before the world is about to end is an extraneous detail, a lingering remainder that cannot be explained or contained by the narrative. Hole 19[5] indicates the presence of an extra absence – one hole too many – an irrecuperable excess in that it is at once too much and nothing at all. The impossible excess of this extra hole is a microcosm of the larger catastrophe. It is the end of the world peeking through a small tear in the fabric. These anxieties about our inability to understand or respond to forces in excess of ourselves are the driving forces behind this book: the ecological crisis forces us to confront our limitations, and films like *Melancholia* imagine what happens when these boundaries are transgressed. Limit cinema in general functions like Hole 19, as an impossible presence/absence that indicates something overwhelming, unexplained and unexplainable in our contemporary relationship with the natural world.

Figure 1 Hole 19, *Melancholia* (Lars von Trier, 2011).

Notes

1 The nonhuman to which I refer throughout this book is different from (though related to) the posthuman. Posthumanism reconsiders what it means to be human in light of accelerating technological shifts that make it increasingly difficult to draw firm boundaries around our bodies and minds. I am similarly invested in reconsidering the self-contained subject of Enlightenment humanism, but while the posthuman is a reconsideration of self in relation to technology and the environment, the nonhuman is radically other from the human and does not relate to it at all (though, as we shall see, the human is always contaminated by the nonhuman through a passive process Bataille calls 'communication'). I explore these conversations in more detail in the introduction.

2 Roland Barthes, 'Diderot, Brecht, Eisenstein', in *Narrative, Apparatus, Ideology: A Film Theory Reader*, ed. Philip Rosen (New York: Columbia University Press, 1986), 173.

3 See Marta Figlerowicz, 'Comedy of Abandon: Lars von Trier's *Melancholia*', *Film Quarterly* 65, no. 4 (2012), 21–6; Briohny Doyle, 'Prognosis End-Time: Madness and Prophecy in *Melancholia* and *Take Shelter*', *Altre Modernita* 9, no. 9 (2013), 19–37; Danielle Kollig, 'Filming the World's End: Images of the Apocalypse in *Epidemic* and *Melancholia*', *Amaltea* 5 (2013), 85–102; Christopher Peterson, 'The Gravity of Melancholia: A Critique of Speculative Realism', *Theory & Event* 18, no. 2 (2015); Sarah French and Zöe Shacklock, 'The Affective Sublime in Lars von Trier's *Melancholia* and Terrance Malick's *The Tree of Life*', *New Review of Film and Television Studies* 12, no. 4 (2014), 339–56; Robert Sinnerbrink, 'Anatomy of *Melancholia*', *Angelaki* 19, no. 4 (2014), 111–26; Robert Sinnerbrink, 'Planet Melancholia: Romanticism, Mood, and Cinematic Ethics', *Filozofski Vestnik* 37, no. 2 (2016), 95–115; Joshua Dienstag, 'Evils of Representation: Werewolves, Pessimism and Realism in *Europa* and *Melancholia*', *Theory & Event* 18, no. 2 (2015); Thomas Elsaesser, 'Black Suns and a Bright Planet: Lars von Trier's *Melancholia* as Thought Experiment', *Theory & Event* 18, no. 2 (2015); Elena Del Rio, *The Grace of Destruction: A Vital Ethology of Extreme Cinemas* (London: Bloomsbury, 2016).

4 Roland Barthes, *Camera Lucida: Reflections on Photography*, trans. Richard Howard (New York: Hill and Wang, 1981), 95.

5 'Hole 19' is also frequently the informal name for the club house at the end of a golf course.

Acknowledgements

I would first like to thank series editors David Martin-Jones and Sarah Cooper, whose support of this project and careful revisions of the manuscript were absolutely invaluable. Katie Gallof and Erin Duffy at Bloomsbury Publishing have also been enormously helpful even while unanticipated obstacles disrupted the final submissions process. David deserves extra thanks, many times over: without him, I never would have opened Meillassoux or even considered ecocriticism as a direction for my thinking. David's characteristic style – wise, intellectually challenging and fair – remains my benchmark for excellent mentorship.

The research underlying this project was made possible by funding from the College of Arts at the University of Glasgow. A version of Chapter 2 was previously published as the article: 'Objectivity, speculative realism and the cinematic apparatus' by Chelsea Birks in *Cinema Journal*, volume 57, no. 4, pp. 3–24 (Copyright © 2018 by the University of Texas Press. All rights reserved). I am grateful to the University of Texas Press for granting permission for its republication here, and I would like to thank Caitlyn Benson-Allott, Marc Furstenau and Shaun Inouye for their feedback on that article.

Timothy Barker and Steven Shaviro made significant contributions to the conceptual framework of this book, and I extend my gratitude for their willingness to share their impressive depth of knowledge about film-philosophy and media theory. I would also like to thank David Archibald, Dmitris Eleftheriotis, Tina Kendall and Karen Lury for their comments and insights at various stages of this project.

Though writing is a difficult, lonely work, it can also be a great joy, especially when the experience is shared. I offer profound thanks to everyone who has participated in various writing groups with me over the years, especially Mike Baker, Andrea Brooks, Lisa Coulthard, Julia Huggins, Lindsay Inouye, Dana Keller, Oliver Kroener, Peter Lester and Su-Anne Yeo.

Finally, thank you to Christine Evans, whose unfailing joy in discussing and challenging a wide range of ideas impacted every single page of this book. Without you, none of this would have been possible.

October 2020

Introduction: Cinema at the limit

The end of the world

Theorists of the nonhuman turn are currently grappling with the devastating implications of climate change and environmental destruction for the humanities and human-centred views of reality. Apocalyptic ideas pervade the discourse: Timothy Morton, for example, argues in *Hyperobjects: Philosophy and Ecology after the End of the World* that the end of the world has already been brought about by global warming, in the sense that the very idea of the 'world' is no longer sustainable due to the humiliating impact of objects that, despite being created by humans, operate on a scale far larger than our anthropocentric mode of perception.[1] The impact of global warming will still be felt in five hundred years, and the half-life of plutonium will extend almost as far into the future as the entire history of the human species extends into the past: for Morton, the task of art at the end of the world is to engage with the 'very large finitude' of these 'hyperobjects', which operate on an enormous scale that is difficult to measure, predict or explain.[2] There is a gap between hyperobjects as they appear to human observers, according to our sense of scale and modes of perception, and as they exist in themselves, excessively distributed across space and time. The difference between appearance and thing – the Kantian distinction that grounds this work and other philosophies of the nonhuman turn – is exaggerated by hyperobjects such as global warming. The task of contemporary art and critical theory is to account for these differences, and this book situates itself at the nexus between art and theory to think about how we might respond to crises that push the limits of comprehension.

The end of the world emphasizes the relative insignificance of the human perspective in comparison to a reality that exceeds us. This works against the general thrust of Western philosophy, which has tended to position humans at the top of a natural hierarchy because of our supposedly superior ability to reason. Western philosophy from Plato to Immanuel Kant largely viewed reason as the highest human faculty, and while it was acknowledged that we might be led astray through the senses or faulty logic, it has generally been agreed that reason allows us to gain knowledge of the world and direct ourselves in relation to it. The philosophies discussed in this chapter, including speculative realism and other theories of the nonhuman turn – as well as my own Bataillean film-philosophy, which I will outline at the end of the chapter – work against this tradition by decentring the human and theorizing realities that exceed anthropocentric frames of reference. Morton's discussion of hyperobjects draws inspiration from speculative realism, a movement inaugurated in 2006 by the publication of Quentin Meillassoux's *After Finitude: An Essay on the Necessity of Contingency*, which argues against the tendency of twentieth-century thought to restrict knowledge to the frameworks of human thought and perception. Meillassoux calls this way of thinking 'correlationism' because it asserts that objects can only be considered as correlates to human thought, and he explains that correlationism relies on the claim that 'thought cannot get outside itself in order to compare the world as it is "in itself" to the world as it is "for us", and thereby distinguish what is a function of our relation to the world from what belongs to the world alone'.[3] Meillassoux argues that both analytic and continental philosophies tend to adhere to the assumption that the correlation between thought and world (rather than the world itself) is the object of knowledge: he writes that 'during the twentieth century, the two principle "media" of the correlation were consciousness and language, the former bearing phenomenology, the latter the various currents of analytic philosophy'.[4] Both types of correlationism explore the world in relation to us, as constructed through consciousness and/or language.

Meillassoux traces correlationism back to Kant's metaphysics in *The Critique of Pure Reason*.[5] The impact of Kant on speculative realism is such that Meillassoux describes his thought as a reaction against the 'Kantian catastrophe';[6] Steven Shaviro writes that speculative realism enacts a return to correlationism's 'primal scene' in the *Critique* in order to renegotiate its terms.[7] In the *Critique*, Kant enacts what he calls a 'Copernican revolution' in philosophy by calling into question the assumption that thought conforms to objects.[8] He argues that this premise results in disagreement rather than secure knowledge and suggests that these differences might be resolved if we looked at things from the other way around. The metaphysics established in the *Critique* is founded on the assertion that apparently necessary features of the external world – cause and effect, for example, as well as space and time – are qualities of our perception rather than of the world in itself. Kant distinguishes between the phenomenal realm of knowable, sensible experience and the noumenal realm of objects as they exist in themselves and argues that the latter is foreclosed from philosophical discussion; in fact, though there are a range of interpretations of the *Critique*, some strongly idealist readings have argued that according to Kantian metaphysics there is no mind-independent reality at all.[9] Regardless of the ontological status of things as they exist in themselves, twentieth-century philosophies, especially those affiliated with the linguistic turn,[10] tend to agree that the only valid object of knowledge is things as they exist for us, subject to human language, observation and understanding.

Shaviro writes in *The Universe of Things: On Speculative Realism* that the speculative realists, troubled by the anthropocentrism of post-Kantian philosophies, 'each propose a different way of stepping outside the correlationist circle'.[11] My book situates itself among these discussions and explores what happens when we try to think outside of ourselves and represent this outside through cinema. Like the speculative realists, I therefore frame my argument in relation to the Kantian primal scene, but rather than trying to step outside of the circle, I argue that we should first try to interrogate its limits. These limits, which form my object of inquiry throughout this work, are the same ones that Kant imposes on reason in the *Critique*: those between the world as it exists for us and the world as it exists in itself. The ecological crisis points to a divide between these two worlds because it forces us to consider how the world might continue to exist in our absence. Meillassoux argues that correlationism cannot properly account for the existence of a world outside of human thought and therefore renders any statement about the existence of matter before human life (the Big Bang, the formation of the earth, evolutionary history) meaningless.[12] Ray Brassier, another founding member of speculative realism, reverses the formula and argues that correlationism cannot properly address the inevitability of human extinction.[13] Both ways of looking at the question suggest that Kantian epistemic limits, which enclose our knowledge of existence within the confines of human thought and language, are becoming increasingly problematic in the face of cosmic questions of origin and the threat of global catastrophe. Speculative realism is therefore part of a larger response to anxieties about human finitude and the end of the world and can be situated among broader discussions about how to address the Anthropocene.

Atmospheric chemist Paul Crutzen popularized the term 'Anthropocene' in 2002 when he argued that human behaviour has impacted the planet to the degree that its effects can be seen in the geological record:[14] we are no longer in the Holocene and have now entered the Age of the Humans. The Anthropocene therefore indicates a frightening paradox, because while humans caused the Anthropocene, the term refers to changes that may (and likely will) outlast human life. We humans have made our mark on the world, but perhaps at the cost of our own extinction. This Anthropocene paradox – of human progress and aggrandizement to the point of self-erasure – suggests a link between the limitations of our human perspective and the potentially impending finitude of our species. Though the Anthropocene remains unofficial – according to the International Union of Geological Sciences we are still in the Holocene – the term has gained currency across the sciences and the humanities as a means of calling attention to threats posed by our tendency to myopically restrict our focus to human interests and concerns. Timothy Clark writes that the Anthropocene requires a reconsideration of scale: 'Phenomena such as ocean acidification, climate change, the general effects of incremental forms of environmental degradation across the planet, global overpopulation and resource depletion do not present any obvious or perceptible target for concern or protest at any one place, or often any immediate antagonist perceptible at the normal human scale.'[15] The Anthropocene therefore raises a number of difficult questions about how to address things that are beyond the scope of our usual modes of engagement. Clark continues: 'One major new effort at work in contemporary literary and artistic practice and criticism is to find some way of usefully or authentically engaging such crucial but elusive concerns, precisely when it is acknowledged that they resist representation at the kinds of scale on which most thinking, culture, art and politics operate.'[16] Criticism in light of the Anthropocene must therefore engage with questions of scale and representation, since part of the problem involves being able to describe and respond to problems and anxieties that exceed familiar frameworks.

I am not suggesting that the limit films discussed in this book answer these problems, but rather that they engage with them by pointing towards a reality in excess of representation. In different ways, they all destabilize the totalizing gaze of the camera and disrupt humanist modes of perception in ways that are useful for the critical reconsiderations made necessary by the Anthropocene. To return to the key example from the preface, *Melancholia* provides a clear illustration of the aesthetics of the end of the world. As mentioned previously, the film's prelude leaves no doubt about its apocalyptic conclusion, as it depicts the slow-motion collision between Earth and the large blue planet

Melancholia. The narrative of *Melancholia* then retroactively dramatizes the end of the world through the disintegration of the relationship between two sisters, Justine (Kirsten Dunst) and Claire (Charlotte Gainsbourg). Despite its focus on planetary destruction, *Melancholia* limits itself to a small cast of characters – Justine's wedding guests – and a single location, the grounds of the mansion where Justine's wedding takes place. These limits are seemingly guarded by strange forces: characters seem unable to leave the grounds on several occasions, as horses balk at its perimeters and cars stop running altogether. But despite its restricted drama, the film envisions its catastrophe globally, seen from the outside in spectacular CGI shots that show the world colliding with Melancholia from space.

This interplay between the subjective and the objective – between planetary and personal disasters – resonates with some of the central questions of this book. How do films represent the ways that we see the universal from the inside? If human thought and knowledge are finite, then how might our limited human perspectives grapple with mind-independent reality? Christopher Peterson argues that *Melancholia* raises questions about decentring the human and writes that *Melancholia* foregrounds tensions between external reality and phenomenal experience. He writes that the film's impending apocalypse event forces Claire to think about her relationship with the world:

> Presumably the cosmos will continue to exist in the wake of earth's destruction, a universe entirely independent and 'indifferent' to her, but for the moment she is still obliged to carry the world as a horizon of perception in anticipation of its utter absence. She has only one world, yet it is not hers. The world has always existed *for* her; it has never existed (solely) for her.[17]

Claire's inability to see beyond her 'horizon of perception' does not stop her from anticipating a universe that continues to exist in her absence. The ending of *Melancholia* is a limit experience because it evokes a subject's confrontation with the possibility of not-being in the face of forces in excess of subjectivity. Limit experiences challenge frameworks of thought and reason and are therefore characterized by paradox and impossibility; they put us in contact with the unthinkable and are therefore resistant to description and explanation. For Bataille, sexuality and death best exemplify this confrontation with the limit because they both call the integrity of the subject into question: in *Erotism*, he writes that 'eroticism always entails a breaking down of established patterns, the patterns … of the regulated social order basic to our discontinuous mode of existence as defined and separate individuals'.[18] This means that for Bataille, eroticism points to the limit between life and death. One of Bataille's favourite examples is a photograph he had in his possession of a torture victim, sentenced to death by *lingchi* (translated variously as death by a thousand cuts, or slow slicing) in 1905.[19] In the photograph, published in *The Tears of Eros*, the victim is strapped to a pole: large swathes of skin have been removed, so that his ribs are exposed, and two men crouch in the foreground as one of them severs the victim's leg above the knee.[20] But the punctum of the photograph for Bataille is the man's expression, with eyes directed upwards in what could be interpreted as transcendent bliss. Bataille writes: 'I have never stopped being obsessed by this image of pain, at once ecstatic(?) and intolerable.'[21] The question mark here indicates a hesitancy, an acknowledgement that there is something unknowable in the photograph that is nevertheless visible and fully present. When I look at the image, I am always similarly struck by a kind of *thereness* of death in the image: my curiosity about what the experience would be like is always met with the realization that knowing would mean that I too had passed beyond a point of no return. The visibility of the limit experience in the photograph recalls the presence of Hole 19 on the golf course in *Melancholia*: both are impossible in that they exceed the bounds of ordinary experience but are also present and perceptible. The *lingchi* photograph captures the moments before death, an experience that can be witnessed but not known; it shows the crossing of a limit when the victim must be aware that it is too late but has not yet reached the other side.

Figure 2 Limit image in *Melancholia* (Lars von Trier, 2011).

Introduction

In the final moments of *Melancholia*, Justine, Claire and Claire's son Leo sit beneath a triangular structure made of sticks, which Justine tells Leo is a magic cave to protect him from the end of the world. It doesn't, of course, and as Melancholia looms on the horizon, its impact is seen before it is heard: debris and waves of water and fire rush towards the three figures, finally swallowing them as the score and sound of the collision coalesce in a thundering roar. This scene depicts a fragile and unsustainable moment right before all sense is enveloped in blackness. Like the *lingchi* photograph, it imagines a point of no return, and every time I watch it, I ask the question: when *exactly* would the three characters die? When does being slip into nothingness, and what does it feel like to have your consciousness extinguished so suddenly? These questions are impossible to answer without imagining a God-like perspective on the action, one that the scene radically undermines by suggesting a universe completely indifferent to human experience. Marta Figlerowicz suggests that the ending of *Melancholia* is a 'radical questioning of how we make ourselves believe our feelings matter',[22] since in the end human agency amounts to nothing more than a tent of sticks. But what interests me most about this final sequence is that fragile moment of *not yet* before the screen cuts to black, a limit experience at once personal and collective: the horizon of perception that ceases to exist belongs both to the individual characters and to humanity as a whole.

The representation of the end of the world in *Melancholia* foregrounds the impossibility of clearly demarcating the locus of transgression between life and death. Though there seems to be a clear difference between being alive and being dead, pointing out exactly when this occurs leads to murkiness and confusion since the distinction can only be drawn from one side of the equation – the point of view of a living subject. As we will see throughout this book, limit images in contemporary cinema similarly unsettle stable categories and call into question the very perspectives from which we are able to pose these categories in the first place. While not all the limit films are as apocalyptic as *Melancholia*, they similarly negotiate the personal and the universal by testing the limits of subjectivity. Morton writes that the Anthropocene necessitates a new kind of thinking 'in which the normal certainties are inverted, or even dissolved';[23] limit films trace these inversions by embracing paradox, impossibility and contradiction, and in so doing they encourage ways of thinking about the end of the world.

Film theory, speculative realism and the nonhuman turn

The film-philosophy outlined in this book belongs to a broader trend in the humanities that attempts to break with the anthropocentrism of post-Enlightenment and particularly twentieth-century thinking. Richard Grusin's *The Nonhuman Turn* argues that the first decades of the new millennium have been characterized by a shift away from humanist modes of analysis and towards new theories influenced by developments in the sciences (such as neuroscience and artificial intelligence) and precursors like actor-network and assemblage theories.[24] Grusin argues that the nonhuman turn, including movements like new materialism and speculative realism, 'insists (to paraphrase Latour) that "we have never been human" but that humans have always coevolved, coexisted, or collaborated with the nonhuman'.[25] Though Grusin acknowledges that questions about the nonhuman have a long genealogy, their renewed emphasis in contemporary philosophy and critical theory indicates that they have become more pressing in light of advancing technologies and intensifying environmental problems.

The immediate context of this book – film studies and more specifically film-philosophy – has kept pace with the nonhuman turn and has recently begun to move away from the questions of human subjectivity that have long been at the forefront of film theory. Theories from psychoanalysis to apparatus theory to cognitivism have paid a great deal of attention to the ways that cinema constructs or impacts processes of identification and subject formation. While there are important precursors to ecocriticism in film theory – Anat Pick and Guinevere Narraway point out that classical film theorists such as Siegfried Kracauer and André Bazin were very much concerned with cinema's ability to represent objects, animals and natural phenomena[26] – recent eco-philosophical engagements with film suggest that questions about nature, animals and technology have become especially pressing in the early decades of the twenty-first century.

At first, film ecocriticism focused primarily on cinema with environmentalist messages or an explicit focus on the natural world (such as wildlife documentaries or films raising awareness about environmental issues).[27] The sub-field has subsequently expanded, however, to cover a range of subjects and methodologies, including not only content-focused discussions of aesthetics and representation but also more expansive considerations of media ecologies.[28] Sean Cubitt, for example, considers cinema in relation to a complex network that includes the agency of humans, technologies and the natural world, and he emphasizes that the ecological crisis demands that we negotiate issues of responsibility within these complex networks.[29] Just as the limit experience at the end of *Melancholia* makes it difficult to differentiate between subjective experience and objective annihilation, Cubitt's argument suggests that ecological catastrophe complicates notions of responsibility: since we are failing to ascribe blame either to individuals or to the system, we should instead ascribe it to our modes of communication because 'agency lies in the field of distribution, the communicative structures operating in the subject-object relation, rather than inhering in either side of said relation.'[30] Communication, as we will see in the following section, is also an important concept for Bataille, who similarly views it as a condition of the distinction between self and other rather than as a consequence of it. This emphasis on communication justifies the consideration of cinema and other media in addressing the ethical issues posed by the Anthropocene: cinema is one way that we communicate ideas about and with nature, and therefore it may help us find new ways of understanding and orienting ourselves in relation to the environment.

Attempting to communicate with the nonhuman sometimes leads to odd and counterintuitive conclusions. Recently, scholars affiliated with philosophies like speculative realism and new materialism have advocated strange new approaches to metaphysical questions, asserting that expanding beyond anthropocentrism means distorting familiar modes of perception and understanding.[31] Jane Bennett, for example, rejects the distinction between living and inert matter and argues that human behaviour and politics are affected more by the agency of supposedly inanimate things than we usually realize.[32] Speculative realism denies the common sense claim that thought must conform to objects – that empirical data corresponds in some way to the actual properties of mind-independent reality – and therefore opens the possibility of a world with rules totally alien to our usual ways of understanding reality: Meillassoux's universe is radically devoid of any necessary physical law,[33] including cause and effect, while Graham Harman's real objects are totally withdrawn and inaccessible to human perception and interaction.[34] By rejecting the premise of correlationism – that metaphysics must account for our modes of access to reality – speculative realism attempts a radical break not only with humanist modes of understanding but even human interests. Ray Brassier's pessimistic realism is most extreme in this regard, insisting on the unavoidable meaninglessness of human existence in light of the inevitability of our extinction.[35] I share with speculative realism the conviction that mind-independent reality is much more bizarre than we can understand, and we similarly understand the limit between human and nonhuman realities according to the Kantian distinction between things-for-us and things-in-themselves; the speculative realists will therefore be frequent interlocutors throughout this book. However, my ontology should not be seen as a continuation or application of speculative realist ideas in the context of film studies, as I disagree with a number of the movement's central motivations. Through Bataille, I will ask many of the same questions as the speculative realists about the possibility of thinking or representing mind-independent reality, but by focusing on how the limit of the human is evoked by cinema I will answer them in a different way.

My major point of disagreement is with the speculative realists' outright dismissal of idealism and constructivist philosophies. Levi Bryant, Nick Srnicek and Graham Harman explicitly position speculative realism as 'a deliberate counterpoint to the now tiresome "Linguistic Turn".[36] Grusin makes a similar claim about the nonhuman turn more broadly: 'Perhaps most powerfully, the nonhuman turn challenges some of the key assumptions of social constructivism, particularly insofar as it insists that the agency, meaning, and value of nature all derive from cultural, social, or ideological inscription or construction.[37] I do not share this sense of fatigue. While I agree with Grusin's point that theory and philosophy need to account for nonhuman agency in their ethics and ontologies – a project rendered difficult by the social constructivism that underlined much of twentieth-century thought – I also think that ignoring the lessons of the linguistic turn means risking arrogance and ideological blind spots. This is in part because the seductive promise of the new can allow us to forget or cover over aspects of thought that are potentially troublesome or reactionary. Though generally approving of the movement, Shaviro warns that 'speculative realism is not without its dangers' since at its worst it is 'a lot like speculative finance, leveraging vast amounts of credit (both fiscal and metaphysical) on the basis of shaky, dubious foundations (or no foundations at all)'.[38] He asserts that, rather than embracing bold new ideas over what Bryant, Srnicek and Harman dismiss as 'stuffy … common sense',[39] a better way to 'outfox correlationism' would be to 'proceed obliquely through the history of philosophy, finding its points of divergence and its strange detours, when it moves beyond its own anthropocentric assumptions.[40] My Bataillean methodology, though different than Shaviro's Whiteheadian approach, seeks just such a detour. I therefore follow Shaviro in thinking that a certain degree of caution towards the new, which might initially appear overly conservative in its return to old ideas, can actually help inoculate against some of the more reactionary aspects of the nonhuman turn. Therefore, while I would agree that not all aspects of reality are socially constructed, it is also relatively uncontroversial to point out that, from a human point of view (which is the only one immediately available to us), a great deal of them are. I therefore think it is misguided to sweep aside concerns about thought, mediation, representation, ideology and language in the bold attempt to speculate about objective, mind-independent reality.

I am overgeneralizing here, because speculative realism at its best is extremely careful and rigorous in its attempts to exceed human thought. However, I *do* think that positioning the nonhuman and speculative turns as reactionary towards or in opposition to the linguistic turn leaves us open to certain problems. The linguistic turn taught us that the same reality can be explained in a multitude of ways: a single phenomenon can be described in terms of ideology, science and subjective experience (and many other ways besides), narratives that are all negotiated in relation to complex systems of power, both human and nonhuman. I do not see a reason to close off avenues of thought, and so my methodology seeks some flexibility between constructivism and realism. This is especially important in dealing with cinema as an object, I think, because as a popular art form it raises questions of ontology and indexicality at the same time as it articulates ideological concepts and negotiates systems of power. I try to engage in analysis on both levels, especially in Chapter 2, which brings together the unlikely combination of speculative realism and Jean-Louis Baudry's apparatus theory. In line with the title of this work, the reader might find it helpful to think of my methodology as somewhere 'at the limit' between linguistic and nonhuman turns. Bataille's work, which bases itself on a 'self-criticism of philosophy in the ambivalence of idealism and realism',[41] is well suited to this more holistic approach to the relationship between human thought and nonhuman reality; philosophies that favour either idealism or realism miss the more general economy that conditions these two positions in the first place.

For now, I will leave this outline of my suspicions and motivations somewhat general; they will be given more sustained engagement in subsequent chapters. But it is worth pointing out that the limit between the linguistic and nonhuman turns is not as stark as some of the theorists of the nonhuman turn would have us think (Harman is most strident in this regard, as he frequently expresses open distaste for constructivist philosophies[42]). For example, though Jacques Derrida is often associated with the constructivism against which the nonhuman turn is supposedly reacting – '*il n'y a pas de hors-texte* (there is no outside-text)'[43] – his thoughts in *The Animal That Therefore I Am* have been enormously influential on critical animal studies, especially in the work of Donna Haraway.[44] Other seemingly anthropocentric theories like psychoanalysis have also been used in nonanthropocentric ways, Slavoj Žižek's turn towards ecology being only one example: in the context of film studies, scholars aligning themselves with posthumanism and/or the nonhuman turn have used Freudian/Lacanian ideas such as desire, the death drive and the uncanny to explore nonhuman elements of films.[45] These examples, though far from comprehensive, suggest that the boundaries between the linguistic and nonhuman turns are already blurry, and my argument here aims to keep these points of connection open. If a central motivation of the nonhuman turn is to avoid binaries between nature and culture, subject and object, and self and other, then I see no reason to close off avenues of thought through rigid distinctions between theoretical approaches.

Bataille, transgression, ecology

This section will introduce my Bataillean eco-philosophy and will argue that, when read from an ecocritical perspective, Bataille's notions of transgression and inner experience offer a particular critique of anthropocentrism that is useful for interpreting human/nonhuman relations in films. The choice of Bataille might seem anachronistic, especially given his marginal position within contemporary philosophy and critical theory. While he remains a key reference for many important twentieth- and twenty-first-century philosophers – Michel Foucault's endorsement on the back cover of *Erotism* claims that 'Bataille is one of the most important writers of the century'[46] – Bataille himself has a reputation for being somewhat outdated, even immature or unsophisticated in comparison to those who source him.[47] There are a number of reasons for this, not least of which being Bataille's obsessive focus on the subjects of transgression, human sacrifice, sexuality and death.

Bataille (1891–1962) was a medievalist who worked for much of his life at the Bibliothèque Nationale in Paris, where he studied medallion collections and published on numismatics. However, as Allan Stoekl points out, 'at the same time … Bataille was living a kind of second life' and 'was far from being a calm and orderly librarian'.[48] Bataille wrote extensively on subjects that range from anthropology to economics to art history to philosophy; he was also a founding

Introduction 13

member of the Collège de Sociologie (1937–9), a lecture series that brought together leading French intellectuals during the interwar period, as well as a more shadowy organization called Acéphale that focused Bataille's central values of 'expenditure, risk, loss, sexuality, death' and even discussed the possibility of conducting a human sacrifice (though they never carried it out).[49] Fred Botting and Scott Wilson suggest that Bataille's interests in the excessive and intolerable are part of the reason for his peripheral status as a philosopher: his thought is focused on 'taking experience beyond every boundary, transgressing every law. Philosophically untenable, it is this aspect of Bataille's work that is most exciting, paradoxical, and difficult, attracting and repelling readers in equal measure.'[50] Beyond Bataille's morbid interests, however, Joseph Libertson attributes Bataille's lack of mainstream popularity to a pronounced sense of privacy in his work and argues that although Bataille frequently engages with thinkers like Friedrich Nietzsche and G. W. F. Hegel, he is less interested in contributing to a specific philosophical framework or school of thought than in struggling with his own conceptual limitations.[51]

I turn to Bataille because of this emphasis on epistemological finitude: his philosophy rests on a critique of subjectivity and anthropocentrism despite recognizing that knowledge inevitably remains within the realm of the human. In *Inner Experience*, he writes that 'we cannot endlessly be what we are: words cancelling each other out, at the same time unwavering joists, believing ourselves the foundation of the world'.[52] Despite the stubborn belief that words can express knowledge about the external world, Bataille argues that this merely gives the impression of objective mastery. Reality always remains in excess of language, and language's attempts to appropriate it always end in inconsistencies and contradictions. Despite these inherent difficulties, we cannot remain within the circular logic of reason that, in trying to escape itself, only ever results in reinforcing its own limits. Denis Hollier explicitly links Bataille's undermining of language with a critique of anthropocentrism: he writes that

> anthropocentrism, indeed, represses dehumanizing and decentering excesses; it is committed to saving 'the world we live in', a world organized around the human subject, against the world of expenditure, which Bataille also calls 'the world we die in', 'a world for nobody, a world from which subjects have been evacuated, the world of the non-I'.[53]

Though language inevitability belongs to the world we live in, which is ordered around the human subject, Bataille's philosophy attempts to trace the limits of thought in order to evoke, without appropriating, what is in excess of human attempts to signify.

While later chapters will explore a number of Bataille's ideas, two concepts in particular are integral to my methodology and will be explained in some detail here: transgression and inner experience. Transgression is the name that Bataille gives to the moment when a limit is crossed, not only in an ethical sense (which is the more usual way of thinking about transgression, as when we transgress a law or taboo) but also an ontological one. The many transgressive acts discussed in Bataille's writing are not merely superficial attempts to shock or disrupt moral sensibilities – though they are intended to do this as well – but also provide ways of enacting this movement, of describing transgression through language while simultaneously giving the reader a way of experiencing it. Bataille's major philosophical texts (including *Inner Experience, The Accursed Share* and *Erotism*, among others) all include chapters on topics such as human sacrifice, sexual taboos and torture, and his erotic fiction (*The Story of the Eye, Madame Edwarda, The Blue of Noon, My Mother, The Dead Man*[54]) describes a number of depraved acts in detail: children copulate next to corpses, a girl masturbates with eggs and human eyeballs, a man has sex with a prostitute who claims to be God, a boy is sexually initiated by his mother. Bataille's intention is not to argue for the permissibility of these acts, as this would domesticate them, thereby stripping them of their transgressive power.[55] Rather, Bataille writes about transgressive acts to comment on their very impermissibility. As Foucault argues, the role of transgression in Bataille 'is to measure the excessive distance that it opens at the heart of the limit and to trace the flashing line that caused the limit to arise'.[56] Bataille works to interrogate rather than eradicate taboo, exposing the ways that interdiction covers over excesses while also giving rise to their very possibility.

What exactly occurs in this crossing of limits? For Bataille, there is nothing for us to cross over into; or, seen from the other direction, transgression is the act of crossing over into nothing. Transgression occurs entirely in the space of this crossing, in an untenable moment that results from 'an *unbearable* surpassing of being'.[57] Bataille's transgressive moments – death as well as the 'little death' of the orgasm – are unbearable in the sense that they cannot be prolonged, because while they occur over a period of time, they must always culminate in the instant when life is extinguished or when mounting sexual pleasure exhausts itself in its release.[58] Neither death nor orgasm crosses over to 'another side', at least not in any positive ontological sense. Beyond death there is nothing; Bataille follows

Nietzsche in affirming the death of God, which implies no external support for human existence. After orgasm there is merely a return to ordinary life. Neither state achieves a sustained 'higher plane', since both eclipse themselves at the same moment that they are experienced.

This temporal understanding of transgression is crucial, as it implies that the experience, either in orgasm or death, can never be pinned down. As Foucault remarks, the relation between limits and transgression is 'situated in an uncertain context, in certainties which are immediately upset so that thought is ineffectual as soon as it attempts to seize them',[59] so that Bataille's attempts to trace these limits are doomed to failure. Transgression itself is not a static entity but rather refers to the thing that slips through at the very moment of seizure; it must be experienced rather than known and as such necessarily remains elusive to thought. Because there is no fixed concept to grasp, the work of theorizing transgression is never over, and Bataille's works are filled with anxious repetitions and failed attempts to provide meaning and context for something inherently unsignifiable. His writings enact their transgressions over and over, each time only briefly touching on something at the limit of human thought. His infamous *Story of the Eye*, for example, is replete with images of round objects, from the eggs that Simone inserts in her vagina at the beginning of the story to bull testicles and a murdered priest's eyeball used in the same way later on. This sexual imagery evinces transgression's temporal elusiveness, as increasing levels of violence are needed to provoke a similar effect; however, despite this apparent progression, the narrative frequently returns to the same symbolism as though unable to move beyond a particular structure of experience. Though the limit films discussed throughout this book are not always transgressive in terms of sex and violence, they similarly touch on a limit that cannot be appropriated. As with *Story of the Eye*, this limit is often conceived of in terms of an inescapable circularity, and circular imagery pervades limit films like *A Field in England* (2013) and *Syndromes and a Century* (2006) (Chapter 1), *Jauja* (2014) (Chapter 2) and *Under the Skin* (2014) (Chapter 3).

While sex and death provide an effective model for understanding transgression, I am less interested in transgressions themselves than in what they can reveal about reality in excess of human experience. Bataille's model of subjectivity involves a desire to overcome the distinction between subject and object while still asserting that interiority can never be transcended. Bataille characterizes the impossible outside of experience in different ways. Often, he describes it as a kind of pure negativity, as in death or the void at the edge of existence. However, he also sometimes describes it as something living, an abject, squirming multitude that writhes underneath the sanitized language of reason. He sometimes frames it in terms of the radical alterity of other people, from which the subject is able to conceive of itself as a singular being in relation to a community of others. But the outside is always in excess of meaning, an 'unknowable immensity' that goes beyond the boundaries of every articulation.[60] Bataille makes excess the fundamental principle of existence, a theory that has profound consequences for not only his metaphysics but also his ethics. Theorizing the world in terms of excess implies that we can never content ourselves with a system of thought; we cannot stay within the limits of our anthropocentric bubble despite our inability to see beyond it.

This paradox between a desire to see beyond subjective boundaries and a complete inability to do so informs Bataille's concept of inner experience, which grounds the theory of subjectivity behind this book. Subjectivity for Bataille is structured through radical alterity, through an 'outside' that can never be accessed except by means of internal experiences, despite the fact that it is irreducible to them. Bataille also conceives of the subject as a complex system that changes through the imposition of differences over time: he writes in *Inner Experience* it becomes impossible to locate the 'being' of the subject in the midst of the web of relations that constitute a person's body and experience. He compares this to a knife that gets a new handle, and then a new blade, and then to a machine that gets a series of new parts, but argues that these examples still do not capture the complexity of 'a man whose constituent parts die incessantly (such that nothing of these elements that we *were* subsists after a certain number of years)'.[61] However, despite the fact that it is impossible to locate a self-contained identity in this web of differences, for Bataille these differences somehow come together to form a singular self, and he writes that the human subject has the ability to 'enclose being in a simple, indivisible element'.[62] He calls this constitutive contradiction of identity-through-difference 'ipseity' (self-identity, selfsameness). Ipseity is what allows us to draw a distinction between what is inside and what is outside of ourselves despite the fact that 'self' is a non-locatable concept, lost in 'a labyrinth in which it wanders endlessly'.[63] The enclosure of being required for ipseity means that the subject in Bataille is founded not on its own internal structure but rather on its relationship to an outside. This paradoxical relationship to the outside from within and the ontological priority of the environment over the subject are both ways of acknowledging that our limits cannot be transcended while simultaneously refusing to restrict existence to the boundaries of human thought.

Introduction

Joseph Libertson writes about subjectivity's relation (or rather, non-relation) to alterity in Bataille: though the subject only exists as a self-enclosed entity because of its vulnerability to an outside, the relation between them is passive and therefore not relational at all. Libertson describes the subject's self-enclosure as a 'non-indifference of … passivity towards the economy which differentiates it'.[64] The subject is passive in that it is not determined by an agency or active sense of self-constitution: it does not draw firm boundaries between inside and outside, but instead differentiates itself through a logic of transgression – it is not an inside, but an inside-out. Libertson calls this asymmetrical non-relation 'communication' and describes a general economy of alterity in which the outside always weighs on the subject but can never be appropriated by it, precisely because it is not the kind of thing capable of being appropriated. The subject is contaminated by an outside that cannot fully arrive but which always 'disturbs' or 'haunts':[65] it is neither positive nor negative but eludes the dialectic entirely. Framing communication and alterity in terms of radical passivity works very much against the tradition of Western Enlightenment humanism, which theorizes subjectivity and otherness according to a logic of agency: 'the West's anthropocentrism is its conception of alterity as a power, an independence or freedom, and an effectivity – that is, as the very image of identity to self'.[66] In contrast to this view of the Other according to our own image, as a separate self-identity with faculties of power and control, Bataille views alterity as something with 'no independence'[67] – not because it is a correlate to human thought but because it operates outside of the differential economy that makes subjectivity possible.

This humiliation of the human subject in relation to an excess that is neither knowable nor eliminable resonates with a number of recent theorizations of subjectivity in posthumanism and film ecocriticism. Anat Pick, for example, argues that passivity is more fundamental to life than agency, and that our ethics ought not to be based on an organism's capacity for reason but on its vulnerability to what Simone Weil calls the 'pitiless necessity of matter'[68] – the caprice and violence of the external world. Like Bataille, Cary Wolfe conceives of subjectivity in terms of exposure to an external environment: in contrast to the humanist model that sees subjectivity as autonomous and self-contained, Wolfe's posthumanism is an attempt to 'take seriously the concept of autopoiesis – that systems, including bodies, are both open *and* closed as the very possibility of their existence (open on the level of structure to energy flows, environmental perturbations, and the like, but closed on the level of self-referential organization)'.[69] This fundamental paradox of 'openness from closure' means that there is no way to conceive of or interact with the environment except from within an internally closed system (such as a subject), but the impossibility of an objective view on reality does not mean it does not exist, or that it does not influence our thoughts or behaviour. For Bataille, Pick and Wolfe, the subject is not a self-enclosed or solipsistic entity, but is instead constituted through a relationship to its outside, and we are subjects less because we can think and act than because we are acted upon. Bataille's notions of transgression and inner experience provide a new way of conceptualizing this (non-)relation between human subjectivity and nonhuman reality, a claim that will be supported in the remaining chapters through analyses of particular limit films.

But why Bataille, when other philosophers already central to the canons of film-philosophy and ecocriticism seem to have much in common with his approach? Before I turn more specifically to how I plan to apply Bataille's ideas to cinema, I want to distinguish my methodology from two more conventional approaches to film-philosophy: Deleuzian and Lacanian. Just as I do not see Bataille as a 'way out' of the constructivist/realist debate but instead as a new way of framing the question, I do not offer Bataille as a radical alternative to previous film-philosophies: he has plenty of points of connection to both Deleuze and Jacques Lacan (and other philosophers besides). Bataille is different in several important respects, however, and these differences offer new critical possibilities for considering the ontology and influence of mind-independent reality on cinematic representation. At first glance, Bataille's theory of subjectivity has a lot in common with Deleuze. They similarly view the subject as composite and unstable, and argue that the apparent unification of the subject is not a condition but the result of experience. There are also commonalities in the ways that Deleuze and Bataille conceive of the unthought or outside, as they similarly make the non-correlationist argument that exteriority conditions existence and that, as Jonathan Roffe summarizes Deleuze's thought, the 'interior is only a selected interior'.[70] These connections are not accidental, since there is a common genealogy of ideas: Deleuze engages extensively with Foucault, on whom Bataille was a major influence, and Deleuze's conception of the outside is drawn from Maurice Blanchot, whose literary theory is intimately linked with Bataille's philosophy.[71] In light of these similarities, what distinguishes the images of limit cinema from Deleuze's time-image, which also emerges from an outside of thought? In other words, what value is there in proposing this new category of image, when Deleuzian analysis and the time-image specifically have received considerable attention as useful categories for the interpretation of cinema?

The primary difference is Bataille's emphasis on the limit between inside and outside, rather than on the outside proper. Although for both thinkers this boundary is porous and unstable, Deleuze is more likely to think that it can be done away with entirely: in the time-image, subject and object 'mark poles between which there is continual passage' so that the distinction between them 'tends to lose its importance'.[72] So, while the time-image operates through 'a principle of indeterminability, of indiscernibility',[73] what I am calling the 'limit-image' – a representation of the unrepresentable outside of thought – functions through a logic of transgression, simultaneously undermining and reinforcing the self-contained nature of subjectivity. Deleuze's philosophy is motivated by a desire to discern 'how the human observer can think beyond its own constituted, habituated and all too human world'.[74] Bataille, on the other hand, is less convinced of our ability to escape our habits; he would insist that the more we think we have exceeded our limits, the more we find we have paradoxically reinforced them. This is exactly what occurs in the process of transgression. I share Bataille's feeling that those forces shaping human subjectivity – ideology, language, consciousness – are difficult or even impossible to shake off, a conviction that seems especially true when cinema is the object of inquiry, since cinema's objective impressions are always articulated in relation to an implied human subject (I will explore this in more detail in Chapters 3 and 4).

If we accept that Bataille's emphasis on the inescapable forces structuring subjectivity differentiates him from Deleuze, however, this seemingly puts him closer to Lacan. For Lacan (and for Žižek, even in his recent ecocritical turn), the Symbolic structures human experience while the Real remains inaccessible, and both Bataille and Lacan characterize the real in terms of elusiveness and paradox. Fred Botting summarizes that for both Bataille and Lacan

> the real remains what *is*, an unspeakable *is*, an impossible, inexpressible, ineffable, and undifferentiated space outside language. The real, then, lies beyond systems of signification; it ex-ists outside Lacan's symbolic order. It is defined as what cannot be defined, that which is alien to or resists signification, that which exceeds symbolization. Utterly Other, the real is Other to subjects of language but has immense effects in its unpresentable in/difference.[75]

But while Bataille and Lacan talk about the real in similar ways – another connection that is far from accidental since, as Botting also points out, Bataille's thought had 'significant bearing' on Lacan[76] – there is an important difference in the ways that they characterize the relation between subjectivity and the real. Lacan's assertion that the world of things is 'only a humanized, symbolized world' aptly exemplifies the kind of correlationist thinking rejected by speculative realism and the nonhuman turn.[77] The Real in Lacan is structured by the Symbolic in that it is what is cast outside of signification rather than what precedes or determines it; the Real and the Symbolic are (with the imaginary) 'fundamental dimensions which, according to Lacan, structure the *human* universe'.[78] Joan Copjec describes the Lacanian Real as 'a by-product or residue of thought [that] detaches itself from thought to form its internal limit',[79] suggesting that while the Real is separate from and disruptive to thought, it is nevertheless conditioned by it. Bataille's insistence on excess as an originary principle reverses the formula, since he argues that a system is determined by expenditure – by what it cannot contain.[80] Though we are foreclosed from this excess, it determines us, and not the other way around.

Bataille's thought is therefore less correlationist than Lacan's. Although they agree that there is no way to see outside of the structuring forces of human subjectivity, Bataille's premise that the outside takes ontological priority is in part a critique against anthropocentric modes of thought that assume the primacy of the human subject. Bataille's ontology is therefore more amenable to ecological questions, while still recognizing the impact of subjectivizing forces (language, law, reason) on human ways of understanding the world. In this way, it might again be helpful to think of my methodology in terms of its in-betweenness: through Bataille, I want to mediate between the solipsistic anthropocentrism that sometimes pervades psychoanalytic discourse and the rhizomatic/relational approach with which Deleuze attempts to exceed human subjectivity. It is far beyond the scope of this work to defend Bataille's ontology against either Lacan's or Deleuze's, or to imply that he is somehow more 'right' in any absolute sense. Nor would I want to do so, as this would elide productive points of connection between these three thinkers, and others besides. Instead, what I am arguing is that Bataille's ideas are *useful* for film ecocriticism, in a way that has been largely overlooked. The cinematic examples in later chapters were chosen because they illustrate this utility of Bataille's ideas. In different ways, these limit films all evoke the boundaries between human and nonhuman realities in ways that resonate with Bataille's notions of transgression and inner experience.

Introduction   21

The impossible imperative

This chapter has seemingly set up an impossible task. Through Bataille, I have characterized the outside of thought as unrepresentable and unthinkable. Attempts at exceeding our limits paradoxically result in our reinforcing them; pinning down the outside inevitably results in failure, paradox and contradiction. I have also begun to suggest that cinema can help us trace the limits of the human, even if we can never finally transcend those limits. But tracing the limits of the human requires that we attempt the impossible and try to think outside of human thought, which raises the question: why grapple with impossibility at all? Though I have framed the limit between human and nonhuman realities in ontological terms, my answer to this question is primarily ethical. The ecological crisis demands that we think of reality in a more holistic way, and that we attempt to overcome challenges such as climate change that have become irreducibly complex and global in scale. The Anthropocene forces us to consider timescales far exceeding those that determine our everyday lives. Humans in the twenty-first century are, as Morton suggests, confronted with the end of the world, not only in the sense of impending apocalypse or extinction but also in terms of our finite abilities to understand and respond to global crises. The end of the world requires a number of ethical reconsiderations in order to recognize the role of humans in a wider ecology, reconsiderations made even more difficult by our finite means of understanding and responding to problems.

I agree with Jonathan Roffe's summation of the Deleuzian ethical project, which aims to 'reconnect with the external world again, and be caught up in its life.'[81] Bataille would add, however, that this reconnection is impossible: 'We are discontinuous beings, individuals who perish in isolation in the midst of an incomprehensible adventure, but we yearn for our lost continuity. We find the state of affairs that binds us to our random and ephemeral individuality hard to bear.'[82] Reconnection with the continuous world only happens at the moment of death, a horizon beyond which we cannot see. Transgression is a way of flirting with this horizon, of attempting to overcome ourselves while recognizing that doing so risks our own annihilation. The above passage suggests that transgression is a compulsion, an impulse to exceed ourselves often against our own better judgement; by theorizing the limit between human and nonhuman realities in terms of transgression, my Bataillean methodology must therefore recognize its own inevitable failure. The Bataillean ethics at stake in this book can therefore, in a reversal of Kant, be called *the impossible imperative*. While Kant's categorical imperative was asserted as a method for ascertaining objective moral truths, the impossible imperative is a recognition of objective moral non-truth; it assumes that objective reality is irreducible to all frameworks – including ethical frameworks – that we attempt to impose upon it. Despite the impossibility of drawing an objective moral framework, however, the ecological crisis insists that we must try, as flawed and partial as those attempts will inevitably be.

Why look to cinema as a place to think through the ethical implications of human finitude? There are two primary reasons for this (as well as a number of other, smaller motivations that will become clearer in subsequent chapters). The first major reason is that art in general has a privileged relationship with excess, a relationship with which philosophy – grounded as it is on structure and reason – has more difficulty. This is not to say that art can access the unthought or outside while philosophy cannot; for Bataille, both art and philosophy are associated with the human world of work and reason and therefore inevitably fail to appropriate what is in excess of human thought and subjectivity. The difference for Bataille is that while philosophy suppresses 'desire' or affect, art embraces it; this makes art 'less the harmony than the passage (or the return) of harmony to dissonance'.[83] This dissonant element to art makes it useful from a philosophical perspective, since it can reveal fault lines in human reason to which philosophy is blind. The second major reason, and the motivation for focusing on cinema specifically (rather than art more generally) is that cinema, as a time-based indexical medium, relies on a unique articulation of subjective and objective perspectives. Cinema can give the impression of an unfiltered access to reality despite perceiving the world in a particular way, one conditioned by human optics and the history of Enlightenment humanism. This contradiction between subjective and objective perspectives makes cinema fertile ground for exploring the limits of the human; I will return to this argument in Chapter 2, where I critique speculative realism through a return to Baudry's apparatus theory.

The limit films chosen in this book disclose or respond to the impossible imperative in a variety of ways. Because the ecological crisis is global, I posit limit cinema as a transnational category, and the examples discussed herein therefore come from a range of national and cultural contexts. Most of them can be loosely categorized as 'global art cinema', which Rosalind Galt and Karl Schoonover describe as narrative films with an 'overt engagement with aesthetic [and] unrestrained formalism' which 'by classical standards, might be seen as too slow or excessive in visual style, use of color, or characterization'.[84] I have not limited myself to narrative films, however, and also incorporate documentaries with similarly excessive styles. I have included as broad a selection of films as space and depth of analysis allowed, but I have also set a few limits on my choices. Because limit cinema represents the relationship between humans and the environment in terms of narrative and formal excess, the category is less easily applied to Hollywood and genre cinemas. This is not to make a taste judgement or dismiss popular cinemas as irrelevant; however, while popular cinemas can also be excessive – horror, action and melodrama especially – these excesses relate to more rigid generic and formal structures, a relationship that I think could serve as the foundation for a whole other project. The films I have chosen here, on the other hand, foreground their excesses more readily; they depart from or destabilize familiar generic patterns to suggest the existence of something beyond the scope of reason. It is this destabilization that I trace through close textual analysis of particular limit films.

Because my argument is situated in a twenty-first-century context, I have also restricted my analysis to films that have been released since the beginning of the millennium. This is not to say that only contemporary art is relevant to the nonhuman turn: film scholars like James Cahill and Jennifer Fay, for example, address current environmental concerns by returning to the archive of film history and reading film-makers like Jean Painlevé and Buster Keaton through an ecocritical lens.[85] Contemporary art, however, can tell us something about what it means to exist in the present. As Boris Groys argues, contemporary art asks us to hesitate and reconsider our position in relation to the past and future: he characterizes the present itself as a kind of limit, since it 'interrupts the smooth transition between past and future';[86] it inconveniently interrupts the progression between the trappings of history and the promise of future progress with an interminable period of hesitation and delay. Understood in Bataillean terms, traversing this limit is a perpetual act of transgression, consisting not of a crossing over – the future inevitably slips into the present – but only ever in the difficult and frustrating act of the crossing itself. By restricting my focus to contemporary films, I am therefore tarrying with the present; I want to explore how cinema relates to reality as it is currently conditioned and made manifest.

This chapter introduced my Bataillean film-philosophy in relation to recent theories such as posthumanism and speculative realism that call attention to the agency of nonhuman things. The method introduced in this chapter will be used to theorize the particular limit films that are the focus of Chapters 2 through

5, which exhibit a wide variety of styles and emerge from diverse national and cultural contexts, ranging from acclaimed auteur cinema like Apichatpong Weerasethakul's *Uncle Boonmee Who Can Recall His Past Lives* (2010) to obscure experimental documentaries like Peter Bo Rappmund's *Tectonics* (2012). My Bataillean approach attempts to avoid homogenizing the diverse ecological perspectives of these contemporary films while simultaneously linking them together through their shared attention to the limits of the human. The examples I have chosen are by no means intended to be comprehensive, but they do cover a range of concerns to do with conceptualizing mind-independent reality. Because my argument explores relations between subjects and objects, I have divided the rest of this book into two parts. Part 1, 'Objectivity', considers the possibility of representing the nonhuman and therefore focuses primarily on questions about the objective. Chapter 1 considers cinematic objectivity in relation to Bataillean notions of the sacred through the films of Apichatpong Weerasethakul and Ben Wheatley. Bataille's sacred is immanent to this world rather than belonging to a transcendent state like God or heaven; I similarly characterize the sacred in Wheatley and Apichatpong, and argue that their films envision human relationships with the sacred in terms of sacrifice (Wheatley) and eroticism (Apichatpong). Chapter 2 engages with objectivity in relation to speculative realism and argues that while speculative realism can provide important insights into the ways that films represent the nonhuman, it has much to learn from film theory. I explore speculative realism in relation to Baudry's apparatus theory in order to argue that the same aesthetic strategy can simultaneously evade and reinforce anthropocentric modes of perception. I apply this claim to two films, *Tectonics* and *Jauja* (Lisandro Alonso, 2014), which both posit spectatorial knowledge as limited in relation to the diegesis, but also simultaneously emphasize the ways that they implicate the spectator through strategies such as single-point perspective. From this, I argue that film ecocriticism cannot do without a theory of cinematic subjectivity, since avoiding the subjective can lead us to overlook some of the ways that anthropocentrism in cinema might either be implicitly reinforced or undermined.

This leads into Part 2, 'Subjectivity', which explores how a Bataillean understanding of cinematic subjectivity might contribute to film ecocriticism. Chapter 3 outlines a nonanthropocentric Bataillean theory of cinematic subjectivity and applies it to the subjectivization of the female protagonists in *Under the Skin* (Jonathan Glazer, 2013) and *Nymphomaniac* (Lars von Trier, 2013). Both films represent subjectivity as an unstable process of turning inside out, which I theorize through Bataille's ipseity and Jean-Luc Nancy's related concept of invagination. Chapter 4 then considers the relationship between the human subject and the unknowable outside of thought in terms of love and looks at *Grizzly Man* (Werner Herzog, 2005) and *Konelīne: Our Land Beautiful* (Nettie Wild, 2016) as examples of how love is an imperfect way of relating to nature, since it always involves problems of projection and subjective bias; through *Grizzly Man* and *Konelīne*, however, I argue that these imperfections can be productively brought to bear on the impossible imperative. This argument builds from the understanding of post-theology explored in Chapter 2 and draws from theological understandings of love to suggest that loving nature is an ever-unfinished process of relating to a world outside of thought. While this process is ambivalent in that it holds potential for both harm and good, *Konelīne* and *Grizzly Man* suggest that love cannot be left out of ecological ethics.

Notes

1 Timothy Morton, *Hyperobjects: Philosophy and Ecology after the End of the World* (Minneapolis: University of Minnesota Press, 2014).

2 Ibid., 60.

3 Quentin Meillassoux, *After Finitude: An Essay on the Necessity of Contingency*, trans. Ray Brassier (London: Continuum, 2008), 4–5.

4 Ibid., 6.

5 Meillassoux clarifies that this argument predates Kant, as it can be found at least since Berkeley's idealism (ibid., 3), but he also points to the *Critique of Pure Reason* as the most influential text on twentieth-century versions of the idea.

6 Ibid., 124.

7 Steven Shaviro, *The Universe of Things: On Speculative Realism* (Minneapolis: University of Minnesota Press, 2014), 68–9.

8 Immanuel Kant, *The Critique of Pure Reason*, 1781, trans. Paul Guyer and Allan W. Wood (Cambridge: Cambridge University Press, 2009).

9 For a helpful overview of the debates and issues raised by Kant's transcendental idealism, see Nicholas Stang, 'Kant's Transcendental Idealism', *Stanford Encyclopedia of Philosophy*, 4 March 2016, https://plato.stanford.edu/entries/kant-transcendental-idealism/. Accessed 26 July 2019.

10 The phrase 'linguistic turn' has been used to describe a wide range of twentieth-century philosophies, both analytic and continental, which put language at the forefront of philosophical inquiry. In the analytic tradition, its forerunners

were Gottlob Frege, Bertrand Russel and Ludwig Wittgenstein. The continental tradition, on the other hand, was largely influenced by Ferdinand de Saussure's semiotics, which inspired both structuralism and the ensuing post-structuralist movement. Thinkers associated with the linguistic turn in continental philosophy include, among others, Jacques Derrida, Jacques Lacan, Luce Irigaray and Michel Foucault. See also Richard Rorty, ed., *The Linguistic Turn: Essays in Philosophical Method* (Chicago: University of Chicago Press, 1967).

11 Shaviro, *The Universe of Things*, 68.

12 Meillassoux, *After Finitude*, 9–27.

13 Ray Brassier, *Nihil Unbound: Enlightenment and Extinction* (London: Palgrave Macmillan, 2007). Brassier has since distanced himself from the movement.

14 Paul Crutzen, 'Geology of Mankind', *Nature* 415 (2002), 23. There is much debate about how to date the beginning of the Anthropocene. Crutzen points to industrialization, while Simon Lewis and Mark Maslin suggest 1610 and link it to the effects of colonialism (Simon Lewis and Mark Maslin, 'Defining the Anthropocene', *Nature* 519 (2015), 171–80; see also David Martin-Jones, *Cinema against Doublethink*, London: Routledge, 2019) ; the Anthropocene Working Group posit 1945 with the testing of the atomic bomb (Jan Zalasiewicz, Jan, Colin N. Waters, Mark Williams, Anthony D. Barnosky, Alejandro Cearreta, Paul Crutzen, Erle Ellis, Michael A. Ellis, Ian J. Fairchild, Jacques Grinevald, Peter K. Haff, Irka Hajdas, Reinhold Leinfelder, John McNeill, Eric O. Odada, Clément Poirier, Daniel Richter, Will Steffen, Colin Summerhayes, James P. M. Syvitski, Davor Vidas, Michael Wagreich, Scott L Wing, Alexander P. Wolfe, An Zhisheng, Naomi Oreskes, 'When Did the Anthropocene Begin? A Mid-Twentieth Century Boundary Level Is Stratigraphically Optimal', *Quarternary International* 383 (2015), 196–203) .

15 Timothy Clark, *Ecocriticism on the Edge: The Anthropocene as a Threshold Concept* (London: Bloomsbury, 2015), x.

16 Ibid.

17 Christopher Peterson, 'The Gravity of Melancholia: A Critique of Speculative Realism', *Theory & Event* 18, no. 2 (2015).

18 Georges Bataille, *Erotism: Death and Sensuality*, trans. Mary Dalwood (San Francisco, CA: City Lights, [1957] 1986), 18.

19 Bataille dates the photograph from 1905 and names the victim as Fou-Tchou-Li; Jérôme Bourgon clarifies, however, that the photograph was of an unidentified victim executed in 1904 (Jérôme Bourgon, 'Photographing "Chinese Torture"', *Chinese Torture/Supplices Chinoises*, http://turandot.chineselegalculture.org/Essay.php?ID=1. Accessed 8 May 2017) . For a detailed analysis of the meanings of *lingchi*, as well as the ways that the West (including Bataille) has misunderstood

the practice, see Timothy Brook, Jérôme Bourgon and Gregory Blue, *Death by a Thousand Cuts* (Cambridge, MA: Harvard University Press, 2008) .

20 Georges Bataille, *The Tears of Eros*, trans. Peter Connor (San Francisco, CA: City Lights, 1961), 204.

21 Ibid., 206.

22 Marta Figlerowicz, 'Comedy of Abandon: Lars von Trier's Melancholia', *Film Quarterly* 65, no. 4 (2012): 21–6.

23 Morton, *Hyperobjects*, 5.

24 Richard Grusin, 'Introduction', in *The Nonhuman Turn*, ed. Richard Grusin (Minneapolis: University of Minnesota Press, 2015), viii–ix.

25 Ibid., ix.

26 Anat Pick and Guinevere Narraway, 'Introduction: Intersecting Ecology and Film,' in *Screening Nature: Cinema Beyond the Human*, ed. Anat Pick and Guinevere Narraway (New York: Berghahn Books, 2013), 2. There has been a recent resurgence of scholarship on Bazin, particularly in an ecocritical context: see Jennifer Fay, 'Seeing/Loving Animals: André Bazin's Posthumanism', *Journal of Visual Culture* 7, no. 1 (2008), 41–64; Seung-hoon Jeong and Dudley Andrew, 'Grizzly Ghost: Herzog, Bazin and the Cinematic Animal', *Screen* 49, no. 1 (2008), 1–12; Laura McMahon, 'Unwinding the Anthropological Machine: Animality, Film and Arnaud des Pallières', *Paragraph* 35, no. 3 (2012), 373–88; Seung-hoon Jeong, 'André Bazin's Ontological Other: The Animal in Adventure Films', *Senses of Cinema* 51 (2009) ; and Anat Pick, *Creaturely Poetics: Animality and Vulnerability in Literature and Film* (New York: Columbia University Press, 2011) .

27 For a comprehensive survey of the first movements in film ecocriticism, see Adrian Ivakhiv, 'Green Film Criticism and Its Futures', *Interdisciplinary Studies in Literature and Environment* 15, no. 2 (2008), 1–28.

28 For an empirical account of the environmental impact of the film industry, see Nadia Bozak, *The Cinematic Footprint: Lights, Camera, Natural Resources* (New Brunswick, NJ: Rutgers University Press, 2012).

29 Sean Cubitt, *EcoMedia* (Amsterdam: Rodopi, 2005).

30 Ibid., 143.

31 Speculative realism has also begun to affect film studies. See Selmin Kara, 'Beasts of the Digital Wild: Primordigital Cinema and the Question of Origins', *Sequence* 1, no. 4 (2014) ; David Martin-Jones, 'Trolls, Tigers and Transmodern Ecological Encounters: Enrique Dussel and a Cine-ethics for the Anthropocene', *Film-Philosophy* 20, no. 1 (2016b), 63–103; and Peterson, 'The Gravity of Melancholia'.

32 Jane Bennett, *Vibrant Matter: A Political Ecology of Things* (Durham, NC: Duke University Press, 2009).

33 Meillassoux, *After Finitude*.

34 Graham Harman, *Tool-Being: Heidegger and the Metaphysics of Objects* (Chicago: Open Court, 2002); Graham Harman, *Object-Oriented Ontology: A New Theory of Everything* (London: Penguin, 2018).

35 Brassier, *Nihil Unbound.*

36 Levi Bryant, Nick Srnicek and Graham Harman, 'Towards a Speculative Philosophy', in *The Speculative Turn: Continental Materialism and Realism*, ed. Levi Bryant, Nick Srnicek and Graham Harman (Melbourne: Re-press, 2011), 1.

37 Grusin, *The Nonhuman Turn*, xi.

38 Shaviro, *The Universe of Things*, 10.

39 Bryant, Srnicek and Harman, 'Towards a Speculative Philosophy', 7.

40 Shaviro, *The Universe of Things*, 9.

41 Joseph Libertson, *Proximity: Levinas, Blanchot, Bataille and Communication* (The Hague: Martinus Nijhoff, 1982), 36.

42 Harman tends to write about his experience as a realist continental philosopher as though he belongs to a persecuted minority that has only recently begun to triumph over those dogmatic idealists who refuse to take reality seriously. In a dialogue with Manuel DeLanda, Harman complains: 'Until quite recently, almost no philosopher who was continentally trained saw anything of value in a realist position. Indeed, in our first correspondence some years ago, you stated accurately that "for decades admitting that one was a realist was equivalent to acknowledging one was a child molester"' (Graham Harman and Manuel DeLanda, *The Rise of Realism*, Cambridge: Polity, 2017, 1–2).

43 Jacques Derrida, *Of Grammatology*, trans. Gayatri Spivak (Baltimore, MD: Johns Hopkins University Press, [1967] 1997), 158. Detractors tend to interpret this phrase as implying that for Derrida there is nothing outside of language (see most famously John Searle, *The Construction of Social Reality*, London: Allen Lane, 1995) , though of course Derrida's meaning is more complex and nuanced and he laments that the phrase became 'a sort of slogan, in general so badly understood, of deconstruction' (Jacques Derrida, *Limited, Inc.*, trans. Jeffrey Mehlman and Samuel Weber, Evanston, IL: Northwestern University Press, 1988, 13) . As Jonathan Basile argues, 'the foundational gesture of New Materialism and Speculative Realism dismisses vast swaths of past philosophy in order to signify their own avant-garde status'; in other words, by uniting a diverse range of post-Kantian philosophies under the term 'correlationism', speculative realism completely ignores the kinds of differences to which Derrida's thought is attuned (Jonathan Basile, 'The New Novelty: Correlation as Quarantine in Speculative Realism and New Materialism', *Derrida Today* 11, no. 2 (2018), 211) .

44 Jacques Derrida, *The Animal That Therefore I Am*, trans. David Willis (New York: Fordham University Press, 2008) ; Donna Haraway, *When Species*

Meet (Minneapolis: University of Minnesota Press, 2007) . See also Jonathan Burt, 'Morbidity and Vitalism: Derrida, Bergson, Deleuze, and Animal Film Imagery', *Configurations* 14, nos. 1–2 (2006), 157–79.

45 See Neil Badmington, *Alien Chic: Posthumanism and the Other Within* (London: Routledge, 2004) ; James Cahill, 'Anthropomorphism and Its Vicissitudes: Reflections on Homme-sick Cinema', in *Screening Nature: Cinema Beyond the Human*, ed. Anat Pick and Guinevere Narraway (New York: Berghahn, 2013), 73–90; and Seung-hoon Jeong, 'A Global Cinematic Zone of Animal and Technology', *Angelaki* 18, no. 1 (2013), 139–57.

46 Bataille, *Erotism: Death and Sensuality*.

47 Bataille was a major influence on important twentieth-century thinkers such as Derrida, Foucault, Julia Kristeva and Jean-Luc Nancy, among others. See especially Jacques Derrida, 'From Restricted to General Economy: A Hegelianism without Reserve', in *Bataille: A Critical Reader*, ed. Fred Botting and Scott Wilson (Oxford: Blackwell, 1988), 102–38; Michel Foucault, 'A Preface to Transgression', in *Bataille: A Critical Reader*, ed. Fred Botting and Scott Wilson (Oxford: Blackwell, 1988), 24–30; Julia Kristeva, *Powers of Horror: An Essay on Abjection*, trans. Leon Roudiez (New York: Columbia University Press, 1982) ; Jean-Luc Nancy, *The Inoperative Community*, trans. Peter Connor, Lisa Garbus, Michael Holland and Simona Sawhney (Minneapolis: Minnesota University Press, 1991).

48 Alan Stoekl, 'Introduction', in *Visions of Excess*, ed. Georges Bataille, trans. Alan Stoekl (Minneapolis: University of Minnesota Press, 1985), x.

49 Ibid., xix–xx.

50 Fred Botting and Scott Wilson, 'Introduction', in *Bataille: A Critical Reader*, ed. Fred Botting and Scott Wilson (Oxford: Blackwell, 1988), 2.

51 Libertson, *Proximity*, 2–3.

52 Georges Bataille, *Inner Experience*, trans. Stuart Kendall (Albany: SUNY, [1954] 2014), 39.

53 Dennis Hollier, 'The Dualist Materialism of Georges Bataille', in *Bataille: A Critical Reader*, ed. Fred Botting and Scott Wilson (Oxford: Blackwell, 1988), 69.

54 Bataille distanced himself from his more literary works, as he published *The Story of the Eye* and *Madame Edwarda* under pseudonyms (Lord Auch and Pierre Angélique, respectively, though a later edition of the latter was published with a preface in Bataille's name); *My Mother* and *The Dead Man* were published posthumously.

55 Some have argued that this has already come to pass: Steven Shaviro argues that Bataille's arguments are outdated and that 'transgression has lost its sting'. Steven Shaviro, 'Come, Come Georges: Steven Shaviro on Georges Bataille's *Story of the Eye* and *Ma Mère*', *ArtForum*, 1 May 2017. See also Linda Williams,

Hardcore: Power, Pleasure, and the Frenzy of the Visible (Berkeley: University of California Press, 1989) and Tina Kendall, 'Reframing Bataille: On Tacky Spectatorship in the New Extremism', in *The New Extremism in Cinema: From France to Europe*, ed. Tanya Horeck and Tina Kendall (Edinburgh: Edinburgh University Press, 2011), 43–54.

56 Foucault, 'A Preface to Transgression', 25.

57 Georges Bataille, 'Madame Edwarda', in *My Mother, Madame Edwarda, The Dead Man*, trans. Austryn Wainhouse (London: Penguin Classics, [1941] 2012), 141.

58 This simplifies matters slightly by ignoring the possibility of multiple female orgasms. But while multiple orgasms complicate the picture by indicating a sexual pleasure that does not immediately exhaust itself upon orgasm, I do not think that they entirely contradict it: in order for them to be experienced as multiple they must be experienced as distinct, which means that at a certain point they must reach a limit.

59 Foucault, 'A Preface to Transgression', 27.

60 Bataille, *Inner Experience*, 88.

61 Ibid., 86. I will return to this analogy in more detail in Chapter 3.

62 Ibid.

63 Ibid.

64 Libertson, *Proximity*, 29.

65 Ibid.

66 Ibid.

67 Ibid., 30.

68 Quoted in Anat Pick, *Creaturely Poetics*, 4.

69 Cary Wolfe, *What Is Posthumanism?* (Minneapolis: University of Minnesota Press, 2009), xxiv–xxv.

70 Jonathan Roffe, 'Exteriority/Interiority', in *The Deleuze Dictionary*, ed. Adrian Parr (Edinburgh: Edinburgh University Press, 2010), 98.

71 See Leslie Hill, *Bataille, Klossowski, Blanchot: Writing at the Limit* (Oxford: Oxford University Press, 2011) ; Patrick ffrench, 'Friendship, Asymmetry, Sacrifice: Bataille and Blanchot', *Parrhesia* 3 (2007), 32–42; and Steven Shaviro, *Passion & Excess: Blanchot, Bataille and Literary Theory* (Gainesville: University Press of Florida, 1990) .

72 Gilles Deleuze, *Cinema II: The Time-Image*, trans. Hugh Tomlinson and Robert Galeta (London: Abalone, 1989), 7.

73 Ibid.

74 Claire Colebrook, 'Introduction', in *The Deleuze Dictionary*, ed. Adrian Parr (Edinburgh: Edinburgh University Press, 2010), 1.

75 Fred Botting, 'Reflections of the Real in Lacan, Bataille and Blanchot', *SubStance* 23, no. 1 (1994), 24 (emphasis original).

76 Ibid., 26.

77 Jacques Lacan, *The Seminar of Jacques Lacan: Book I Freud's Papers on Technique 1953–1954*, trans. John Forrester (Cambridge: Cambridge University Press, 1988), 87.

78 Slavoj Žižek, *The Plague of Fantasies*, 2nd edn (London: Verso, 2009b), 222, my emphasis.

79 Joan Copjec, *Imagine There's No Woman: Ethics and Sublimation* (Cambridge, MA: MIT Press, 2002), 3.

80 Georges Bataille, *The Accursed Share: Vol. I*, trans. Robert Hurley (Brooklyn: Zone Books, [1967] 2012).

81 Roffe, 'Exteriority/Interiority', 98.

82 Bataille, *Erotism*, 15.

83 Bataille, *Inner Experience*, 61.

84 Rosalind Galt and Karl Schoonover, 'Introduction', in *Global Art Cinema: New Theories and Histories*, ed. Rosalind Galt and Karl Schoonover (Oxford: Oxford University Press, 2010), 6.

85 See James Cahill, 'Forgetting Lessons: Jean Painlevé's Gay Science', *Journal of Visual Culture* 11, no. 3 (2012), 2–36 and Jennifer Fay, 'Buster Keaton's Climate Change', *Modernism/Modernity* 21, no. 1 (2014), 25–49.

86 Boris Groys, 'Comrades of Time', *e-flux* 11 (2009), https://www.e-flux.com/journal/11/61345/comrades-of-time/. Accessed 15 November 2019.

Part 1

Objectivity

1

Sacrifice and the sacred in Apichatpong Weerasethakul and Ben Wheatley

Introduction

In the previous chapter, I argued that certain contemporary films confront us with the limits of the human, and I contextualized this claim within recent discussions in the humanities and film studies more specifically about how to break with anthropocentric modes of thought. This chapter, the first half of Part 1 on Objectivity, will consider the possibility of representing nonhuman reality through cinema in relation to Bataillean notions of the sacred. Bataille distinguishes the sacred from the profane world of work and reason, which he argues betrays the nature of existence by imposing truth and meaning. The sacred, on the other hand, is what is excluded by or in excess of the human: 'There is in nature and there subsists in man a movement which always exceeds the bounds, that can never be anything but partially reduced to order.'[1] Though the sacred is external to human modes of thought, it nevertheless 'subsists' in our behaviour and manifests itself through irrational drives such as sexual desire and self-destruction. Because the sacred resists reason, Bataille characterizes it as irrational, contradictory and ambivalent; the sacred is also associated with nature, since despite its exteriority to human thought it is immanent to this world rather than belonging to a transcendent world beyond. This Bataillean understanding of objectivity – of a world outside the particularities of the human perspective – will be explored in relation to the works of two film-makers: Ben Wheatley[2] and Apichatpong Weerasethakul. I will argue that the films of Wheatley and Apichatpong evoke two kinds of relationship with the sacred: Wheatley's films emphasize death and sacrifice, while Apichatpong's films envision an erotic communion with nature.

The films of Apichatpong and Wheatley differ greatly in terms of cultural context and aesthetic approach, but this chapter will draw connections in the ways that both film-makers explore tensions between contemporary society, related to suburban and urban spaces, and a pagan or animist history that inheres in the natural landscape. Apichatpong is a prolific artist and a prominent favourite on the international film festival circuit, especially after his Palme d'Or-winning *Uncle Boonmee Who Can Recall His Past Lives* (2010); he makes films that are slow-paced and narratively obscure and has been linked to other contemporary 'slow cinema' auteurs such as Béla Tarr, Abbas Kiarostami and Lisandro Alonso. His art house aesthetics, however, are infused with a love of pop culture, even kitsch: Thai pop songs feature prominently on his soundtracks, and the supernatural elements of his films are often referencing sci-fi and horror as much as Buddhist and animist folklore. Wheatley, a British film-maker who has been extremely prolific since the release of his first feature, *Down Terrace*, in 2009, is similarly interested in supposedly low-brow genres such as horror and science fiction. His films straddle the line between genre and art house cinema, as they experiment with generic structures through narrative ambiguity and formal excess. Wheatley's films often stage human relationships in the midst of natural landscapes characterized by irrationality and violence, representations that serve as counterpoints to the comparatively gentler but no less incomprehensible junglescapes in Apichatpong.

While Wheatley insists on violence and death by focusing on male brutality and pagan sacrifice, in Apichatpong's work the dissolution of the rational is staged as erotic, evidenced in the frequent sexual encounters of humans in nature or even of humans with nature (inter-species sex is a common trope in his cinema). Reading Apichatpong and Wheatley through Bataille will allow me to see them as two sides of the same coin, because eroticism and death for Bataille are the two ways by which we can confront the limits of the human. As I outlined in the previous chapter, both sex and death culminate in a transgression of/at the limits of thought: both acts risk the dissolution of the self into an ecstatic communion with alterity. Complementary representations of eroticism and death in the films of Apichatpong and Wheatley will help to elucidate – as much as possible, given its resistance to thought and language – the Bataillean sacred. I will start by exploring the negative post-theology of Wheatley's *Kill List* (2011) and *A Field in England* (2013), which I argue are structured by a sacrifice-for-nothing that emphasizes the radical aporia of death. Building from this, I will move towards the erotic encounters with nature in Apichatpong's *Tropical Malady* (2003), *Syndromes and a Century* (2006) and *Uncle Boonmee*. Wheatley's evocations of the sacred are violent and nihilistic, while Apichatpong's are more optimistic and life-affirming; however, rather than insisting on one of these versions of the

Sacrifice and the Sacred in Weerasethakul and Wheatley 37

sacred over the other, I argue that holding positive and negative notions of the sacred in suspension is essential for the ethical project made necessary by the Anthropocene.

Wheatley, post-theology and the sacrifice of sacrifice

Like Bataille, Ben Wheatley's films are obsessed with death and sacrifice. *Down Terrace* ends with the protagonist murdering his parents with the help of his girlfriend; *Kill List* culminates in the ritual sacrifice of the protagonist's family, unknowingly committed by the protagonist himself; *A Field in England* contains the repeated death and resurrection of a central character; the romantic holiday in *Sightseers* (2012) ends with a woman allowing her boyfriend to fall to his death in a thwarted double suicide. Rather than answering questions or resolving narrative tensions, these deaths raise more questions than they answer as they coincide with the gradual disintegration of generic structure towards an increasingly obscure and excessive aesthetic. This gradual collapse into irrationality and excess correlates with the central tension between Christian rationalism and a repressed pagan violence that Wheatley views as central to the British cultural imaginary. This concern with pagan history is nothing new to British cinema, and Wheatley borrows extensively from horror films such as The *Wicker Man* (Robin Hardy, 1973) and *Witchfinder General* (Michael Reeves, 1968) that focus on themes of witchcraft and human sacrifice. What differentiates Wheatley from other British folk horror is that the sacrifices in his films no longer serve an authority but rather inhere in the structure of his films as a sacrifice of form itself. Sacrifice in Wheatley serves nothing: there is something in it that cannot be recuperated to serve the structuring forces of law, god or truth. The sacred evoked by sacrifice in Wheatley inheres in the landscape itself, a landscape that is bereft of higher meaning but that structures human existence as its very limit.

Bataille provides an effective framework for considering Wheatley's treatment of sacrifice, as he also envisions a sacrifice-for-nothing that has radical potential to disrupt authoritarian forces. This notion of sacrifice attests to the pervasiveness of sacrificial logic despite the impossibility of sacrifice serving a higher truth after the death of God. Christopher Watkin argues that 'to think in the West today is to think after God, with concepts and a tradition bequeathed by theology and theologically informed thinking, and even if the aim of such thinking is to be atheological it cannot avoid the task of disengaging itself from the theological legacy'.[3] Watkin continues that post-theology recognizes that the death of God does not rid us of God's impact on metaphysics; thinking beyond God requires that we recognize the influence of theology on the construction of thought and language.[4] Sacrifice in Wheatley serves a similar function by undermining generic conventions and frustrating attempts at interpretation or meaning.

Sacrifice holds a central place in the foundations of Western thought, culminating in Christianity's notion that humankind could only achieve salvation by sacrificing God. Post-theology argues that, despite the absence of God, this way of thinking persists in secular culture, and that sacrifice remains implicated in the ways that we understand and work towards truth. As Dennis King Keenan explains, the notion of truth has explicit ties to sacrifice in the Western philosophical tradition because 'sacrifice has come to be understood as a necessary passage through suffering and/or death (of either oneself or someone else) on the way to a supreme moment of transcendent truth. Sacrifice effects the revelation of truth'.[5] This process is thwarted by the lack of possibility for transcendence, since there is no higher truth to attain; while sacrificial logics persist, their grounding has become obsolete, resulting in what King calls the need for sacrifice to sacrifice itself.

Keenan locates this movement towards the sacrifice of sacrifice in thinkers like Julia Kristeva, Nancy and Bataille (among others); Bataille, he argues, effects this by emphasizing 'the irreducible undecideability of the double meaning of death articulated by that moment when death as possibility turns into death as impossibility'.[6] Death is aporetic in that, at the very moment that it can be apprehended, the possibility for apprehension ceases to exist; it remains a 'not yet' until the moment when speaking the not-yet becomes impossible.[7] Sacrifice for Bataille is a means of relating to this impossibility at a distance because, through the communal witnessing of the death of another, we can share an experience of death without dying. The impossible subjective experience of death is turned into an objective event, which in turn can only be experienced in fragments of individual subjective experiences. Sacrifice is therefore the name Bataille gives to the compulsion to go beyond the self, to break the boundaries of ego and to experience alterity: it is a way of explaining the 'necessity of throwing oneself or something of oneself out of oneself',[8] a necessity that exceeds the rational and requires the ecstatic communion of a group. He continues that this compulsion to exceed oneself 'in certain cases can have no other end than death';[9] the urge to break the boundaries of the self is an inherently self-destructive one, though that destruction can be mitigated through the deferred, mediated experience of witnessing.

Sacrifice in Bataille is also a means of breaking with anthropocentric rationality. Human sacrifices and other offerings to gods are useless expenditures that exceed the profane logic of work and reason because, as waste, sacrificed objects are no longer subordinated to use and cannot be contained by the restricted systems of human labour and productivity.[10] By exceeding profane human logic, Bataille argues that sacrifice can form a paradoxical relation to the sacred outside of thought. This duality between the sacred and the profane is another way of naming the divide between the human and that which exceeds it: since the profane for Bataille is structured by labour and encompasses everything related to human activity and production – from philosophy to language to trade – the sacred is everything in excess of this sphere. It is the 'beyond' of experience, implied by the structure of the profane and conditioned by its limits. This 'beyond' encompasses alterity in all forms, including the mind of the other and the impossible experience of death; but most importantly for my purposes the sacred is also associated with nature, the unknowable outside of human consciousness. While we cannot move beyond our limits, Bataille argues that through sacrifice we can exceed the narrow logic of the profane and form a paradoxical relation to what is outside of human thought. Sacrifice is one of the ways that we can break from the logic that allows us to conceive of nature as subordinate to human reason.

Bataille's assertion of sacrifice as an ethical act is not meant to be taken literally and, in fact, one of his philosophical motivations is to avoid catastrophic expenditures such as war in favour of more ethical forms of sacrifice. One of the ways of doing this is by performing sacrifice through dramatization and art. Aesthetics also requires distance and mediation, so art, like sacrifice, allows us to witness the horror of death at a distance. He describes this connection between art and sacrifice in 'The Cruel Practice of Art':

> It is true that sacrifice is no longer a living institution, though it remains rather like a trace on a streaky window. But it is possible for us to experience the emotion it aroused, for the myths of sacrifice are like the themes of tragedy, and the Crucifixion keeps the image of sacrifice before us like a symbol offered to the most elevated reflections, and also as the most divine expression of the cruelty of art. However, sacrifice is not only this repeated image to which European civilization has given a sovereign value; it is the response to a secular obsession

among all the peoples of the globe. Indeed, if there is any truth to the idea that human life is a trap, can we think – it's strange, but so what? – that, since torture is 'universally offered to us as the bait,' reflecting on its fascination may enable us to discover what we are and to discover a higher world whose perspectives exceed the trap?[11]

This question remains, though the possibility of answering it is foreclosed to us after the death of God; instead of finding our way out of the trap, the practice of sacrifice can only trace the trap's edges. The obsessive return to sacrificial violence through art indicates an ache for transcendence, a longing for the sacred despite the impossibility of achieving or even conceptualizing it. Bataille's atheistic appropriation of sacrificial logic enacts what King calls the sacrifice of sacrifice in that Bataille colonizes sacrificial thought in order to break it apart. This fracturing of sacrificial logic leaves room for a new, non-transcendent kind of sacred, an excess of the rational that undermines its very structure and also exists not in some conceptualizable space beyond reason (like God or heaven) but only at the very limits of thought. The sacrifices in Wheatley's cinema also serve to sacrifice sacrifice, as they are enacted not in the name of a higher authority but rather as a disruptive force that breaks apart narrative formal logic in order to open onto something else. This deconstruction of narrative logic occurs through the central conflict between Christian rationalism and Pagan violence, a central theme that Wheatley borrows not only from history but also from traditions in British cinema. Wheatley's films effect a sacrifice-of-sacrifice that is cinematic rather than philosophical, appropriating the narrative logics of previous films in order to undermine their patriarchal and theological assumptions.

Paganism and British folk horror

Wheatley has been hailed in the popular press as 'one of British cinema's most singular voices,'[12] and scholarly interpretations of his work tend to read him in relation to familiar codes of genre and national identity. As a result, Wheatley's films are characterized as distinctly British and familiar in their appropriations of generic conventions.[13] However, these familiar patterns are destabilized in a number of ways, and Wheatley's films subvert audience expectations by undermining established interpretive frameworks; Adam Lowenstein goes as far as to suggest that 'we often wish we could find our way back to familiar cinematic spaces and genre codes to which we are accustomed, but Wheatley has gleefully erased the map and set the house on fire'.[14] Wheatley's cinema, then, interrogates a number of tensions central to British cinema and culture: genre convention and formal innovation, realism and excess, and romanticism and modernism. Rather than resolving these conflicts, however, Wheatley's cinema radically destabilizes them by undermining their associated expectations. If, as Andrew Higson argues,

> 'to identify a national cinema is first of all to specify a coherence and a unity'[15] – a process that Higson points out is necessarily fraught since this unity is continually contested by internal conflicts and contradictions – then Wheatley's cinema exploits the sense of unity suggested by familiar generic and aesthetic codes in order to obliterate any stable sense of meaning.

Reading Wheatley in relation to British cinema as a whole is beyond the scope of this book; however, reading his films in terms of their reinterpretation of folk horror will help to contextualize the theme of sacrifice in *Kill List* and *A Field in England*. Robert Macfarlane associates Wheatley, especially *A Field in England*, with a trend in contemporary British media towards a new 'English eerie' that works against the British pastoral tradition by provoking 'ideas of unsettlement and displacement'.[16] Macfarlane writes that the representation of the English countryside in *A Field in England* (and a number of other contemporary art works) reflects an unsettled relationship with history as well as anxieties about climate change and ecological catastrophe. The eeriness associated with the landscape in *A Field in England* is a way of reminding us that past violence cannot be buried under the earth, and that 'the skull beneath the skin of the English countryside' will always re-emerge.[17] While eeriness associated with the landscape in British media is nothing new – Macfarlane traces its historical lineage to writers MR James, Alan Garner and Susan Cooper, and to films such as *The Wicker Man* – he argues that there is something significant about its contemporary manifestations, which take on anxieties associated with the increasing threat of climate change in the twenty-first century. As such, Macfarlane's new English eerie gives an ecological slant to the broader trend of 'uncanny landscapes' in British film and media identified by Peter Hutchings; Hutchings writes that these landscapes unsettle pastoral codings of the countryside and express an uneasy relation between the past and present.[18] In

Wheatley's cinema, this takes the form of a conflict between modern masculine rationality and a repressed, violent paganism.

Kill List obviously borrows directly from *The Wicker Man*, and the general obsession with paganism in Wheatley's cinema is in part a nostalgic throwback to the folk revival of the 1960s and 1970s.[19] As Marcus Harmes discusses in his extensive survey of British horror from that period, folk horror resonated with the anti-authoritarian ideals of hippie culture at the same time as it expressed anxieties about the loss of social order represented by those ideals.[20] With *The Wicker Man*, for example, while it might seem as though 'the authority represented by Sergeant Howie (Edward Woodward) of the Highland Police is defeated by the sexualized paganism of the islanders of Summerisle',[21] in fact the Christian rationalism represented by Howie is merely replaced by a more potent pagan authority in Lord Summerisle (Christopher Lee). Howie's sacrifice at the end of the film is therefore performed not as an act of anti-authoritarian rebellion but rather in the service of a more primordial and sinister patriarch. A number of folk horror films from the period, including *Witchfinder General*, *Cry of the Banshee* (Gordon Hessler, 1970) and *The Blood on Satan's Claw* (Piers Haggard, 1971), were set during the English civil war, a period when authority was radically called into question; however, rather than affirming the liberating possibilities offered by the collapse of law and return to paganism, these films long for a return to the stabilizing influence of Christian paternal authority.[22] *Kill List* and *A Field in England* pick up on the anxieties central to folk horror, but rather than reaffirming the patriarchal authorities these earlier films call into question, Wheatley's films conclude with a radical sense of indeterminacy.

Irrational violence in *Kill List*

Given the resonances between folk horror and Wheatley's cinema, the obsession with paganism in Wheatley's films is a reference not only to Britain's pre-Christian history but also to the folk revival of the 1960s and 1970s. Wheatley, who grew up during this era and who explicitly states it as an influence, takes up the problematization of authority from the earlier cycle but revises it by radically undermining its re-repression of destabilizing forces. Thus, Wheatley's films can be read as post-theological in that they hold no nostalgia for the lawfulness of the past, nor do they look forward to the establishment of new forms of order. Existence in Wheatley is godless and groundless, subject not to higher powers but to the irrational contingency of the natural landscape. The sacrifices in Wheatley's films therefore *serve nothing*, because there is nothing for them to serve: rather than resolving narrative tensions or exposing truth, their sacrificial logics collapse the structures of narrative and meaning. Comparing *Kill List* with *The Wicker Man* clearly demonstrates this, because although the sacrifice that concludes the former was obviously inspired by the latter, it radically revises the formula by refusing the reassertion of patriarchal authority.

In *Kill List*, retired hitman Jay (Neil Maskell) is hired to do one last job. Jay and his partner Gal (Michael Smiley) follow the orders of a group of violent men with mysterious motivations and are given a 'kill list' that includes The Priest, The Librarian and The Member of Parliament. *Kill List* initially seems to follow the conventions of the contract killer genre, but it gradually begins to deviate from the formula and dissolve into chaos. The film hints at this descent towards disorder and violence in the beginning when, during a dinner party Gal's girlfriend Fiona (Emma Fryer) carves a cultish symbol – a cross with a triangle meeting at the top point, surrounded by a circle – in the back of the bathroom mirror. There are other ominous indications that the job is part of something more sinister than Jay and Gal first expect: Jay is coerced into signing his contract in blood, a deep wound that festers throughout the film; their victims appear to know Jay and thank him before they are killed; Jay's doctor is replaced by a strange man who also appears to know him and gives him cryptic advice rather than fixing his hand; and Jay's cat is killed and hung from his doorway after Gal and Jay try to back out of the mission. Unnerved by these unexplained events, Jay becomes increasingly agitated as he and Gal work through the list, and he strays from the cool professionalism of a hired gunman towards paranoia and psychosis.

The meaning of the symbol carved in the back of the mirror at the beginning of the film is revealed in the end, when Jay and Gal approach the home of the MP, their final target. The film's final act abandons the urban and suburban spaces of previous scenes as Jay and Gal head out into the countryside where the politician's mansion is located, and – as with all of Wheatley's films – this journey to nature is associated with pagan ritual and unbridled violence. Gal and Jay emerge from the woods surrounding the MP's mansion to find a group of masked cultists walking in procession towards a triangular structure resembling the cult symbol from the mirror. Their masks, made of broken twigs, are an obvious reference to the titular structure in *The Wicker Man* – an allusion that foreshadows the human sacrifice that follows. A noose hangs from the point of

Figure 3 Sacrifice in *Kill List* (Ben Wheatley, 2011).

the triangle, and the cultists look on as a robed young woman is hung from it. Jay, disturbed by the ritual, opens fire on the cultists. In the chaos that follows, Gal is disembowelled and Jay shoots him out of mercy; he then runs back to the house where his wife and son are hiding before being knocked unconscious. He wakes to find himself back in the woods, surrounded by cultists who hand him a knife and urge him to combat a cloaked figure called the Hunchback. After he stabs the figure repeatedly in the hump and chest, the cultists remove their masks, revealing Jay's employers, the doctor and Fiona. They remove the cloak and mask from the Hunchback, exposing Jay's son riding piggyback on his wife – a revelation that was foreshadowed in an earlier scene where Jay's son rode piggyback on Shel and pretended to battle Jay with a plastic sword. Shel, caked in blood, looks up at Jay and laughs as the cultists applaud and crown Jay with a circle of branches. The cult symbol flashes onscreen again before the title of the film appears and the credits roll.

The violence that concludes the film does not serve a clear purpose but rather plunges the film into narrative obscurity. By contrast, the sacrifice of Sergeant Howie at the end of *The Wicker Man* solves the mystery that structures the film: the girl whose disappearance Howie was investigating turns out to be alive, and Howie learns that she was not the victim of human sacrifice as he had begun to suspect but rather bait to lure him – their real target – to the island. The sacrifice of Howie also restores the status quo of the village, as its aim is to bring back a bountiful harvest and reinforce the leadership of Lord Summerisle. In *Kill List*, on the other hand, the sacrifice only further obfuscates the mystery and strips the central father figure of his power. Jay's unknowing sacrifice of his wife and son nihilistically undermines the family structure that serves as the impetus for the entire narrative – Jay's motivation to take up the job was to provide for his wife and son – and Shel's laughter at the end contradicts earlier images of her readying to do battle with the cultists. Was she in league with them all along? Was she convinced, or coerced? Why did the cultists select Jay? Did Gal know, since he thanks Jay before he dies just like the other victims? What does the cult want to gain through Jay's sacrifice of his family? While answers to these questions are possible (a Google search of '*Kill List* explained' reveals a number of plausible theories – it was all a dream, Jay is the Antichrist and so on), the film itself refuses to settle on a meaning. There are too many gaps and too many conflicting pieces of information for an easy interpretation, and the ending frustrated a number of viewers and critics who saw its violence and refusal of resolution as a pointless shock tactic.[23]

Rather than adhering to the linear progression of genre cinema, *Kill List*'s structure is doubled and symmetrical (a format that I will examine again in relation to Apichatpong, whose films also tend to be laid out in a two-act structure). Wheatley reveals in interviews that the hammer torture scene, which occurs midway through the film's runtime, forms a break in the narrative, after which events in the film begin to echo the first half: 'You've got a fold in the middle, the hammer attack at the 45 minute mark, and you've got the two hunchbacks at the beginning and end.'[24] Gal and Jay roughhousing during the dinner party is mirrored in a scene towards the end where they fight after discussing plans to kill the MP; the cultists in the woods recall an earlier scene where Jay and Gal encounter a group of Christians at dinner; Gal's protruding intestines evoke the eviscerated rabbit on Jay's lawn found earlier in the film. But *Kill List*'s symmetry is disrupted by small narrative and visual gaps as well as stylistic excesses that do not fit neatly into the film's balanced structure. Black frames are used as ellipses throughout the film, repeatedly giving the impression of missing information. Brutal violence is sometimes elided and sometimes shown in graphic detail, and the shock of the latter is intensified because the viewer is left uncertain about what is going to be shown and what is going to be concealed.

In the hammer scene, for example, Jay and Gal discover videotapes containing unseen horrors in the possession of the Librarian. While the contents of the videotapes are concealed from the viewer – the television screen faces away from the camera while the two men watch – the torture that follows is shown in graphic detail. After burning the Librarian with a cigarette, Jay takes a hammer out of the toolbox on the table, and the camera cuts to his face as he begins

46   *Limit Cinema*

hammering the Librarian in the knee; the camera then tilts down to reveal the impact before tilting back up again to show the Librarian's reaction. This rhythm of graphic onscreen violence followed by a reaction shot continues for several moments, but when Jay eventually hammers the Librarian's head in, there is no interluding cutaway or tilt, and this break in the rhythm intensifies the shocking effect of bone and brain matter spraying up from the Librarian's skull. Describing the scene, Wheatley says that this editing pattern was intended to betray the spectator's expectations and trust:

> The main idea from all that was from seeing *The Orphanage* [Juan Antonio Bayona 2007], when they run over the old lady in the beginning and they do the cut away from it, you don't see it and you go: 'Oh, that's okay, we're not going to see it.' And then they cut back a little bit and you go: 'Okay, I've seen this now, they won't go back for another go on this.' And then they cut back and when her jaw falls off, it's just like: 'Oh f**king hell, no! Why did you do that? You already told the story of the woman being dead, you didn't have to do that!' But it's so clever, because it basically says: 'Alright, we've shown you this, we can basically show you anything now.'[25]

By creating tension between revealing and obscuring the shock of unrestrained violence, *Kill List* gives rise to a frightening sense of possibility. The escalation of violence following the Librarian scene exploits this tension and gives the impression that the film has spiralled out of control; the film's violence is excessive not only in terms of its graphic representation but also in its disruption of the film's narrative structure. By refusing to re-repress these excesses in the form of a satisfying narrative resolution, *Kill List* insists on the shocking irrationality of violence rather than providing it with a framework that would grant it validation or meaning.

Because *Kill List*'s doubled events and images refuse in the end to be reconciled into a singular meaning, the film concludes with a frustrating and uncanny sense of circularity. Uncanniness is the Freudian term for the familiar-turned-unfamiliar, and potentially accounts for many of the frustrated reactions to the film's ending: while the first act leads the viewer to expect the logic and linearity of genre, what we end up with is the irrational circularity of dream logic. (Wheatley compares his non-linear approach to David Lynch, whose films operate similarly in this respect.[26]) The rationality implied by the generic framework that guides the first half of the narrative as well as by the titular idea of the 'list' is subverted in the last half, replaced by the uncanniness of empty

Sacrifice and the Sacred in Weerasethakul and Wheatley 47

repetition. As in a dream, repeated events do not gesture towards an overarching explanation but rather to a disturbing feeling of something being amiss in a way we do not understand; Freud links the uncanny to repeated events and the recurrence of random numbers, which give the sense of a foreclosed meaning though none can rationally be discerned. This narratively unsatisfied insistence on doubled events and images finds resonance in Bataillean dualist materialism, which also insists on holding two sides in suspension:

> Dualism itself, as a doctrine, never relinquishes the untenable position it imposes upon the one enticed by it, keeping him in a never resolved dissatisfaction. According to Bataille, this simply results from the fact that one must choose between a perfection which, satisfying the mind, definitely puts it to sleep, and the awakening which requires an ever unresolved dissatisfaction.[27]

Wheatley makes a similar point when he expresses his distaste for exposition, asserting that 'if you give additional context where it isn't needed people just shut off'.[28] While a satisfying reading of *Kill List* is not impossible, doing so domesticates the excesses that make the ending so impactful, and the fact that multiple interpretations are possible undermines any efforts to find a singular underlying truth. What we are left with, then, is an irrational and violent excess associated with pagan ritual.

In contrast to Christian eschatology, paganism finds the sacred in the material. The pantheistic theology characteristic of many types of European paganism identifies the divine with nature, foreclosing a realm beyond this one and instead locating the sacred in the natural environment. This folding inward of the sacred and its association with nature rather than a singular god provides a form of resistance to the rationalist view that subjugates nature to human will and understanding. If we locate a force in this world beyond human comprehension, then there will always be something about reality that evades us, and pagan pantheism resonates strongly with the Bataillean conception of the sacred as found not in a realm beyond this one but rather at the limits of human thought. This is not to conflate Bataille or Wheatley with pagan mysticism, however, since such a reading reduces aporetic dualism into a singular positive theology; the point is not to replace Christian salvation with the divine presence of nature, but to set these systems against each other to frustrate any claim to underlying truth. In directing itself towards the pagan landscape, Jay's sacrifice of his family subverts the Western/Christian conception of sacrifice as transcendent or meaningful. But the sacrifice has no clear link to a non-transcendent positive outcome either, unlike the sacrifice in *The Wicker Man*, which is performed in order to ensure a successful autumn harvest and thereby re-subsume nature under human control. By refuting clear links to truth, salvation or resolution, Jay's sacrifice directs itself instead towards a terrifying and groundless excess that cannot be contained or domesticated.

Circularity in *A Field in England*

The circular logic of *Kill List* and the trope of sacrifice-for-nothing carry over into *A Field in England*, which does not slip gradually into irrationality and violence but rather begins in a state where law and order have already collapsed. The film is set in the mid-seventeenth century, and Wheatley has stated that he is interested in the period because 'at that moment in England, anything could have happened. Everyone was starving, and they were basically killing God, because they were killing the king, God's representative; they were writing their own rules.'[29] If *Kill List* takes its cue from *The Wicker Man*, then *A Field in England* follows from *Witchfinder General*, a film that similarly explores the lawlessness of the English civil war. But while *Witchfinder General* remains resolutely (albeit nihilistically) humanist in its insistence on evil as an explainable human phenomenon – the witch-hunt in the film is an assertion of patriarchal misogyny rather than a response to natural forces spun out of control – *A Field in England* expands its scope beyond the violence underlying human interactions. Rather than staging its conflicts between two sides of a war or between the oppressed and their oppressors, the central opposition in *A Field in England* is between humans and their landscape. Comments from the characters like 'there are no sides here' and 'forward is back, tis all the same' suggest that the field where the film takes place is beyond human power structures, a location where the rules can be turned upside down. The collapse of civilization in *A Field in England* is not a precursor to revolution where tensions might be resolved and new rulers (even cruel ones) instated, but is rather an event that leaves room for forces in excess of human reason to surge up through the cracks.

A Field in England follows a group of army deserters as they traverse a field in search of an alehouse. Cowardly alchemist's assistant Whitehead (Reece Shearsmith) escapes from his commander and encounters Jacob (Peter Ferdinando) and Cutler (Ryan Pope). Cutler convinces the men to desert and follow him to an alehouse over the hill, and at the mention of ale a nearby corpse – named Friend (Richard Cutler) – regains consciousness. The men, except for pious Whitehead, eat a stew laced with psilocybin mushrooms and then summon sinister Irishman O'Neil (Michael Smiley) by pulling on a long rope attached to a carved rowan pole. O'Neil coerces the men into digging for a treasure he believes is buried in the field, and the film's logic becomes increasingly obscure as characters converse about God, descend into violence and come back from the dead. Eventually, the treasure is revealed to be nothing but a skull and all but Whitehead are brutally killed. Perhaps because of its more anarchic setting, *A Field in England* is Wheatley's most artistic film in that it strays the furthest from generic conventions and engages the most in visual and formal experimentation. The black-and-white cinematography frequently pauses on natural details: there are close-ups of insects crawling up dewy leaves, slow-motion shots of long grass blowing in the wind, and extreme long shots dwarfing human characters in a wide landscape of field and sky. The aesthetic appeal of these shots is undercut by a sense of menace and brutality, and low thrums on the soundtrack and frequent eruptions of graphic violence evoke a landscape that is anything but pastoral. The field in *A Field in England* where the entirety of the action takes place is a liminal space where the rules of time and causality do not apply, a location that at once strictly limits the actions of the characters and also opens limitless possibilities because it is beyond law and order. The hedgerow that Whitehead crawls over at the beginning of the film while attempting to escape his commander contains the space of the narrative and eventually proves to be inescapable: in the film's final moments, Whitehead attempts to cross back over the hedgerow only to re-emerge in the field with his deceased comrades standing before him. A shot of Cutler and Friend recalls an apparition from the beginning of the film, of two figures standing in a cloud of dust. Whitehead had dismissed that vision as 'only shadows', and its echo in the end implies that the field is delimited and circular both in terms of time and space, as the past appears inexplicably haunted by future events. This unsurpassable limit conditioned by irrational nonhuman forces is an effective image of the sacred because the field characterizes nature as in excess of reason but only conceivable within certain inescapable boundaries.

The editing and framing of *A Field in England* call attention to the nonhuman by destabilizing relations between human figures and the field that surrounds them. Shot scale often moves abruptly between extreme close-ups of details in the landscape and extreme long shots that diminish the human figure in relation to a wide horizon and open sky. In his essay 'Uncanny Landscapes', Jean-Luc

Nancy associates the framing of figures lost in landscapes with post-theology and the disappearance of the gods. He writes that 'landscape begins when it absorbs or dissolves all presences into itself: those of gods or of princes, and also the presence of the peasant'.[30] Landscape painting for Nancy is inherently post-theological in that it is 'an affirmation that the divine, if it presents itself in some way, certainly does not present itself as a presence or as a representation, nor as an absence hidden behind or within the depths of nature (another form of presence), but as the withdrawal of the divine itself'.[31] There is no hidden meaning in the landscape; for Nancy it is written entirely on its surface, which evokes a groundless landscape that swallows up the human figure. The extreme long shots in *A Field in England* are similarly disorienting in that they do not clarify space or anticipate action, nor are they based on human scale.

Positioned in relation to an environment that exceeds them, the characters fall prey to forces beyond comprehension and, within the boundaries of the field, strange occult forces begin to manifest and drive the characters towards confusion and violence. O'Neil is characterized as the darker pagan counterpart to Whitehead's pious Christianity: Friend refers to him as the devil, he threatens to use spells on the men to turn them into frogs, and he uses a scrying mirror and divination spells to control the men and find the treasure. His hat, billowing cloak and buttoned waistcoat are a subtle reference to Michael Hopkins (Vincent Price) from *Witchfinder General*, an association that aligns him with masculine evil: *A Field in England* subverts traditional links between nature, paganism and femininity, an association that *Witchfinder General* exposes as being easily exploited in order to subjugate women. Women are entirely absent from *A Field in England* – though like most of Wheatley's films it was written by a woman, his partner Amy Jump – and the film troubles masculine power to the point of absurdity rather than exposing or rewriting its systems of domination. Unlike its predecessor, *A Field in England* does not allow for the troubling reassertion of a violent patriarchal system but rather undermines masculinity by framing its struggle in relation to an indifferent landscape. Whitehead captures O'Neil only to have O'Neil turn it around and capture Whitehead instead; Friend aligns himself with Whitehead and Jacob, but after being killed and resurrected again he betrays their location to O'Neil; Cutler turns against O'Neil after the treasure is revealed to be nothing but 'dirt and old bones' and O'Neil shoots him in the face in retribution. The state of nature where the men find themselves is Hobbesian in its brutality and senselessness, and their petty battles mean nothing when framed in the absurd circular logic of the field.

The film's irrational logic draws on the influence of the mushroom circle, a reference drawn from British folklore. According to Wheatley, 'within [a mushroom circle] time moves at a different speed. The lore is that if you go into a circle it takes four men and a rope to pull you out and although you feel that weeks may have passed – it could be minutes in real time'.[32] After being pulled from a mushroom circle, O'Neil remarks that 'the world is turned upside down', a comment that applies equally to the political state in England as well as the formal logic of the film: shots are inverted, the 180-degree rule is repeatedly broken and at one point there is a long psychedelic sequence where past and future images from the film are looped together in kaleidoscopic patterns. This suspension of cinematic and narrative laws leads not to a utopic sense of infinite possibility, but rather, as with *Kill List*, a menacing sense of circularity. The disorientation created by non-continuity editing and the layering of past and future events enhances the sense of being delimited by forces beyond comprehension, a feeling emphasized by the film's circular conclusion. *A Field in England* creates the sense of being trapped within an inescapable space and beholden to forces beyond what we can understand, which is an apt metaphor for the problem of anthropocentrism.

The irrational, circular logic of *A Field in England* intensifies the senselessness of the sacrifice that structures it. The death and repeated resurrection of the character Friend establishes him as a kind of Christ figure, an association strengthened further by the metaphoric weight of his name and the repeated references to God and the Bible throughout the film. However, this association

Figure 4 Disorientation and nonhuman scale in *A Field in England* (Ben Wheatley, 2013).

with Christ, the ultimate Western sacrificial figure, is also turned upside down and rendered radically senseless. Friend is a thoroughly ambiguous figure, at once endearing for his stupidity and detestable for his cruelty. When he is accidentally shot by Cutler, he asks Jacob to deliver a message to his wife, but instead of passing on his love, he asks Jacob to tell her that he hates her, and that he loved her sister – whom he had 'many times, from behind like a beautiful prize sow'. Further, Friend is resolutely an earthly figure with no link to a transcendent beyond; when asked by Whitehead if he knows about celestial bodies, 'those things that hang above us', Friend replies that he has never looked up because it sounds badly paid. If the seventeenth century was a time when God was dead, then the potential for salvation was rendered impossible; the death and resurrection of Friend, like the sacrifice of Jay's family in *Kill List*, is therefore an empty, repetitive gesture.

The only revelation effected by sacrifice in *A Field in England* is death. After Friend is killed for the second time, Whitehead drags his corpse through the field and sees an ominous black orb growing in the sky. Cutler digs frantically in the hole for the treasure, and a loud clang is heard as he hits a skull with his shovel. This 'skull beneath the skin of the English countryside' (to recall Macfarlane) refers back to another folk horror, *The Blood on Satan's Claw*, in which a skull unearthed in a village incites demonic possession among the villagers. While that film rids the village of the curse by destroying the bones of the satanic beast, in *A Field in England* there is no escaping death. The empty repetition of sacrifice only defers it; the 'not yet' is approached at a distance but never quite appropriated, never granted meaning because death is the moment when meaning is lost. It is this endless deferral of meaning through sacrifice that I argue is the image of the sacred found in Wheatley. Without external grounding or justification, sacrifice loses its meaning – or, rather, it is the very loss of meaning. *Kill List* and *A Field in England* embrace the terrors of this collapse into senselessness; however, a post-theological understanding of the sacred need not be so pessimistic. While the beautiful imagery of *A Field in England* and Wheatley's other films hint towards some of the creative possibilities of Bataillean aesthetics by adding an element of positive affect to otherwise very bleak narratives, the emphasis on death and violence through the theme of sacrifice prevents Wheatley's films from making any positive statement about our post-theological condition. The films of Apichatpong, on the other hand, demonstrate that post-theological aesthetics need not be so pessimistic. The loss of any external truth leaves open the opportunity to

Sacrifice and the Sacred in Weerasethakul and Wheatley   53

create our own ways forward, and Apichatpong's films pose an alternative to Wheatley's nihilism through an excessive aesthetic of eroticism.

Ambivalent Apichatpong

Apichatpong's cinema, like Wheatley's, is characterized by destabilizing stylistic and narrative excess. While the English landscape in Wheatley's films differs radically from Apichatpong's untamed jungle, both film-makers oppose traditional pastoral/romantic notions of their respective nations' countryside and instead evoke the natural as an irrational force beyond human control. A number of scholars have commented on a quality of 'in-betweenness' in Apichatpong's cinema tied to his construction of landscape, taking note of the ways that his films move between the margins of city/country, animal/human, Buddhism/animism and East/West. As David Teh argues, these wanderings construct an 'itinerant cinema' that reflects on the cultural and political history of Thailand, particularly the north-eastern Isaan region where Apichatpong lives and grew up.[33] Teh argues that Apichatpong's ambiguities, more than merely constituting an aesthetic refusal of meaning, reflect a deep political ambivalence while also evoking the marginal identity of Isaan, which is 'buffeted between three spheres of influence: Khmer to the east; Lao kingdoms to the north (with whom it has close ethno-linguistic ties); and the central Siamese lowland powers, shifting south from Sukhothai (thirteenth to fifteenth centuries), through Ayutthaya (fifteenth to eighteenth centuries), to Thonburi and Bangkok (1768 to the present).'[34] While Apichatpong avoids explicit political commentary, Teh argues that the narrative ambiguities of his films are tied to this cultural history of marginalization, and that Apichatpong combines Surrealist strategies with Thai storytelling conventions to obfuscate straightforward readings: 'his [Apichatpong's] subjects tend not to represent one or the other position, but usually both, an imbrication of identities that short-circuits attribution to a singular ethnicity or political stance.'[35] Other scholars have read liminality in Apichatpong through an ecocritical rather than political lens: Seung-hoon Jeong argues that the shifting perspectives in Apichatpong evoke nature as 'not simply organic in its totality or antagonistic to humans, but deeply antagonistic and even indifferent to itself' and reads Apichatpong's work as largely functioning through negativity;[36] Una Chung, on the other hand, reads Apichatpong's work more positively, arguing that it 'moves beyond horror' through reincarnation and transformation.[37] That Apichatpong's work can be read as constructing either a negative project (Jeong) or a positive one (Chung) is testament to a profound ambivalence inherent in his aesthetics, and all of the above scholars see Apichatpong's films as evoking a boundary or border zone.

While these scholars emphasize the political stakes of Apichatpong's ambiguity by tying it to self/other relations (human/animal, Isaan/Bangkok), I want to shift the focus to discuss *how* exactly this relation operates. Relations between self and other in Apichatpong's films are staged in erotic terms, and this eroticism has only been tangentially considered in the scholarship on Apichatpong thus far. While Wheatley stages the relations between humans and their landscapes in terms of violence, Apichatpong envisions these interactions as sensuous and intensely erotic. Sex in Apichatpong is always outdoors and often interspecies, and his films represent the erotic encounter as an experience that blurs boundaries between the human and the natural. As with Wheatley, these interactions between humans and their environment are framed in religious terms: for Apichatpong, modern Buddhism is interlaid with earlier folk traditions that inform the representation of the natural landscape. Apichatpong uses Buddhist themes and imagery but places them in a resolutely earthly, quotidian context. Reading the religious themes of Apichatpong's films alongside their erotic content, I argue that the sacred in Apichatpong is linked to an erotic encounter with nature. Focusing in particular on *Syndromes and a Century*, *Tropical Malady* and *Uncle Boonmee*, the following sections will explore the ways that nature is represented as sacred but non-transcendent, linked to human experience and memory of the natural landscape.

Most of Apichatpong's films take on a bisected structure that operates along a nature/culture divide. His first film to take this approach, *Blissfully Yours* (2002), begins with an extended city sequence, and only after the two central characters enter the countryside forty-five minutes into the film do the opening credits appear. While the city sequence is shot in comparatively drab tones, the jungle sequences are sensuous and lush: the sun creates deep shadows in the green foliage where characters sleep, eat, swim and have sex. This erotic sensuality tied to the jungle is also apparent in *Tropical Malady*, but the jungle becomes more than a stage for human sexual relationships: the second half of the film envisions an erotic encounter not between humans but rather between a human and the jungle itself. Apichatpong has linked the two-act structures of his films to Buddhist reincarnation, and the doubled storylines of his films reflect on themes of memory and embodiment. These themes explore what Apichatpong refers to as the transmigration of souls: 'I like the idea of the transmigration of souls,' he explains, 'but I can't say I believe in something until it's proven.'[38] As Chung suggests, instead of shocking us into recognizing irrecuperable alterity, Apichatpong's alternative aesthetic of transformation and reincarnation moves between 'the viral passage among human, animal, machine, god, and ghost, who appear through the action of birth, death, and rebirth.'[39] The two-act structures of Apichatpong's films represent impossible encounters through an erotic aesthetic that emphasizes affect and sensuality, and in *Tropical Malady*, the bisected structure can be read as depicting two versions of the same love story: in the first, soldier Keng (Banlop Lomnoi) meets Tong (Sakda Kaewbuadee), a quiet boy from the village where Keng is stationed; in the second, a soldier also played by Banlop Lomnoi chases a tiger spirit – who sometimes appears as Sakda Kaewbuadee in tiger make-up and sometimes as a real tiger – deeper and deeper into the jungle.

The two sets of relationships reflect in different ways on the difficulties of love, as the fascination with the other in Apichatpong is necessarily predicated on difference and unknowability, and is always transient or impermanent. At the end of *Blissfully Yours*, a title card reveals that the film's central couple – Roong (Kanokporn Tongaram), a young factory worker, and Min (Min Oo), an illegal Burmese immigrant – have split up and Roong has gone back to her previous boyfriend. The end of the first section of *Tropical Malady* ends with Tong's disappearance and Keng's attempts to locate him, while the second section ends with Keng staring down the tiger-ghost, caught in suspension between killing him or being eaten; a monkey speaking from a tree in an earlier scene had instructed Keng to either 'kill him to free him from the ghost world, or let him devour you to enter his world'. The Hegelian struggle-to-the-death that marks the end of *Tropical Malady* is left in a state of indeterminacy: neither the man nor the ghost is dominated, and in the end, both are left exposed to the other, trembling in the dark and caught in each other's gaze. If, for G. W. F. Hegel, self-consciousness depends on the outcome of the struggle – on the recognition of the other – then *Tropical Malady* concludes right at the limit of this self-consciousness, the instant before the subject is complete and aware. This zone of indeterminacy is the Bataillean erotic moment, which desires 'to bring into a world founded on discontinuity all the continuity such a world can contain'.[40] The erotic for Bataille is always impermanent and dangerous, and, because it longs to join the discontinuous subject with a continuous world, eroticism cannot be sustained without risking the death of the subject. While the erotic is dangerous, however, for Bataille it is also necessary, to the point where Bataille argues that a theory of humankind cannot be constructed without it. Eroticism is one of the names Bataille gives to the problem of inner experience: he writes that 'we fail to realize this because man is everlastingly in search of an object *outside* himself but this object answers the *innerness* of the desire'.[41] The longing to overcome oneself and become continuous with the world – the Bataillean version of the death drive in that its complete accomplishment is the annihilation of the subject – is the basis for the desire to connect with another, either physically through sex or more abstractly through communication.

The impossibility of this desire is the result of the paradox of inner experience: the desire to be outside the self can only come from within it, since the self is the very thing that constructs the limit between inside and outside. Once the desire is fulfilled, there is no longer a subject to desire it. We can only grasp shadows of this exteriority in the moments when the integrity of our self-hood is risked, either at the moment of death or at the moment when we encounter the other. While this process is dangerous, it is also intensely life affirming, and Bataille argues that the broadest definition of eroticism 'is assenting to life up to the point of death'.[42] The erotic encounter with alterity paradoxically affirms the subject as self-enclosed because, as discussed in the last chapter, ipseity or self-identity can only occur as conditioned by an outside (non-identity). During the erotic encounter, the subject confronts the limit between inside and outside, and is therefore suspended between the affirmation of its self-enclosure and its negation in the presence of the other. This limit can only be held temporarily before it falls back on one side or the other: either the paroxysm subsides and the subject retreats back into its self-enclosure or the limit is transgressed and the subject is annihilated.

These paradoxes of inner experience and the subject's encounter with alterity are reflected in the ambiguous ending of *Tropical Malady*, which refuses to settle the question of kill-or-be-killed. Jeong writes that this ambiguity articulates a nonanthropomorphic ethics of the animal, arguing that the tiger's 'animal gaze destabilizes the frame of nature vs. culture and seemingly addresses the man in an unheard inhuman voice'.[43] The ethics of this encounter, which the film suggests can only be resolved when the man kills or is eaten, are cyclical: as Jeong points out, the tiger-ghost that Tong has become is presumably the same tiger that was implied to have eaten him in the city sequence.[44] By conflating romantic love with the relationship between humans and nature, *Tropical Malady* suggests that the stakes of eroticism are ecological as well as intersubjective: the loss of the self in the other is analogous to humankind's relationship with the natural world. Bataille, too, draws this comparison, as he begins his theory of human sexuality with the reproduction of single-celled organisms and continues to draw parallels between erotic desire and the birth, death and decay of animal populations.[45] As a name for a non-rational encounter with alterity, eroticism provides a way of thinking beyond anthropocentrism: it acknowledges that the limits demarcating nature from culture are always constructed from within.

The shadowy ambiguities of the erotic encounter are reflected in *Tropical Malady*'s jungle aesthetics. The boundaries between Keng's body and the surrounding jungle begin to blur as he tracks the tiger-ghost through the forest: the camouflage of his fatigues blends in with the sun-dappled foliage, and as he stalks deeper into the jungle, he becomes more exposed and permeable to his environment. As Keng's body responds to the jungle humidity, the artificial pairing between his army fatigues and the forest generally fades into a moister, more organic indistinction – he sweats, defecates and becomes muddy. But while this porous exchange between Keng's flesh and his environment is sensuous, even erotic, it is also dangerous: his body is penetrated by the bites of insects, sharp branches and rocks, and red trickles of blood mingle with beads of sweat and caked-on mud. This intense affectivity contrasts with the more reserved city sequences, and the restrained static long shots in the first half are replaced in the second by a wandering camera that spreads into the space of the jungle and pauses often in close-up on various sensual details. This increasing sense of intimacy also affects the relationship between Keng and Tong, and while their romance in the first half is shy and tentative, in the second half they are drawn together more viscerally: 'He can smell you from mountains away', the monkey tells Keng. Keng's confrontations with the tiger spirit are marked equally by fascination and violence and, at one point, Keng runs into the spirit in his anthropomorphic state and chases him into a clearing; the two figures are shot from a distance, the outlines of their bodies blurred and ghostly as they grapple with each other in the long grass. Keng is eventually thrown down a cliff, rocks and earth tumbling around him; the spirit then looks down at him from above as he examines his bloodied palms. If we read the second half as an echo of the first – a transmigration of the men's souls – then these interactions can be seen as a way of making explicit the risk of annihilation at the heart of erotic desire, and the tentative back and forth of sexual attraction is paralleled with a mutual fascination between predator and prey. Consummation becomes consumption; the more metaphorical expenditure of being that constitutes the sexual act is paralleled by the literal expenditure of killing and eating that characterizes animal existence in the jungle.

This emphasis on the permeability of the body that simultaneously enhances awareness of the body's boundaries is evoked not only visually but also through sound. Philippa Lovatt calls attention to the ways that *Tropical Malady* de-emphasizes the voice and heightens ambient sounds to increase their affective impact: 'the sound of the environment is often so dominant that it dismantles our reliance on the verbal or linguistic to ground our understanding of what is happening in the narrative, and instead encourages (or rather insists upon) an embodied, phenomenological engagement with the scene'.[46] For Lovatt, sound in Apichatpong helps bring us outside of ourselves; in Bataillean terms, this process is erotic in that the hapticity of heightened ambient sound is linked to the desire for continuity between body and world. This haptic reading suggests that sound can bring the spectator in more immediate contact with the outside world represented on film. As with everything that brings us outside, however, sound also brings us right back in, reverberating off the limits of our experience; Timothy Morton draws from this paradox in *Ecology Without Nature* to analyse the effects of ambient noise: he writes that the intimate qualities of sound waves, which 'vibrate air, which vibrates the body',[47] promise a more immediate interaction with the environment; however, because sound

Figure 5 Blending in with the jungle in *Tropical Malady* (Apichatpong Weerasethakul, 2004).

Sacrifice and the Sacred in Weerasethakul and Wheatley   59

is necessarily experienced sensually, 'ambient art misses the genuine unknown, which would consist of radical non-identity'.[48] The outside brought to sensory experience inevitably turns inward, losing what characterized it as external in the first place. The ambient noises in *Tropical Malady* reflect this aporia, because by destabilizing the rationalizing framework of the voice they call attention to a sensuous reality in excess of the human; however, the very sensuousness that evokes this reality emphasizes that we can only experience the outside world in human terms. The recognition of this aporia is the basis for Morton's ecological ethics, and *Tropical Malady* hangs on the limit between these perspectives by stopping its narrative right at the point before the inside turns outside – at the moment before death.

Desublimating the sacred

The ambiguities of embodiment and desire in *Tropical Malady* map onto the divide between the human and the animal; these lines become fluid as the two halves of the film divide from each other and reconverge through repeated themes and images. Themes of reincarnation and memory across Apichatpong's cinema indicate an ambiguity between not only the human and the animal but also the real world and spirit world. The spirit world in Apichatpong's cinema is always folded into this reality rather than being pushed beyond its boundaries, and ghosts are often a metaphor for how the past is embedded in the present. Apichatpong's films reflect this folding-inward of the sacred by desublimating religious imagery and bringing the spiritual into the everyday. Apichatpong's ghosts inhabit the same world as his people and animals and are generally shot in the same way, indicating that the sacred is material, folded into this world rather than being deferred to one beyond. This conception of the sacred as immanent to this world rather than transcending it reflects the animist traditions from which Apichatpong borrows: for animist cosmology, there is no separation between the real and the spiritual, and nonhuman entities in the world possess a spiritual nature beyond what we can understand. Animism also implies the possibility of engaging with the sacred on a sensual rather than rational or spiritual level, and the erotic encounters between humans and animals in Apichatpong's films reflect this possibility by providing an alternative method for engaging with the natural world, one predicated on an ecstatic, irrational, sensuous exchange rather than on use and subordination.

60   *Limit Cinema*

Apichatpong links the animist influences of *Uncle Boonmee* to north-eastern Thailand and says that its traditions differ from mainstream Thai culture:

> Before Siam became Thailand the country had several communities, tribes, and the north-east has more the influence of Laos and Cambodia. It's a very animistic society, more Hindu. More about magic, sorcery, witchcraft. For this film I use a dialect of the area, very close to Laotian. So if you showed this film in Bangkok, many or most people might not understand.[49]

A number of scholars have expanded on the links between Apichatpong's films and north-eastern animist folklore. Teh writes that while Western commentators are quick to draw out the Buddhist influences on Apichatpong's work, they miss the more complex regional history where Buddhism was imposed 'somewhat against the grain of an animist substrate',[50] and that the opposition between matriarchal-syncretic animism and patriarchal-monological Buddhism provides a more nuanced framework for considering Apichatpong's films. May Adadol Ingawanij argues that Apichatpong's animism indicates an alternative cinematic ontology – a new realism – which draws on 'the property of film image as trace, or a material record of contingent details in excess of the narrative system' to construct the world as a constant flux of disparate parts.[51] Both scholars tie Apichatpong's animist aesthetics to the conflicted politics of north-eastern Thailand, a legacy picked up in Apichatpong's films through frequent references to war and anti-communist violence that have marked the region's recent past. As Ingawanij points out, Apichatpong evokes these political issues obliquely, 'training his gaze lower and further to the ground';[52] his emphasis on the materiality of the everyday insists on contingencies that refuse to be subordinated to a totalizing grand narrative.

The materiality of the natural world in Apichatpong's cinema is inflected with forces beyond reason, an excess of style and narrative that emits from the landscape and resists straightforward interpretation. *Uncle Boonmee* begins with a picture of murky twilight, the 16mm image blurring together the lush jungle blues and greens. A cow stands tethered to a tree and impatiently resists its rope. It escapes and wanders through the forest until it is found by a farmer; the silhouette of an ape-like creature with glowing red eyes observes as the cow is led back towards the farm. The titles appear, after which we do not see the cow again. The connection between the cow sequence and the central narrative, which focuses on Boonmee's encounters with the ghosts of his family before he dies, is left unclear, as are the relationships between other side stories throughout the film. The cow might be Boonmee in a past life, or it might be another inhabitant of the jungle surrounding his house where the monkey ghosts live. It might simply be a reminder of the animal gaze. In *Uncle Boonmee*'s crepuscular jungle, the animal world interpenetrates the human; it is depicted as utterly alien and yet inexorably connected to human activities and perspectives.

Two later scenes similarly highlight the interpenetration of the human and the animal, and explicitly reinforce the eroticism of such engagements. In the first, a princess (who is unconnected to the central narrative) stops at a pool underneath a waterfall. There, she meets and is seduced by a catfish, who swims between her legs as she tilts her head back in ecstasy. In the second, one of the monkey creatures from the opening scene arrives on Boonmee's porch and explains that he is Boonmee's long-lost son, Boonsong; Boonsong recounts that he transformed after mating with a monkey ghost he had followed into the jungle. Boonsong's story makes literal the erotic dissolution of self into other because, in coming to know the monkey ghost, he grew to forget his humanity. Both of these erotic encounters with nature provide a model based on sensuous exchange rather than subordination. Eroticism is the impossible desire to know the other, but such an exchange is only approachable if we risk being exposed to the other in turn, and this exposure is a (non)relation to the outside – a form of communication with the sacred. The final shot of the princess interlude alludes to this nonhuman economy: the princess's jewellery, shot from the catfish's

Figure 6 Crepuscular jungle in *Uncle Boonmee Who Can Recall His Past Lives* (Apichatpong Weerasethakul, 2010).

62   *Limit Cinema*

perspective, sinks to the bottom of the pool. As sacrificial objects, these jewels are wasted and therefore rendered sacred, divorced from the human logic of production.

The fluid natural world of *Uncle Boonmee* contrasts with the rigid linearity of *Syndromes and a Century*. *Syndromes*, like Apichatpong's other works, takes on a two-act structure split between rural and urban spaces. Both sections of the film contain the same actors playing the same sets of characters, which include two doctors (one man, one woman), a dentist, an old monk and a young monk. The parts each begin the same way, with Dr Toey (Nantarat Sawaddikul) interviewing Dr Nohng (Jaruchai Iamaram) for a position in the hospital. Her questions and his answers remain more or less identical; only the settings and perspective are different, as the first takes place in a comfortable country office surrounded by lush gardens, and the second takes place in a sleek white high-rise office with a city view and stainless-steel fixtures. The first sequence is shot primarily from Dr Toey's point of view as Dr Nohng answers her questions; the second sequence reverses the gaze as Nohng observes Toey's reactions to his responses. The repeated events give the uncanny impression of an echoed memory or a dream – a feeling of déjà vu without a clear narrative purpose. As with *Uncle Boonmee*, it is unclear how the different parts of the story are connected: they seem to be separated by time as well as space, as though the characters have been transposed into the future only to be irrevocably connected to their past. *Syndromes and a Century* is narratively structured not through clear cause and effect but rather through the idea of reincarnation, as traces of the past are left on the present and characters shift perspectives but circle back through their earthly existences.

Circles and straight lines make up most of the diegetic world of *Syndromes*, in sharp contrast to the unruly wildness of Apichatpong's previous films. When asked about his favourite shape, Dr Nohng replies 'a circle', round and smooth like the bottom of a glass, and both halves of the film feature a number of circular images: a solar eclipse, the mouth of a pipe, a remote-control flying saucer. These images are poetic and metonymic, linking the two halves of the film by association rather than cause and effect. In both halves, the mise en scène is characterized by the stark rigid lines of long hallways: people stand upright and move in straight lines, or else they sit in rigid chairs, unlike in Apichatpong's previous films, in which characters frequently crouch, kneel, look upwards and lay down. As though unsettled by these new linear environments, the camera moves more than it usually does in Apichatpong's cinema, swinging from side to side and frequently wandering away from the action. Just as the camera resists the linearity of the hospital environment, a wild orchid growing in the country hospital stands as a small symbolic reminder of the disorder of nature: an orchid seller explains to the hospital director that the orchid is precious precisely because it is 'not so pretty' and 'seems to lack form and order'. This contrast between smooth lines and unruly disorder is not a dialectical relation of opposites; instead, the human and the natural interpenetrate each other, like the roots of the orchid growing up through the hospital walls.

Syndromes is quiet and contemplative, and it is therefore perhaps surprising that it was the most controversial of Apichatpong's films upon its release in Thailand. The film was released as a new censorship law was being drafted with a restrictive ratings structure that allowed the government to maintain the right to censor and ban films, and *Syndromes* drew national media attention as Apichatpong protested the censorship of four scenes, and then refused to screen it in its censored state (it was later screened with the four scenes replaced by black screens and silence of equal duration). While *Syndromes* was met with shock and outrage, the scenes at issue are resolutely mundane, censored not because they represent excessive violence or sexuality (according to Apichatpong, the fact that one of the monks is gay was not a factor[53]) but rather because they bring what is supposed to be sacred within everyday contexts. Teh makes a similar claim when he argues that Apichatpong's transgressions work through domestication and desublimation rather than shock value: he writes that 'while Buddhist symbols appear frequently in his work – as in everyday life – he avoids the sacral zones of religious life, instead framing the clergy (sangha) in profane and quotidian contexts'.[54] In contrast to Wheatley's brutal nihilism, Apichatpong's quiet transgressions are evidence that the sacred need not be evoked through brutality or bloodshed. The perceived desecration of Buddhist imagery in a scene where a monk quietly plays guitar at a small gathering, or a group of monks play with a remote-control flying saucer, provides an alternative mode of transgression. While transgression is generally thought of as a way of breaking moral laws to reveal a chaotic or violent excess, *Syndromes* does the opposite: it brings the sacred back within the confines of the human, revealing a disorder growing quietly within established boundaries. Both kinds of transgression cross the limit between the sacred and the profane, simultaneously articulating and subverting distinctions between the everyday human world and the unknowable sacred world. Apichatpong's desacralized religious images, however, expose the ways that inside and outside are always intertwined. By drawing the sacred into the material, *Syndromes* quietly interrogates the distinction between the linear human world and the disordered natural one and reveals how the two are mutually inflected.

Conclusion

The films of Apichatpong Weerasethakul and Ben Wheatley approach the nonhuman from very different perspectives. Apichatpong's cinema is more life-affirming in its emphasis on eroticism and sensuousness, while Wheatley's cinema is more negative in that it foregrounds cruelty, death and violence. By theorizing Wheatley and Apichatpong through Bataille's ontology of the sacred, I have framed their differing approaches not as opposites but as two sides of the same coin; in contrast to the linearity of the profane human world, the sacred is ambivalent and its contradictions must be held in suspension rather than resolved or domesticated. Engaging with the sacred means pushing our limits and putting ourselves at risk, and Apichatpong and Wheatley provide two models for accomplishing this. The endless deferral of meaning through sacrifice-for-nothing at the heart of Wheatley's project deconstructs the notion of sacrifice itself, which I argued is central to Western conceptions of truth. There is something in the sacrificial violence of Wheatley's films that cannot be recuperated into structuring forces, something in excess of the narrative that cannot be made to mean without losing the force of its impact. Rather than undermining the possibility for positive meaning, Apichatpong's films envision an excess of the human in terms of erotic interpenetration: in the space of the jungle, the boundaries of the human are destabilized as they come into contact with natural forces. Both filmmakers depict the sacred natural world as beyond the bounds of human rationality, and therefore as a risk to the integrity of human self-hood; however, while the process of engaging with it is inherently dangerous, it is also a necessary part of the process in disrupting anthropocentrism.

The cinemas of both Wheatley and Apichatpong insist on immanence, of a sacred inhering in this world. Both film-makers frame this in terms of a pagan return to nature: Christianity and Buddhism are pulled aside to reveal a pagan or animist substrate, one that exists simultaneously to dominant rationalizing narratives. For pagan cosmology, there is no moving beyond this world: the sacred is enfolded into it, at the limits of the human but not beyond the bounds of material existence. Apichatpong and Wheatley's cinemas envision existence as circumscribed and finite, and the circularity that characterizes their narrative approaches reinforces the idea that there is something in excess of understanding inherent to the physical world. The loss of God eliminates the possibility for transcendent truth as well as for singular structuring narratives, but the limit cinemas of Wheatley and Apichatpong suggest another way forward – one that paradoxically involves circling back around to re-examine our fraught relationship with the natural world.

Notes

1 Bataille, *Erotism: Death and Sensuality*.

2 While I am reading art cinema through an implicitly auteurist framework throughout this book by associating films with their directors, it is worth noting the limitations of this approach, especially in the case of Wheatley. Wheatley's films are extremely collaborative: as mentioned later in this chapter, he frequently works with the same cast and crew, and his writing partner Amy Jump's influence on his work is such that she is best described as a co-author. I do not align myself with the modernist tradition of authorship (famously championed by film critics François Truffaut, Alexandre Astruc and Andrew Sarris), which views the individual auteur as a stamp of quality and guarantor of interior meaning. Instead, my position is more in line with postmodern or post-structuralist readings, which view the author as an identifiable discursive pattern in a text, one that is often associated with but whose function and legibility exceed the person/people who created the artwork. See Michel Foucault, 'What Is an Author?', in *Language, Counter-Memory, Practice: Selected Essays and Interviews*, ed. Donald Bouchard (Ithaca, NY: Cornell University Press, 1997), 213–38.

3 Christopher Watkins, *Difficult Atheism: Post-theological Thinking in Alain Badiou, Jean-Luc Nancy and Quentin Meillassoux* (Edinburgh: Edinburgh University Press, 2011), 12–13.

4 Post theology and post-secularism have recently received some attention as frameworks for interpreting film; see John Caruana and Mark Cauchi, eds, *Immanent Frames: Postsecular Cinema between Malick and Von Trier* (New York: SUNY Press, 2019). I also owe the connection between Apichatpong and immanent ideas of the sacred to a conference paper presented by Mark Cauchi at the Film-Philosophy Annual Conference in 2014, 'Post-Secular Lux: Illuminating New Worlds in Recent Cinema with Nancy and Taylor.' Although his framework and conclusions were different from my own, Cauchi's

interpretation of the cave sequence in *Uncle Boonmee* sparked some of the ideas and research that eventually became this chapter.

5   Dennis King Keenan, *The Question of Sacrifice* (Bloomington: Indiana University Press, 2005), 10.

6   Ibid., 45.

7   Ibid., 50–1.

8   Georges Bataille, 'Sacrificial Mutilation and the Severed Ear of Vincent Van Gogh', in *Visions of Excess: Selected Writings, 1927–1939*, ed. and trans. Allan Stoekl (Minneapolis: University of Minnesota Press, 1985), 67.

9   Ibid.

10 See Bataille, *The Accursed Share: Vol. I.*

11 Georges Bataille, 'The Cruel Practice of Art', 1949, trans. Supervert32C, http://supervert.com/elibrary/georges_bataille/cruel_practice_of_art. Accessed 2 August 2019.

12 Mark Kermode, 'Ben Wheatley: "Financing a Film as Crazy as This Takes Good Casting," *The Guardian*, 6 March 2016. https://www.theguardian.com/film/2016/mar/06/ben-wheatley-interview-high-rise-jg-ballard-mark-kermode. Accessed 2 August 2019.

13 See the 2016 special issue of *Critical Quarterly* (58, no. 1) dedicated to Wheatley's work, which was published to coincide with the release of *High-Rise* (2015).

14 Adam Lowenstein, 'A Cinema of Disorientation: Space, Genre, Wheatley', *Critical Quarterly* 5, no. 1 (2016), 5.

15 Andrew Higson, 'The Concept of National Cinema', *Screen* 30, no. 4 (1989), 37.

16 Robert Macfarlane, 'The Eeriness of the English Countryside', *The Guardian*, 10 April 2015. https://www.theguardian.com/books/2015/apr/10/eeriness-english-countrysiderobert-macfarlane. Accessed 6 August 2019.

17 Ibid.

18 Peter Hutchings, 'Uncanny Landscapes in British Film and Television', *Visual Culture in Britain* 5, no. 2 (2004): 27–40.

19 Michael Bonner, '"The Blood in the Earth": An Interview with *A Field in England* Director Ben Wheatley', *Uncut*, 3 July 2013. https://www.uncut.co.uk/features/the-blood-in-the-earth-an-interview-with-a-field-in-england-director-ben-wheatley-.21055/. Accessed 4 March 2021.

20 Marcus K. Harmes, 'The Seventeenth Century on Film: Patriarchy, Magistracy, and Witchcraft in British Horror Films, 1968–1971', *Canadian Journal of Film Studies* 22, no. 2 (2013), 64–80.

21 Ibid., 68.

22 Ibid., 75.

23 Scott Tobias compares the ending to that of *Lost* (2004–10), arguing that *Kill List* evokes more mysteries than it can handle, causing it 'to collapse in a bloody, calamitous heap' (Scott Tobias, 'Cult Horror, Plus some Hatred on the Homefront', *NPR.org*, 2 February 2013. https://www.npr.org/2012/02/02/144620067/cult-horror-plus-some-hatred-on-the-homefront. Accessed 4 March 2021). Blogger Dan Gillette is less charitable in his summation of responses to the film: 'Now as for audiences, the majority who have seen it are like "WTF? What a piece of shit!"' (Dan Gillette, 'Kill List Explained', *CinemaDan.com*, 13 March 2012. http://cinemadan.com/blog/kill-list-explained/. Accessed 4 March 2021). Customer reviews of the DVD on the Amazon echo this sentiment: 'Raw and Crude, Occasionally Effective' (Mark C. Jones), 'Great Setup, Very Disappointing Ending' (Baudelaire), 'Good First Half, Bad Second Half' (Gabriel), 'Confusing' (hoozon), https://www.amazon.com/Kill-List-Region-Neil-Maskell/product-reviews/B007749J0Y?reviewerType=all_reviews. Accessed 6 August 2019.

24 Ross Lincoln, '"Kill List" Director Ben Wheatley Talks "End Deniers"', *Pro. BoxOffice.Com*, 12 February 2012. http://cms.pro.boxoffice.com/articles/2012-02-kill-list-director-ben-wheatley-talksend-deniers?q=Paranoia. Accessed 6 August 2019.

25 Rob Carnevale, 'Kill List: Ben Wheatley Interview', *indieLondon*, 2012. http://www.indielondon.co.uk/Film-Review/kill-list-ben-wheatley-interview. Accessed 6 August 2019.

26 Lincoln, 'Kill List'.

27 Hollier, 'The Dualist Materialism of Georges Bataille'.

28 Lincoln, 'Kill List'.

29 Alex Godfrey, 'Ben Wheatley: Master of the Macabre', *The Guardian*, 22 June 2013. https://www.theguardian.com/film/2013/jun/22/ben-wheatley-field-in-england. Accessed 4 March 2021.

30 Jean-LucNancy, 'Uncanny Landscapes', in *The Ground of the Image*, trans. Jeff Fort (New York: Fordham, 2005), 58.

31 Ibid., 60.

32 Wheatley, Ben, 'An A-Z of the World in *A Field in England*', *AFieldinEngland.com*, 2014. http://www.afieldinengland.com/masterclass/historical-terms/. Accessed 6 August 2019.

33 David Teh, 'Itinerant Cinema: The Social Surrealism of Apichatpong Weerasethakul', *Third Text* 25, no. 5 (2011), 595–609.

34 Ibid., 600.

35 Ibid., 602. See also Natalie Boehler, 'The Jungle as Border Zone: The Aesthetics of Nature in the Work of Apichatpong Weerasethakul', *Australian Journal of South-East Asian Studies* 4, no. 2 (2011), 290–304.

36 Jeong, 'A Global Cinematic Zone'.

37 Una Chung, 'Crossing Over Horror: Reincarnation and Transformation in Apichatpong Weerasethakul's *Primitive*', *Women Studies Quarterly* 40, nos. 1–2 (2012), 211–22.

38 Ibid.

39 Ibid., 221.

40 Bataille, *Erotism*, 19.

41 Ibid., 29.

42 Ibid., 11.

43 Jeong, 'A Global Cinematic Zone', 146.

44 Ibid., 148.

45 Bataille, *Erotism*, 11–25.

46 Philippa Lovatt, ' "Every Drop of My Blood Sings Our Song. There Can You Hear It?": Haptic Sound and Embodied Memory in the Films of Apichatpong Weerasethakul', *New Soundtrack* 3, no. 1 (2013), 62.

47 Timothy Morton, *Ecology without Nature: Rethinking Environmental Aesthetics* (Cambridge, MA: Harvard University Press, 2007), 95.

48 Ibid., 96.

49 Nigel Andrews, 'Nigel Andrews Talks to Thai Filmmaker Apichatpong Weerasethakul', *Financial Times*, 12 November 2010, https://www.ft.com/content/6c477c26-ede9-11df-8616-00144feab49a?mhq5j=e1. Accessed 15 November 2019.

50 Teh, 'Itinerant Cinema'.

51 May Adadol Ingawanij, 'Animism and the Performative Realist Cinema of Apichatpong Weerasethakul', in *Screening Nature: Cinema Beyond the Human*, ed. Anat Pick and Guinevere Narraway (New York: Berghahn, 2013), 92.

52 Ibid., 101.

53 Andrews, 'Nigel Andrews Talks'.

54 Teh, 'Itinerant Cinema', 602.

2

Objectivity, speculative realism and the cinematic apparatus

Introduction

In the previous chapter, I tackled the question of objectivity – of mind-independent reality – in terms of the Bataillean distinction between the sacred and the profane. Rather than conceiving of the sacred in terms of transcendence, I have, following Bataille, characterized it as those things in the world left out of human frameworks of truth and rationality. The sacred in Bataille is always in dynamic relation with human ways of understanding reality, but remains irreducible to them. This chapter, the second half of Part 1 on 'Objectivity', will tackle questions about objectivity and cinema's ability to represent the outside of thought from a slightly different direction; Bataille will move somewhat into the background, though the ontology established in the previous chapters will continue to undergird my philosophical assumptions here (his relevance will re-emerge more explicitly in Chapter 3). Because my understanding of the relation between human and nonhuman reality has much in common with speculative realism (see the introduction), this chapter will engage with some central ideas from speculative realism about how to access mind-independent reality. Questions about subjectivity, mediation and reality are pivotal for classical as well as 1970s film theory, and the contemporary debate surrounding speculative realism is recontextualized here through relevant ideas from André Bazin, Siegfried Kracauer and Jean-Louis Baudry.

In particular, Baudry's apparatus theory – explored in various essays from the mid-1970s – contains several insights relevant to contemporary debates about how to conceptualize and relate to nonhuman reality. Notably, apparatus theory complicates speculative realism's claim that we can think about reality outside of human thought. Although I agree with the speculative realists that we must attempt to think beyond the limits of the human perspective, I simultaneously maintain that such a task is impossible. This impossible imperative – we cannot, but we *must* think beyond the limits of the human – forms the basis of a new ecological ethics that recognizes the limits of human perceptions and concepts but also asserts the existence of a world beyond them (see also Chapter 4). The complex interplay of subjective and objective forces in cinema can provide a model for understanding the relationship between human subjectivity and nonhuman reality at issue in speculative realism. Such capacity is apparent in two films that self-reflexively engage with questions of subjectivity, objectivity and nature: Peter Bo Rappmund's 2012 experimental documentary *Tectonics* and Lisandro Alonso's 2014 historical drama *Jauja*. The self-reflexive gestures of these two films expose the limits of the cinematic apparatus and gesture to a world beyond representation, one that can be related to only in fraught, unstable and contradictory ways.

Following Bataille, one of the central claims of this argument is that reality – the world in itself rather than the world as it exists for human beings – may not align with human ideas of coherence and rationality; analysis of the two films discussed here embraces impossibility and contradiction. The structure of this chapter therefore works through two conflicting positions without resolving the arising tensions, as the tensions themselves expose something crucial about the limits of the human. The next section, 'Speculative realism and film theory', provides an overview of relevant concepts from speculative realism as well as their application to film studies before critiquing speculative realism's position through a rereading of apparatus theory. The following two sections then look at conflicting functions of *Tectonics* and *Jauja*, approaching the question of nonhuman reality from opposing perspectives: the section on 'Objectivity and nature' looks at how *Tectonics* and *Jauja* call attention to a nonhuman reality in excess of human perception, and then 'Subjectivity and apparatus' examines how both films simultaneously expose ways that cinema must always stage nonhuman reality in relation to a human spectator. Both films assert the importance of nonhuman reality on the level of content while inevitably bringing this reality back to human perception on the level of form. This tension supports a more general claim about the impossibility of breaking with anthropocentrism, as the same idea can undermine it on one level while affirming it on another. This impossibility need not condemn us to despair over our imprisonment within the phenomenal bubble but rather can form the basis of a more nuanced ecological ethics.

Speculative realism and film theory

Speculative realism is a movement in contemporary philosophy that, though diverse in approach and conclusions, is united through a desire to get past the boundaries of the phenomenal bubble in which it claims Continental philosophy has been encased at least since Immanuel Kant. Speculative realism, which rejects the Kantian limit on knowledge to things as they appear to us (rather than things as they are), has recently begun to influence film studies, and scholars such as Selmin Kara, David Martin-Jones and Christopher Peterson have employed, engaged and critiqued the ideas of speculative realism in relation to cinema. Kara argues that films such as *The Tree of Life* (Terrence Malick, 2011) and *Beasts of the Southern Wild* (Benh Zeitlin, 2012) exemplify a new 'speculative realist aesthetic' in that they are similarly concerned with questions of origin and extinction; Martin-Jones critiques speculative realism as an overly Eurocentric approach to ecocinema and argues for a more world-historicized approach to film-philosophy through the work of Enrique Dussel; Peterson argues that, contrary to the claims of speculative realism, we cannot do without the human as our epistemological grounding point, using insights from *Melancholia* (Lars von Trier, 2011) and *Gravity* (Alfonso Cuarón, 2013) to bolster his claims.[1] That these discussions have arisen within film studies makes sense, given that film theory – like speculative realism – often addresses questions about the relationship between reality and perception.

There are significant insights to be gained from speculative realism and its application to film studies, yet film studies also has significant contributions to make to speculative realism. Speculative realism often skips over the warnings of twentieth-century philosophies (especially postmodernism and poststructuralism) about the difficulties in ascertaining objective truth, and, as Steven Shaviro argues, at its worst it can 'bespeak a contemptuous arrogance, implicitly suggesting that "everyone else is deluded, but I know better"'.[2] The dangers posed by the arrogance of the 'new' can be mitigated somewhat by following Shaviro's advice and returning to old ideas that are generally ignored or forgotten by new theoretical approaches;[3] he advocates a return to the process philosophy of Alfred North Whitehead, whereas I take a somewhat different approach by returning to classical and 1970s film theories.

Bringing film theory, and particularly apparatus theory, into conversation with speculative realism demonstrates that the latter has something to learn from not only the written discourse of film studies but also films themselves – that is to say, their medium-specific mediation of reality. This chapter therefore contributes to a long tradition in film theory of making an argument about the relationship between human subjectivity and the formal properties of cinema.[4] This position has a number of detractors, most famously Noël Carroll and David Bordwell.[5] Despite my return to 'grand theory' and its focus on medium specificity and subject formation, I take Carroll's point that our understanding of mental processes is far from secure enough to form the basis of a meaningful analogy with cinema.[6] The film analysis that follows is therefore more concerned with negative and limiting factors: what mind and cinema have in common is that they are similarly partial and deficient in their perspectives on reality. Film theory's scepticism about our ability to breach these limitations remains relevant in this new context of speculative realism and film ecocriticism.

A brief overview of the history and motivating concepts of speculative realism shows how the movement can benefit from film theory's meditations on human and nonhuman perception. Speculative realism takes its name from a conference held at Goldsmith's College, London, in 2007 that was inspired by the publication of Quentin Meillassoux's *After Finitude*. Speakers at the first event included Meillassoux, Ray Brassier, Graham Harman and Ian Hamilton Grant, and although these thinkers are quite different in their approaches (ranging from object-oriented ontology – or OOO – and process philosophy to panpsychism and nihilism), they nonetheless share a critique of correlationism, the idea that 'thought cannot get *outside itself* in order to compare the world as it is "in itself" to the world as it is "for us," and thereby distinguish what is a function of our relation to the world from what belongs to the world alone.'[7] Speculative realism expresses frustration with post-Kantian Continental philosophy's tendency to examine reality only in relation to human concepts and discourse, as a product of language, power structures, texts, ideological systems and/or consciousness.[8] By correlating existence with human thought, correlationist philosophy turns its attention away from reality and towards the question of our access to it. Acknowledging that everything we know is conditioned by the way that we know it, correlationism (represented by philosophers as diverse as Martin Heidegger, Jean-Paul Sartre, Edmund Husserl, Maurice Merleau-Ponty and Michel Foucault) turns ontological questions into epistemological ones and maintains the Kantian position that things-in-themselves are beyond the bounds of knowledge and reason. Speculative realism calls this premise into question, pointing out that correlating everything we know about the world *to*

Objectivity, Speculative Realism and Cinematic Apparatus

us inevitably results in a problematic anthropocentrism by placing humans in a privileged position at the centre of the universe. The position asserted in this chapter acknowledges the need to move past anthropocentric correlationism while still remaining sceptical of the speculative realists' claims that they are able to grasp mind-independent reality in previously unconsidered ways.

Although I am critical of speculative realism and seek a more nuanced view of the relation between thought and reality, I share its concern with the ethical consequences of anthropocentrism. As Bryant, Harman and Nick Srnicek explain in the introduction to their edited volume *The Speculative Turn*, the motivation to question antirealist philosophies came about at least in part because of ecological concerns: 'In the face of the looming ecological catastrophe, and the increasing infiltration of technology into the everyday world (including our own bodies), it is not clear that the anti-realist position is equipped to face up to these developments.'[9] According to this view, antirealist thought is coming under pressure from the real. In the form of present and looming disasters, reality is impinging on our ability to stay comfortably within the anthropocentric circle of human thought and consciousness; the time has come to consider reality independent of human perception. This is not the same as saying that we should return to a pre-Kantian realism, or what Meillassoux calls 'the "naïve" stance of dogmatic metaphysics'.[10] As Steven Shaviro explains it, 'The basic speculative realist thesis is the diametrical opposite of the "naïve" assertion that things in themselves are directly accessible to us; the key point, rather, is that the world in itself – the world as it exists apart from us – cannot in any way be contained or constrained by the question of our *access* to it.'[11]

Acknowledging the difficulties of thinking the unthought (the outside of thought, or what Meillassoux calls the absolute), speculative realism asserts the importance of *speculating* about it. It tends to argue that a nonanthropocentric, noncorrelational picture of reality looks stranger than pre-Kantian versions of reality because we can no longer assume that the world adapts to our concepts of it. To that end, Graham Harman passionately defends speculative realism against charges of being old-fashioned or reactionary.[12] He writes that 'usually, the main problem with the term realism is that it suggests a dull, unimaginative appeal to stuffy common sense. But this connotation is exploded in advance by the "speculative" part of the phrase, which hints at starry landscapes haunted by poets and mad scientists.'[13] All the speculative realists are committed to *reality itself* rather than to representations or mediations of it, and although their answers differ as to how we can know anything positively about reality, they agree that such positive knowledge is bound to be quite different from traditional realist notions of a knowable external world.

A potential problem with speculative realism is that it cannot sufficiently account for ethics despite being motivated in part by ethical concerns. Several film scholars have already suggested ways that film points to more ethical alternatives than the ontology offered by speculative realism: Martin-Jones argues that speculative realism's metaphysical focus risks ignoring historical and political factors, which is a problem given that our current ecological situation is largely the result of the exploitative and exclusionary logics of modernity and colonialism.[14] Peterson criticizes speculative realism in relation to cinema from a different angle by arguing that we cannot do without the human as the basis for our encounters with the world. While Peterson praises speculative realism – specifically Graham Harman's OOO and its 'unrelenting displacement of human exceptionalism' – he contends that pointing out that we are not special does not grant us access to perspectives beyond our own.[15] Peterson argues that OOO grants equal ontological value to all things, a so-called flat ontology that amounts to 'an impossible view from nowhere'.[16] Peterson writes that we are inevitably grounded in our own point of view, a position that he argues is not unethical or metaphysically untenable but rather the very starting point of ethics. The notion of the impossible imperative that underlies the ethics of my own book expands on these ethical critiques of speculative realism by pointing out ways that cinema exposes (without resolving) tensions between subjectivity and objectivity.

Ecological metaphysics is, in part, the recognition of perspectives other than our own, a way of negotiating with the other. It is unclear if the internal battles of the speculative realists, who often cannot even agree among themselves, can provide us with an adequate methodology for negotiating between human and nonhuman perspectives.[17] If the aim is to produce positive knowledge of the absolute, then the radically different ontologies that this aim has inspired stand testament to the difficulties inherent in doing so. Antirealism risks the arrogance of anthropocentrism by forgetting about spheres beyond human concepts and understanding, whereas speculative realists risk the arrogance of mistaking their own particular insights for objective truth. Ideas from film theory about the interconnections between subjective and objective forces in the construction of cinematic perspective can provide something of a middle ground.

Questions central to speculative realism about reality, mediation and perception have been part of film theory since its inception. In their introduction to *Screening Nature*, Anat Pick and Guinevere Narraway discuss early realists as important precursors to studies of ecology in cinema, noting that the 'link between film and the physical world has been a central theme in the study of film and film theory, most notably the classical theories of cinematic realism of Siegfried Kracauer and André Bazin. Each in his way … argued for the affinity between film's photographic ontology and the reality it captures.'[18] Speculative realism poses similar questions about the relationship (or lack thereof) between reality and perception, but film theory's answers are more attuned to the difficulties involved in distinguishing subjective impressions from objective reality.

Kracauer's *Theory of Film* explicitly argues for film as a medium uniquely capable of revealing and recording physical reality, in contrast to the traditional arts, because 'the world of film is a flow of random events involving both humans and inanimate objects'.[19] For Kracauer, film can both mimic our modes of perception to represent a realistic scene and penetrate aspects of reality that are normally hidden from us (e.g. by slowing down movements too fast for us to see or enlarging small details with close-ups). Kracauer's theory of film is a kind of object-oriented metaphysics *avant la lettre*, as he argues that film as an art is uniquely capable of representing those aspects of reality that escape our notice or are beyond our abilities to perceive.

Bazin similarly argues for the realist capabilities of cinema, asserting that film's capacity to objectively record physical reality is the basis of its artistic merit. Bazin was heavily influenced by phenomenology (especially the work of Merleau-Ponty), and so his thought is perhaps more at odds with speculative realism than Kracauer's, despite his commitment to cinematic realism. Although Bazin asserts that film is capable of reproducing 'the object itself, the object freed from the conditions of time and space that govern it'[20] – a sentence that could just as easily have been written by Harman describing his object of inquiry – he also acknowledges that this reproduction of reality is possible only through artifice and mediation.[21] Cinema is objective in the sense that it reproduces an image of reality through an automatic photochemical process rather than 'the creative intervention of man', but this does not amount to OOO's 'impossible view from nowhere' because it remains anchored to a particular viewpoint – that of the camera.[22]

Bazin is not trying to argue that the 'creative intervention of man' is entirely absent from cinema; of course film-makers choose what objects are to be photographed and how.[23] Rather, he is pointing out that the actual process of reproduction differs from arts like painting and literature in that it is not filtered through a human subject. For Bazin the objectivity of cinema is based on our psychological impressions of reality because the camera sees more or less as we see, but the automatic, mechanized process involved in representation works to conceal cinema's basis in subjective impressions. Bazin's realism therefore rests not on the simplistic idea that cinema is able to give us direct access to objective reality but on the fact that it provides a subjective impression of objectivity; cinematic realism depends on the contradictions between (rather than the resolution of) nature and artifice, human and machine, subjectivity and objectivity. These oppositions do not cancel out or bracket off the real (as speculative realism would argue about phenomenological versions of realism) but rather are the very condition of cinema's relationship to reality. Cinema might represent a desire to produce a perfect reproduction of reality (Bazin calls this the 'myth of total cinema'), but it will always fall short because of the particularities of its perspective. Like ours, cinema's view of the world is only partial, deficient and incomplete. Its objectivity does not imply totality: to borrow the logic of speculative realism, the reality reproduced by cinema is not exhausted by the camera's access to it. This does not imply that cinema bears no relationship to reality, just as our subjective perception of the world does not undermine the existence of a world outside of those perceptions.

From an ecocritical point of view, what is interesting about realists like Bazin and Kracauer is that they discuss perspective not only in relation to human subjectivity but also as mediated through a nonhuman entity. Their work suggests that cinematic perspective is objective not in the sense of being omniscient or ungrounded, but rather because it is literally the point of view of an object. Baudry continues this line of thinking by arguing that our encounter with cinema is a subjective impression of an objective perspective, as we identify with a camera that sees things in a way similar to but not identical with the way we perceive (much as we might identify with another person). He argues that 'the spectator identifies less with what is represented, the spectacle itself, than with what stages the spectacle, makes it seen, obliging him to see what it sees; this is exactly the function taken over by the camera as a sort of relay'.[24] Seen in this way, cinema becomes relevant for speculative realism because it highlights the ways that our perspectives are shaped by and come into contact with not only other humans but also nonhuman things. Because cinema is a technology invented by humans, it is of course bound to be related to us in some way, but that relationship does not only go in one direction: we both affect and are affected by cinema.

Objectivity, Speculative Realism and Cinematic Apparatus 77

Crucially, however, cinema also reveals that these encounters are never neutral or uncontaminated by human perspectives and ideological structures. The apparatus of cinema establishes a mode of perception before the spectator encounters any specific impressions of reality on-screen, and this mode of perception is conditioned by both the material objects involved (camera, projector, screen) and the ideological structures that gave rise to those objects. Baudry's apparatus theory explains cinematic realism by looking at subjectivity and objectivity in relation to each other; although unlike speculative realism it cannot do without a theory of subjectivity, it also cannot do without the mechanical elements involved in cinematic representation. The ideological effects of cinema have a material basis, as they are not imposed on it from the outside but are part of its material functioning as a technical apparatus.

Baudry would probably object to being compared to early realists like Bazin and Kracauer, as during the 1970s he – along with other thinkers informed by Althusserian Marxism (e.g. Jean-Louis Comolli, Stephen Heath, Jean Narboni) – famously partook of the 'Bazin-bashing [that] became widespread and even fashionable in French, British and U.S. film theory and scholarship'.[25] More recent readings of Bazin assert that his argument was more nuanced than Baudry or his contemporaries realized, however, and that his definition of realism is more complex than the traditional concept of an objective external world.[26] Further, although there are significant differences between Bazin's realism and Baudry's apparatus theory, speculative realism would categorize them both as correlationist, as they both rely on assumptions drawn from phenomenology (Merleau-Ponty for Bazin, Husserl for Baudry).[27] Baudry argues that cinema is a 'phantasmatization of objective reality (images, sounds, colours) – but of an objective reality which, limiting its powers of constraint, seems equally to augment the possibilities or the power of the subject'.[28] For Baudry, cinema enables the spectator to enjoy an illusion of objectivity because the apparatus works to conceal its own ideological basis.

Baudry argues that one cannot consider reality in the cinema without considering the subject, because the ways that reality is staged for the spectator take precedence over any particular impressions of reality on-screen. It is true that film is 'objective' in the sense that it mechanically reproduces physical reality, but apparatus theory reminds us that this objectivity is conditioned by ideological and subjective forces. The subject remains 'the active centre and origin of meaning' even though the mechanisms of cinema work to repress cinema's subjective origins.[29] We cannot consider the objective effects of cinema without an account of its subjective workings, although this does not mean (as speculative realism would have it) that we cannot consider reality at all. Cinema represents a desire to exceed the limits of subjectivity and occupy an objective position, and it simultaneously bears witness to the impossibility of doing so. The following sections bolster these claims by providing examples from particular films that interrogate the tensions between subject and reality, spectator and screen. By rejecting speculative realism's claims for newness and returning instead to theories such as Baudry's that assume medium specificity, I am making a claim about the cinematic apparatus in general; however, my cinematic examples complicate such a totalizing approach by demonstrating how individual films can push against the limitations of the medium.[30] *Jauja* and *Tectonics* both expose conflicting truths: on one level they draw attention to an objective world in excess of the human (thereby resisting the phenomenological basis of the apparatus), but on another they self-consciously indicate the ways that this world is necessarily framed in a subjective way.

Objectivity and nature

Peter Bo Rappmund's *Tectonics* contextualizes human activity against a broader environment while simultaneously interrogating the position of the spectator through its use of perspective. Its sixty-minute runtime consists of a series of static shots of the landscape surrounding the Mexican-American border; but while it stages the images for a motionless camera – and by extension viewer – it represents the environment as vibrant and uncannily alive through time-lapse techniques and a sense of discord between image and sound. *Tectonics* follows the border from the Gulf of Mexico to the Pacific Ocean through a style reminiscent of James Benning's experimental documentaries, which also often use static shots of landscape to comment on environmental issues or undermine anthropocentric modes of perception (e.g. *California Trilogy*, 2000–1; *Ten Skies*, 2004; *Nightfall*, 2013; *BNSF*, 2013).[31] However, unlike in Benning's films, in *Tectonics* the image has obviously been digitally manipulated and animated in a number of ways, and the manipulations give a sense of vitality and rhythm to the environment that prevent it from seeming passive or inert.

The film begins with a black screen and a low electronic hum; the sound of the ocean rises as we begin to see the blue-green outline of waves shuddering against a black shore. The colours are enhanced and artificial, and the movements of the waves are sped up and altered so that they appear jerky and unnatural. The soundtrack, by contrast, is more continuous, and the sound of waves rolls over a fade to black. This is followed by another ocean scene, this time in natural colours. Waves pulse onto a sandy shore as seagulls group and disperse mid-frame, and in the distance a group of three people seem to be conversing next to a parked car; a lighthouse stands immobile on a rocky outcrop.

The actions of the birds are sped up and looped as they cluster, disperse and repeatedly fade away. The movements of the human figures are more restrained; they huddle together and shuffle back and forth. All these actions are jerky and unnatural, similar to the motions of the waves in the previous shot. By contrast, the accompanying sounds of the birds and the ocean seem natural and continuous, immersing the spectator in the ambient environment of the seascape. The opening scenes establish the aesthetics of the film as a whole, which exhibits a range of movements and patterns. Shots vary in length and are arranged in unpredictable, organic rhythms; the soundtrack sometimes bridges shots and other times cuts abruptly. Black frames periodically punctuate the images. Although the overall structure of *Tectonics* is straightforwardly linear – east to west, Atlantic to Pacific – it tangles and snags time along the way, pausing to loop and repeat details that viewers might otherwise ignore.

Tectonics makes visual associations between various geographical features, from sun-drenched hills and rivers to ramshackle houses on dusty roads. Humans are not entirely absent from the film, as several shots feature tiny figures that appear and disappear in the distance. They are never foregrounded in the frame, however; *Tectonics* takes on an alternative scale, modelled on features of the landscape rather than the human body. There is only one face shot in close-up in the entire film. On a billboard beside a parked border patrol van are posters with the faces of wanted men, and there is a cut to one of these faces in close-up; the paper is so wrinkled and water damaged that it becomes its own geography. Enlarged in the frame, the image becomes as much a landscape warped by ridges and valleys as the green hill in the shot that follows.

Tectonics examines a politically charged topic, one that has become even more contentious in the wake of the 2016 US election and President Trump's promise to build a wall along the Mexican-American border. (The film reveals the absurdity of this project, as many scenes demonstrate that the border is already marked by numerous walls, fences and otherwise prohibitive landscapes, such as mountains and cliff faces.) However, the film addresses its subject matter with an ecological eye that expands beyond the scope of human interactions that we

Figure 7 Face as landscape in *Tectonics* (Peter Bo Rappmund, 2012).

might ordinarily associate with the border. Issues of surveillance and violence are not elided, as evidenced by shots of blimps, border crossings, cameras and police cars. At one point we see a row of small American flags fixed to a painted blue wooden board; a close-up reveals a message on one of the flags: 'You can't have too much border security. Only too little as we have now.' From these images, one can easily imagine a different documentary about the same subject, where shots of the landscape are intercut with talking head interviews of people on either side of the border discussing their experiences. In light of the weight of its subject matter, it is significant that *Tectonics* instead frames its more politically charged images in relation to a broader ecological context.

This choice hints towards an alternative ecological politics, attuned to what Jane Bennett calls the vibrancy of matter. Bennett argues that distinctions between living and non-living things are problematic because we can observe vitality in matter of all kinds; she writes, 'By vitality I mean the capacity of things – edibles, commodities, storms, metals – not only to impede or block the will and designs of humans but also to act as quasi agents or forces with trajectories, propensities, or tendencies of their own.'[32] Viewing the world in terms of the distinction between active living things (with humans at the top, given their perceived superior agency and free will) and inert matter means that we overlook the multitude of ways that nonhuman matter motivates human behaviour and affects the world in which we live, and Bennett argues that opening ourselves up to the vitality of matter will have profound consequences for the ways we view and interact with our environment.

Tectonics supports Bennett's point that we must account for nonhuman agency (although the following section advocates scepticism about our ability to fully understand such agency). The film suggests that we cannot conduct a politics of the border without considering the actual, physical place: the line between Mexico and the United States is explored not merely as an abstract concept, delineating a political distinction between countries and ethnicities, but in its real material consequences. Contemporary geopolitical concerns are placed in the context of nonhuman timescales, as the title of the film calls attention to geological time – the slow movement of tectonic plates – and suggests that things that might appear static, such as canyons and mountains, are active and that their movements become visible given a long enough timeline. *Tectonics* makes the earth come alive, as the motions of things both tiny and large are enhanced and multiplied: plants move twitchily, seemingly of their own accord; a stream trickles through a canyon; people drive cars, erect fences, build houses. The ecologically attuned aesthetics of *Tectonics* views humans as another force shaping the landscape, just like rivers and tectonic plates.

Jauja similarly calls attention to nonhuman agency, using both narrative and framing to undermine the subjugation of nature by humans. The film's critique of anthropocentrism is waged in part by problematizing colonialism, especially its attitude towards nature as something to be conquered and exploited. *Jauja* is set in the 1880s in Argentina, and it follows Captain Gunnar Dinesen (Viggo Mortensen) as he chases his runaway daughter Ingeborg (Viilbjørk Malling Agger) through the Patagonian Desert. Although Dinesen's presence in Patagonia is not fully explained, and his role in the military operation is never made explicit, the film is set during the Conquest of the Desert (1870–84), a military campaign to secure Patagonia against invasion from Chile and to exterminate or displace the Indigenous peoples who controlled the region at the time. *Jauja* loosely employs iconography and narrative tropes from the western – including a lone wanderer on horseback, hostile natives, desolate desert landscapes – but it displaces them to a new context and renders them unfamiliar and uncanny. While the western genre's relationship to colonial ideology (whether supportive or critical) has historical roots in the American frontier, *Jauja* draws from the genre to critique colonialism in a broader global context. The film offers a commentary that extends beyond the scope of human interactions to consider the relationship between colonial ideology and the natural world.

While the Conquest – which resulted in the genocide of more than a thousand Indigenous people and the displacement of thousands more – is only obliquely referred to, its racist project is made evident in the statements by various officers during the film's opening scenes. Pittaluga, an arrogant man whom we first see masturbating in a tidal pool with his military medals gleaming on his bare chest, describes the Indigenous people as 'coconut heads' during a conversation with Dinesen; when Dinesen protests that this designation does little to help them understand their enemy, Pittaluga replies that they do not need to understand them, only exterminate them. Pittaluga tells Dinesen that their mission in the desert – building a country – is a difficult business, but that 'one must embrace an idea and push ahead with it' because 'that's what sets us apart from the coconut heads'. Such linearity is revealed to be at odds with the landscape, which disrupts and disorients any straightforward trajectory, and Dinesen's mission unravels the farther he gets away from camp and its associated colonial logic.

Jauja's critique of colonialism through the construction of space and landscape builds on Alonso's previous films, which represent Argentina's wilderness as enigmatic and in excess of any allegorical reading. Jens Andermann argues that the wilderness in Alonso's cinema is always related to Argentina's complex

Figure 8 Pittaluga in *Jauja* (Lisandro Alonso, 2014).

Objectivity, Speculative Realism and Cinematic Apparatus 83

colonial history as well as its cinematic heritage; in Alonso's films, however, these histories are divorced from any clear allegorical meaning. Andermann situates Alonso's work (particularly *Los muertos* [*The Dead*, 2004]) in the context of other recent Argentinean and Brazilian films (e.g. Mariano Donoso's *Opus* [2005]; Andrea Tonacci's *Serras da desordem* [*The Hills of Disorder*, 2006]) and argues that these films refer to histories that they simultaneously work to cloud or forget:

> Instead of endowing place with hegemonic and affective density … these recent films from Argentina and Brazil approach the rural interior as what at first appears to be an exercise in oblivion. By stripping it of its previous inscriptions, these films invest landscape with an enigmatic nature, which, however, is often the effect of a staged ingenuity on the part of the cinematic narrator, who misreads or pretends to ignore the previous archival codings of the rural interior.[33]

Andermann maintains that these films simultaneously refer to and dismiss the ways that previous films (especially Cinema Novo from the 1960s and 1970s) treated cinematic landscapes as a means of critiquing Argentina's oppressive colonial history.[34] Films like *Los muertos* therefore bear ambiguous traces of these histories that refuse to be settled into an overarching narrative: landscapes are 'exhausted' of allegorical meaning despite their excesses of signification.

This expansion towards a wider reality that cannot be appropriated by the camera is supported on a stylistic level by Alonso's framing. His 'lonely man' films – *Los muertos, La libertad* (*Freedom*, 2001) and *Liverpool* (2008) – all feature sequences in which the camera comes untethered from the central protagonist, who otherwise completely anchors the perspective. In *La libertad*, the camera follows the movements of a woodcutter (Misael Saavedra) until he retreats to his hut for a nap; while the woodcutter sleeps, the camera wanders away from the hut without him and tracks through the surrounding forest. Towards the end of *Liverpool*, Farrel (Juan Fernández) leaves the remote village where his mother lives; the camera does not follow him but stays for a moment on the empty winter scene before cutting back to the lives of the family he has left behind. *Los muertos* opens with an out-of-focus shot that tracks over lush foliage in the jungle until it lands on the bloodied corpses of children; this shot is never contextualized, and thus might represent a dream, prolepsis or memory. The end of *Los muertos* repeats this puzzling gesture by staying outside the hut where Vargas (Argentino Vargas) reunites with his family, panning down to the dirt rather than following Vargas to settle the question of whether he intends to murder his family. These wandering shots emphasize that landscapes in Alonso's films exceed their function as backdrop for human action.

Jauja makes explicit the political and historical stakes of Alonso's previous films by directly addressing Argentina's complex colonial history while still refusing any straightforward allegorical reading. *Jauja* also features several shots in which the camera lingers on spaces that characters have left; these similarly construct the Argentinian landscape as full of phenomena but empty of determinate meaning. This simultaneous plenitude and lack also makes it a sacred space in a Bataillean sense, since it can only be described in contradictory terms; Bataille described the sacred as 'the prodigious effervescence of life that … the order of things holds in check' as well as 'the passion of an absence of individuality, the imperceptible sonority of a river, the empty limpidity of the sky'.[35] Ingeborg emphasizes this paradoxical nature of the sacred when she tells her father that she loves the desert because it fills her, a description that contradicts common notions of the desert as barren, empty, a wasteland. By pausing on features of the landscape such as horses, grasses and mountains rather than following characters that exit the frame, *Jauja*'s cinematography undermines the importance of the human figure and calls into question the latter's domination over the image. Like *Tectonics*, *Jauja* stages its political critique through a more holistic aesthetic that positions humans in relation to a wider ecological context, which is related to the representation of the landscape as something in excess of human reason or purpose.

Because what is at issue is linear colonial rationality – wherein 'one must embrace an idea and push ahead with it' – *Jauja*'s narrative works to undermine any straightforward, sensible reading. *Jauja* begins as a more or less uncomplicated period drama with a clear narrative direction: Dinesen must leave his camp at the coast and go into the desert to retrieve his daughter, who has eloped with a young soldier named Corto (Misael Saavedra). However, the film's narrative logic begins to unravel as Dinesen wanders into the wilderness. The film begins with a title card that explains that Jauja is a 'mythological place of abundance and happiness' that has inspired many expeditions and increasingly exaggerated legends; the title card continues that the 'only thing that is known for certain is that all who tried to find this earthly paradise got lost along the way'. In this respect, Jauja becomes a structuring absence of the film, a non-place that leads the characters to get lost rather than providing a goal for their wanderings. Dinesen journeys away from the camps at the coastline into the desert and encounters various unexplained acts of violence before his horse gets stolen and

Objectivity, Speculative Realism and Cinematic Apparatus · 85

he falls asleep on a mountain under the stars. Upon waking, Dinesen finds a wolfhound that leads him to a cave on the mountain, where he encounters an old woman who seems somehow to be his daughter. Although Dinesen ostensibly reaches his goal by finding Ingeborg, the discovery accomplishes little in terms of narrative resolution. The woman undermines Dinesen's entire project by telling him: 'All families disappear eventually, even if it takes a long time. They're wiped off the face of the earth. The desert swallows them up. I think it's for the best.' These statements imply that the various questions raised over the course of the narrative – including the whereabouts of Ingeborg and the motivations for acts of violence – are meaningless, ambiguous or rendered indeterminable by the desert. The human dramas that focused the narrative to this point are spun out of control, overcome by the expansive irrational logic of the wilderness.

Following this conversation, Dinesen wanders back to the desert and disappears into the rocks as the old woman asks in voice-over, 'What is it that makes a life function and move forward?' This linearity of human life is then problematized as the film suddenly jumps to a Danish mansion in the present day. A girl played by the same actress as young Ingeborg wakes up and walks through the house and into the yard, where she converses with a man leading a pack of wolfhounds. The man explains that he has been treating an infection on one of the dogs, who contracted it because he had been scratching on account of anxiety about the girl's long absence. The girl takes the dog for a walk in the neighbouring woods, where she finds a wooden soldier. The wooden soldier is a recurring motif in the film, as Ingeborg sees it in the beginning floating in the ocean and shows it to her father, who later discovers it along the path to the old woman's cave. After the girl finds the soldier, she hears the dog howl in the distance and follows the noise to find a small pond with a still-rippling surface, as though something has just fallen in. She tosses the wooden soldier into the water before a transition to the final shot of the film, of the Patagonia seaside populated with seabirds and seals.

As with the cave sequence, the baffling final sequence bears an excess of meaning that refuses to be answered in any straightforward way. Did the girl dream all the events of the film? Did the dog somehow become her father after falling into the pond and being transported to nineteenth-century Patagonia? Had she fallen into the pond previously, accounting for her long absence and the dog's anxiety? Or is it the wooden soldier that symbolizes Dinesen? *Jauja*'s narrative explores the woman's question – what is it that makes a life go forward? – by examining lives that do anything but. The events of the film fold over each other through metonymic rhythms and repeated images rather than a clear narrative trajectory. By calling the linearity of time and progress into question, *Jauja* dismantles the anthropocentric colonial logic that motivates the presence of the army in the desert. The old woman's assertion that the desert swallows up all families and all countries unsettles the boundaries of the narrative and places the film in the context of a broader timescale, one that outlasts the parameters of human lives and generations. The desert renders Dinesen's search for his daughter and the army's claim on Patagonia contingent and fleeting, tiny in comparison to a vast and incomprehensible wilderness.

Subjectivity and apparatus

As demonstrated in the previous section, both *Jauja* and *Tectonics* call attention to a reality beyond human representation and reason through an emphasis on natural landscapes and geological time. Although these ecological concerns are central to *Tectonics* and *Jauja* and should not be ignored, they are not the only possible conclusions. There are also important considerations to make about the ways that the camera positions the spectator in relation to the landscape depicted in both films. These formal elements might be overlooked if one were to consider only the ecological relationships established within each diegesis. Indeed, one must examine the ways that both films stage their ecological awareness for a human spectator and consider not only what is represented on-screen but also some of the processes that allow for these representations – especially the ideological processes involved in the construction of perspective, an aesthetic aspect of cinema that *Tectonics* and *Jauja* foreground in interesting ways. Although their emphasis on perspective complicates claims to objectivity or any kind of holistic ecological awareness, it is precisely this disruption of objectivity that makes these films important from an ecocritical perspective.

Baudry writes that within the cinematic apparatus, it is the lens of the camera that occupies the position between the inside and outside (the subjective and objective):

> The lens, the 'objective,' is of course only a particular location of the 'subjective.' Marked by the idealist opposition interior/exterior, topologically situated at the meeting point between the two, it corresponds, one could say, to the empirical

Objectivity, Speculative Realism and Cinematic Apparatus

organ of the subjective, to the opening, the fault in the organs of meaning, by which the exterior world may penetrate the interior and assume meaning.[36]

Baudry is drawing here on a play on the French word *objectif*, which can mean both 'lens' and 'objective': he argues that the lens is the point within the process of making a film where the exterior world comes to meet subjective apprehension. It marks the limit between inside and outside, which, as Baudry argues, is an idealist distinction, meaning that it can be drawn only with reference to human consciousness. (Baudry's camera lens is therefore autopoietic in that its openness to external reality is conditioned by its function as a closed system; it also aligns with Bataillean inner experience in that it can only assume meaning in relation to a human subject.) Within the cinematic apparatus – including everything from profilmic reality to camera to projector to exhibition space to spectator – it is the lens that Baudry argues forms the first encounter between inside and outside.

It is significant that Baudry does not locate the first instance of subjective differentiation between inside and outside within a human subject. It would be more obvious to suggest that the point of this encounter happens when the image meets the spectator's eye, but instead, Baudry externalizes the process by arguing that it takes place through an object – the camera. He argues that this externalization of subjective processes leads the spectator to assume an objective position in relation to the cinematic image. Crucially, however, this objectivity is an illusion, and one that is possible only because of the ways that the cinematic apparatus relates to subjective experience and produces the subject position occupied by the spectator. Baudry argues that although realist theorists of cinema tend to rely on formal analyses about devices within particular films to explicate the relationship between cinema and the real, doing so overlooks a more crucial question about why cinema is able to have realistic effects at all:

> The key to the impression of reality has been sought in the structuring of the image and movement, in complete ignorance of the fact that the impression of reality is dependent first of all on a subject effect and that it might be necessary to examine the position of the subject facing the image in order to determine the *raison d'être* for the cinema effect.[37]

Considering the form of individual films is not enough for Baudry: understanding cinema's realistic effects involves broadening the scope to include all elements of the cinematic apparatus as well as their ideological underpinnings.

88 *Limit Cinema*

All of these, Baudry argues, support the subjective illusion of objectivity, an illusion that can be explicated only through a theory of subjectivity.

Cinema for Baudry looks 'real' only because it is modelled on our psychic structure; it is therefore necessarily correlational even if it evinces a genuine encounter between internal and external forces. The camera is modelled on the human eye, but externalizing its mode of representation allows it to give an impression of objectivity by repressing its subjective origin. He writes that the body, which he describes as another apparatus, is forgotten while we watch a film and that the subjective position established by the cinematic apparatus occupies the whole frame rather than a particular point within it.[38] Cinema grants the illusion of a masterful gaze by centring the image on the spectator as well as allowing the spectator to temporarily forget his or her particular, limited perspective. Baudry suggests that this process is influenced by the entire history of Western art since the invention of perspective during the Renaissance and argues that perspective in art comes at the same historical moment and through the same technology as Galileo's refutation of geocentrism and decentring of the human in relation to the universe. Baudry writes that Western science originates with

> the development of the optical apparatus. … But also, and paradoxically, the optical apparatus *camera obscura* will serve in the same period to elaborate in pictorial work a new mode of representation, *perspectiva artificialis*. This system, recentring or at least displacing the centre (which settles itself in the eye), will ensure the setting up of the 'subject' as the active center and origin of meaning.[39]

We can see his point more clearly by imagining alternatives. Baudry points out that previous modes of representation did not stage their images for an imagined observer from a set position; Greek theatre, for example, was 'based on a multiplicity of points of view, whereas the paintings of the Renaissance will elaborate a centred space'.[40] Perspective unifies the image for a singular viewpoint, thereby establishing the spectator as the subject for whom the entirety of the representation is staged. The centring of the subject through perspective carries through Western art to cinema, and although it appears natural to filmgoers, the fact that alternative models are possible indicates that it arose from a particular, contingent history of ideas. Perspective is therefore imbued with ideological baggage, and the use of it in cinema cannot be said to be neutral or objective.

I am less concerned here with the particular framework Baudry provides for explaining this ideological baggage (he relies heavily on Marxism and

Objectivity, Speculative Realism and Cinematic Apparatus

89

psychoanalysis) than with the more general point that we cannot subtract the subjective effects of cinema to access an objective reality existing underneath. Although it is a correlationist claim, it does not necessarily trap Baudry within a problematic anthropocentrism. As one can see in *Tectonics* and *Jauja*, perspective can give film-makers the tools to undermine correlationism from within. Baudry's observation that the camera obscura emerged at the same time as Galileo's theory of heliocentrism – centring and decentring the subject at the same time – suggests the difficulties involved in breaking with anthropocentrism, because the same idea can be both more and less implicated in its logic. The way out of this trap is not to set aside the issue of subjectivity altogether in favour of objects, as speculative realists generally do, but rather to subvert our perspective from within subjective boundaries to open up the possibility of touching on a reality larger than ourselves. Because there is no outside position from which to approach objective reality, the only other possibility is to disavow the limit between self and world – an act of repression that Baudry reminds us amounts to narcissism.[41] Rather than attempting to set these limits aside, we are better off calling attention to them in order to find the places where their logic breaks down. Analysing the ways that particular films push against the limits of their own systems of representation can suggest ways of undermining (without escaping from) anthropocentric modes of perception.

Tectonics enacts such a deconstruction, because its emphasis on perspective calls attention to the apparatus while also evoking a reality irreducible to its representation. The ecological awareness elicited by the film indicates that such a deconstruction need not myopically remain within the realm of human perception; it can evoke a wider reality while still acknowledging that it represents this reality for a human observer. *Tectonics'* repeated visual emphasis on straight lines fading into the distance interrogates this tension by emphasizing the ways that cinema always addresses itself to a spectator. Lines open up from a centred point towards the edges of the frame, inviting the spectator into the image. This self-conscious form of address points to the ways that the subject facing the screen is always included in the image and necessary for its process of signification.

Tectonics also calls attention to structuring gaps and absences in the image by simultaneously working with and against the unifying effects of cinema. The jerky movements of elements within the frame disrupt the smooth progression of time; parts of the frame suddenly appear and disappear, their absences perceptible for only a brief moment that becomes emphasized as the image is looped. One shot,

Figure 9 Single-point perspective in *Tectonics* (Peter Bo Rappmund, 2012).

for example, overlooks a hilly village with small, brightly coloured buildings; we see cars and people moving up and down the streets in the distance, and smoke billows from several rooftops. There are small gaps between the movements of the people and cars, and the effect is something like the fragmented movements of time-lapse photography; the image is then looped so that the motions are repeated again. This emphasis on absence calls attention to what is not seen. At the same time, it makes aspects of the frame perceptible that might otherwise be ignored, as the spectator is drawn to meditate on patterns of movement and the relations between them rather than viewing time and space in terms of linear progress. These absences are like crevices in the topography of the image, so that rather than being continuous and whole, *Tectonics* is rippled and cratered with tiny holes. The perspective on the Mexican-American border in *Tectonics* is partial and incomplete, despite its representation through a medium that usually establishes space as comprehensible and consistent.

The tiny absences in the frame also call attention to broader gaps in our knowledge: what is unrepresented and unseen. Because the camera remains static, the spectator is never given a contiguous sense of space. We never see what is off-screen; each shot is a discrete tableau, more like a moving painting or photograph than part of a film. To recall the Roland Barthes passage from the preface, 'the tableau (pictorial, theatrical, literary) is a pure cut out segment with clearly defined edges, irreversible and incorruptible; everything that surrounds it

Objectivity, Speculative Realism and Cinematic Apparatus

is banished into nothingness, remains unnamed, while everything that it admits within its field is promoted into essence, into light, into view'.[42] The tableau presents a perspective that renders everything that is excluded irrelevant, which reinforces the mastery of the spectator's gaze since everything present comes 'into light'.[43] *Tectonics* suggests that this process of representation is predicated on exclusion and absence; by working these two modes of representation against each other – cinema and tableau – the film exposes the structuring absences of each. While a still tableau evokes a sense of wholeness by seeming like a partial view of a complete universe, *Tectonics* provides a succession of moving tableaux that resist being connected to a coherent, contiguous space; they are partial glimpses that refuse to suggest a totality. The stasis of the camera works against the movement of the image over time to destabilize the unifying effects of cinematic representation.

It is crucial to note that this destabilization of the image occurs not through a radical break with its mode of representation but rather as a result of engaging with cinema's inherent logic. *Tectonics* uses perspective, movement and time to investigate the limits of cinematic representation. This does *not* result in an erasure of the boundary between human and nonhuman realities or a complete break from the ideological trappings of perspective (which would be impossible) but in a complex interrogation of the relationships among reality, the image and the spectator. The undermining of the human in each frame is contradicted by these emphatic assertions of the spectator's position outside of the frame, but it is through this very contradiction that the relationship between nonhuman reality and a human observer is articulated. *Tectonics* makes visible the gap between reality and representation by pointing out its own inability to exceed subjective boundaries; the observer cannot be subtracted from the image, but *Tectonics* also reminds us that this relationship between image and observer is insufficient in accounting for the reality we perceive.

As with *Tectonics*, *Jauja*'s ecological project is related not only to an expansion beyond the human within the diegesis but also to the way that the film self-consciously appeals to an observer. At the same time that the spectator's attention is drawn away from human figures within the frame, the 1.33:1 aspect ratio and restricted construction of space emphasize the limits of perception. The restricted framing gestures towards the position of the spectator, emphasizing the spectator's relationship to the image in a way similar to the use of single-point perspective in *Tectonics*. But because *Jauja* is implicated in the logic of cinema, its attempts to break from anthropocentrism are necessarily limited by the subjective workings of the apparatus. Rather than ignoring or overcoming these limitations, *Jauja* draws attention to them in order to call the spectator's mastery over the image into question.

If we recall the claim from the previous section that the same idea can simultaneously implicate us more and less in the logic of anthropocentrism, then Alonso's use of the wandering camera can be understood as performing two conflicting gestures at the same time. While these shots do function to expand awareness of a world beyond the human, as was argued in the previous section 'Objectivity and nature', they also reinforce that this awareness always belongs to the spectator and is therefore inevitably subjective. Alonso's wandering camera sequences tend to mark a break in stylistic logic, given that his films generally limit perspective to a single protagonist; the result is unsettling and alienating, as the spectator's identification with the lone male wanderer is interrupted and attention drawn instead to the camera itself. In the scene from *La libertad* when the camera veers away from the woodcutter as he sleeps, for example, the shot is obviously handheld, implying the somewhat unsettling presence of a definite but unseen observer. Perspective is untethered from the narrative but crucially is not objective, and the effect is voyeuristic in part because it seems limited to a single, unknown observer. This voyeuristic effect calls attention back to the position of the spectator, emphasizing that such a position was always implicit in the image. Although shots like this might be able to expand perspective beyond the human characters, they cannot expand beyond the camera and therefore inevitably remain 'subjective' in that, to recall Jean-Louis Baudry, they maintain the spectator as the 'active centre and origin of meaning'.[44]

But while the subjective position of the camera cannot be overcome, it can be undermined from within. The mastery over the image that Baudry argues is a central aesthetic effect of cinema exposed as illusory; in Alonso's films it does little to clarify narrative events. We are often denied essential information because the camera veers away from actions that might provide narrative resolution, as with the ending of *Los muertos*, when the camera tracks away from Vargas just when he is reunited with his family, or the final shot of *Liverpool*, when the camera tilts away from the face of Farrel's daughter as she examines the keychain he had given her, shielding her emotions from view. In *Jauja* the sense of mastery over the image is initially even more pronounced than in Alonso's previous films because of the self-contained framing and 1.33:1 aspect ratio. Every shot is balanced, like a tableau or a painting, and all elements fit neatly within the nearly square frame – a marked contrast from westerns that make use of widescreen formats to provide panoramic views of spectacular landscapes (e.g. *The Big Sky* [Howard Hawks, 1952], *The Big Country* [William Wyler, 1958], *How the West Was Won* [John Ford, Henry Hathaway and George Marshall, 1963]). This makes the wilderness in *Jauja* seem at first to be smaller and more controlled, a feeling emphasized by the deep-focus cinematography used throughout: everything remains visible and attention is rarely drawn towards off-screen space. But this totalizing gaze is increasingly problematized as the film progresses, because the excesses of information contained in each frame cannot easily be integrated into a coherent, linear narrative. And although we often see the entirety of the action within a scene, this generally does not help us interpret it. Actions are often seen from too far away to make out clearly, as with a scene in which we witness the murder of a man in extreme long shot with Dinesen in the foreground and the figures barely visible amid poles on the hill in the horizon; our more holistic view of the event paradoxically precludes us from understanding it. The spectator's apparent mastery over the image is emphasized to draw attention to its limitations, as there is not enough information to construct a contextualizing framework for the events that unfold in front of the camera. The universe of *Jauja* appears to extend beyond the confines of the frame and operate according to a logic to which we are given only partial access.

Figure 10 Riding towards the camera in *Jauja* (Lisandro Alonso, 2014).

While cinema conventionally constructs space horizontally across the frame – especially in the widescreen formats often employed by westerns – space in *Jauja* is constructed backwards, limited laterally by the square sides of the frame and expanding away from the spectator towards the horizon. Actions within the frame tend to occur from back to front rather than from side to side. As Pittaluga masturbates in the pool, for example, we see Dinesen approach a log in the background; the shot is later reversed as Dinesen sits on the log in the foreground and Pittaluga emerges from the pool behind him. A particularly striking shot observes Dinesen riding up from the distance towards the camera before reversing to watch him ride away and fade into the desert landscape. This emphasizes single-point perspective in a manner similar to *Tectonics*. Actions occur in straight lines towards and away from the camera, gesturing towards the position occupied by the spectator. However, although we view each action in its entirety from multiple angles, these shots do not clarify space; rather, they enhance the sense of disorientation created by *Jauja*'s puzzling narrative. The space of the desert remains mysterious, as it is never made entirely clear in which direction Dinesen is heading: he may be riding in circles or back and forth, towards and away from the camera. This enhances the sense that actions are divorced from any clear direction or aim, that Dinesen's decision to heed Pittaluga's advice and push forward into the desert is at odds with the irrational, nonlinear logic of the wilderness. The spectator is lost along with Dinesen, and as the narrative progresses, the framing reinforces that information is limited by the narrow confines of the screen. The diegetic universe exceeds the boundaries of the image but remains inaccessible to the spectator because of the limited perspective of the camera. This marks not a radical departure from cinematic aesthetics but rather a use of cinema's inherent logic against itself in order to question its construction of a totalizing gaze.

As with *Tectonics*, *Jauja*'s attempts to gesture towards a broader ecological reality must be read alongside the way that the film directs itself towards a human spectator. The diegesis is self-consciously staged for us, but our ability to interpret it is radically called into question. Within the diegesis, *Jauja* expands its awareness beyond the human to give presence to the landscape, but our access to this reality necessarily remains partial and limited. Although Alonso's films draw attention towards a natural landscape emptied of characters within the frame – thereby disrupting the correlation between humans and space within the diegesis – they simultaneously underscore the spectator's relationship with the screen, emphasizing that on the level of the apparatus the correlation is impossible to escape. The tension between an expanded ecological awareness and the limits imposed on it by the cinematic apparatus is not settled or overcome but rather remains central to Alonso's aesthetics; *Jauja* cannot escape the trappings of the cinematic apparatus, but by interrogating its own limits, it can disrupt the spectator's mastery over the image. It gestures towards a reality in excess of representation that remains forever clouded from us, pushed outwards and subsumed by the blackness at the edge of the frame.

Conclusion

I have argued that although the ecological crisis impels us to recognize a world beyond the human, we are in the end unable to transcend the limits of our finite human perspectives. Using insights from film theory, especially Jean-Louis Baudry's apparatus theory, I critiqued speculative realism's assertion that we can think outside of the correlation between human thought and world. Although there is indeed a world independent of human thought, as speculative realists argue, our ability to relate to that world is limited by the boundaries of our perception. This need not enclose us within the anthropocentric bubble, but it shows us where we might find points of contact between human subjectivity and nonhuman reality. Hence speculative realism has something to learn not only from written discourses within film theory but also from cinema itself. The cinematic apparatus is a complex system comprising both human and nonhuman elements, and it negotiates tensions between subjectivity and objectivity in ways that can be productively brought to bear on issues central to speculative realism. Although cinema can provide an illusion of objectivity, the ideological underpinnings of the apparatus reveal that this sense of objectivity is conditional on cinema's subjective effects. It is only by positioning the human subject as the centre and origin of meaning that films are able to appear realistic or objective. Rather than falling on one side of this contradiction or the other – emphasizing subjectivity or objectivity– it is more productive for ecological thinking to maintain these oppositions in order to trace the limits between them. *Jauja* and *Tectonics* explore these tensions in that both films call attention to a wider reality while simultaneously emphasizing the ways they frame that reality for a human spectator. Both films use cinema's logic against itself to point out the limits of their own representations, thereby undermining the totalizing effects of cinema and gesturing towards a world outside of image and thought. A nuanced ecological ethics can neither shed the subjective trappings of the human perspective nor take that perspective for everything. Despite the impossibility of seeing beyond human concepts and perceptions, we must continue to push against our limits, searching them for fractures and inconsistencies that might open onto the unknown wilderness beyond.

Phenomenology and ecology must be considered together, and ecological ethics cannot do without a theory of subjectivity. Questions remain about how a theory of cinematic subjectivity might contribute to ecocriticism and an ethics of the Anthropocene, and so the second part of this book will flip the terms of this relationship and consider how cinema can represent the subject as conditioned through and contaminated by external reality. The next chapter will introduce an ecological theory of cinematic subjectivity through Bataille's ontology of the subject in *Inner Experience*. For Bataille, the subject is finite but constantly desires to exceed itself, and this tension between finitude and excess can help us find the locus of transgression: the limit between human and nonhuman realities, the unstable boundary between inside and outside.[45]

Notes

1 Kara, 'Beasts of the Digital Wild'; Martin-Jones, 'Trolls, Tigers and Transmodern Ecological Encounters'; Peterson, 'The *Gravity* of *Melancholia*'.

2 Shaviro, *The Universe of Things*, 9–10.

3 Ibid., 9.

4 I owe this connection to Marc Furstenau, who acted as mentor for the version of this chapter published in *Cinema Journal* and provided detailed comments during the review process.

5 See David Bordwell and Noël Carroll, eds, *Post-Theory: Reconstructing Film Studies* (Madison: University of Wisconsin Press, 1996); for focused critiques on the medium specificity thesis and mind-film analogies, respectively, see Noël Carroll, 'The Specificity of Media in the Arts', *Journal of Aesthetic Education* 19, no. 4 (1985), 5–20 and Noël Carroll, 'Film/Mind Analogies: The Case of Hugo Munsterberg', *Journal of Aesthetics and Art Criticism* 46, no. 4 (1988), 489–99.

6 Carroll, 'Film/Mind Analogies', 497.

7 Meillassoux, *After Finitude: An Essay on the Necessity of Contingency*.

8 Bryant, Srnicek and Harman, 'Towards a Speculative Philosophy', 3–4.

9 Ibid., 3.

10 Meillassoux, *After Finitude*, 3.

11 Shaviro, *Universe of Things*, 66.

12 I am not convinced that speculative realism is an entirely new kind of realism. This statement from Bryant, Srnicek and Harman evidences a contradiction between old and new that remains unresolved in speculative realism (but can be rethought via film theory): 'By contrast with the repetitive continental focus on texts, discourse, social practices, and human finitude, the new breed of thinker is turning once more toward reality itself.' Their claim that they are 'turning once more toward reality' indicates a reactionary return to traditional metaphysics that they disavow by claiming to be a 'new breed of thinker'. Bryant, Srnicek and Harman, 'Speculative Philosophy', 3.

13 Graham Harman, 'On the Undermining of Objects: Grant, Bruno, and Radical Philosophy', in *The Speculative Turn: Continental Materialism and Realism*, ed. Levi Bryant, Nick Srnicek and Graham Harman (Melbourne: Re-press, 2011), 21.

14 Martin-Jones, 'Trolls, Tigers, and Transmodern Ecological Encounters', 83.

15 Peterson, '*Gravity* of *Melancholia*', 2.

16 Ibid., 4. Harman insists that all things, human or otherwise, are equal, at least insofar as they relate to each other in the same way; Levi Bryant, another proponent of OOO, calls this the 'democracy of objects'. See Levi Bryant, *The Democracy of Objects* (Ann Arbor, MI: Open University Press, 2011).

17 Harman describes a fantasy about a future where different camps of speculative realists fight to the death:

> No longer reduced to alliance under a single banner, the speculative realists now have a chance to wage friendly and futuristic warfare against one another. Intellectual fault lines have been present from the start. At the Goldsmiths event two years ago, I played openly with scenarios in which each of us might be isolated against a gang attack by the other three on specific wedge issues. In my new capacity as a blogger, I have turned this into a scenario of outright science fiction, in which the continental landscape of 2050 is made up solely of warring clans descended from the various branches of 2007-era speculative realism.

Harman, 'On the Undermining of Objects', 22.

18 Pick and Narraway, 'Introduction', 2.

19 Siegfried Kracauer, *Theory of Film: The Redemption of Physical Reality* (Princeton, NJ: Princeton University Press, 1960), 1.

20 André Bazin, *What Is Cinema?*, trans. Hugh Gray (Berkeley: University of California Press, 2005), 1:14.

21 Ibid., 2:26.

22 Ibid., 1:13; Peterson, '*Gravity* of *Melancholia*', 4.

23 Bazin, *What Is Cinema?*, 1:13.

24 Jean-Louis Baudry, 'Ideological Effects of the Basic Cinematographic Apparatus', in *Narrative, Apparatus, Ideology: A Film Theory Reader*, ed. Philip Rosen (New York: Columbia University Press, 1986), 295.

25 Philip Rosen, *Change Mummified: Cinema, Historicity, Theory* (Minneapolis: University of Minnesota Press, 2001), 8.

26 See Dudley Andrew's *What Cinema Is!* (Oxford: Wiley Blackwell, 2010); Dudley Andrew and Hervé Joubert Laurencin, eds, *Opening Bazin: Postwar Film Theory and Its Afterlife* (Oxford: Oxford University Press, 2011); and Rosen, *Change Mummified.*

27 Baudry's apparatus theory is of course indebted to and implicated in a broader debate than the phenomenological lineage through Husserl that I trace here. Baudry theorizes human subjectivity through a complex framework including not only Husserl but also Freud, Althusser and Marx. My point is that, regardless of any theoretical nuances we might recognize in the ways that Baudry and Bazin respectively theorize subjectivity and its relationship to the cinematic apparatus, speculative realists would immediately reject both positions (fairly or unfairly) for their correlationist assumptions. Both thinkers would be immediately eschewed for their indebtedness to phenomenology (Merleau-Ponty for Bazin, Husserl for Baudry), while Baudry's theory is doubly reprehensible for its reliance on psychoanalysis.

28 Baudry, 'Ideological Effects', 292.

29 Ibid., 286.

30 *Tectonics* and *Jauja* complicate totalizing claims about medium specificity in other ways as well. *Tectonics*, for example, has been distributed and exhibited in a number of formats: it was screened at film festivals in 2012, including the Locarno International Film Festival, the Vancouver International Film Festival and the New York Film Festival, and it has played in various museums as an art installation; in 2016 it was featured on the video-on-demand website Mubi and acquired by educational distribution label Torch Films.

31 For an analysis of the nonanthropocentric aesthetics of *BNSF*, see Samuel Adelaar, 'A World in the Making: Contingency and Time in James Benning's *BNSF*', *Film-Philosophy* 21, no. 1 (2017), 60–77.

32 Bennett, *Vibrant Matter*, xii.

33 Jens Andermann, 'Exhausted Landscapes: Reframing the Rural in Recent Argentine and Brazilian Films', *Cinema Journal* 53, no. 2 (Winter 2014), 55.

34 Ibid., 53.

35 Georges Bataille, *Theory of Religion*, trans. Robert Hurley (New York: Zone Books, 1992), 50–2.

36 Baudry, 'Ideological Effects', 297.

37 Jean-Louis Baudry, 'The Apparatus: Metapsychological Approaches to the Impression of Reality in the Cinema', in *Narrative, Apparatus, Ideology, A Film Theory Reader*, ed. Philip Rosen (New York: Columbia University Press, 1986), 312.

38 Baudry, 'Ideological Effects', 291; Baudry, 'Apparatus', 313.

39 Ibid., 286.

40 Ibid., 289.

41 Baudry, 'Apparatus', 313.

42 Barthes, 'Diderot, Brecht, Eisenstein', 173.

43 This reading also applies to the three *tableaux vivants* in *A Field in England* (see Chapter 2), which similarly undermine the anthropocentric gaze of the camera. In the tableaux, the actors stand motionless as the camera cuts between them, their expressions visibly trembling as they try to hold their faces still; these emphatically unnatural pauses in *A Field in England*'s narrative highlight the artificiality of the cinematic image and its reliance on human scale. They also reference seventeenth-century art: 'the tableaux came out of looking at woodcuts that reflect that time period, obviously flat and two dimensional. It was a way to reference those but also a way of using a film language that wasn't traditional.' Ben Wheatley, 'An A-Z of the World of *A Field in England*', *AFieldinEngland.com*, 2014. http://www.afieldinengland.com/masterclass/historical-terms/. Accessed 6 August 2019.

44 Baudry, 'Ideological Effects', 286.

45 This chapter was originally published as 'Objectivity, Speculative Realism and the Cinematic Apparatus', *Cinema Journal* 57, no. 4 (2018), 3–24, and is reprinted with permission from the University of Texas Press.

Part 2

Subjectivity

3

Eco-consciousness in *Under the Skin* and *Nymphomaniac*

Introduction

I suggested at the end of the previous chapter that film ecocriticism cannot do without a theory of subjectivity. Theorizing the nonhuman in cinema requires that we recognize the subjective underpinnings of the apparatus which – drawing from Jean-Louis Baudry – I argued always directs itself towards a human subject, even if this subjective position can be deconstructed or undermined from within. While previous chapters have focused on what is in excess of the human – what Quentin Meillassoux calls 'the great outdoors',[1] or reality independent of human thought – this chapter will explore how human subjectivity is constituted by this excess and attempt to provide a more ecological way of reading cinematic subjectivity. This does not mean that the subject takes ontological priority: according to Bataille, while humans can only have knowledge within a limited sphere, our existence is conditioned by an unknowable wider reality. Therefore, while this chapter might sometimes appear to take a step back from the broader ecocritical concerns of this book by focusing at length on the structure of human subjectivity, the argument here is integral to my overall methodology. Since human subjectivity cannot merely be subtracted from our metaphysics or modes of film analysis, as I demonstrated in the last chapter, in what follows I will attempt to work through subjectivity as a way of accessing what exceeds it. Human subjectivity will therefore be characterized as related dynamically to a multitude of external forces.

To theorize human subjectivity as limited and beholden to broader forces, I will draw primarily from Bataille's notion of ipseity (or selfhood, individuality), which he conceives as a paradox between continuity and discontinuity: human subjects perceive themselves as discrete, self-contained beings, discontinuous from nature, despite the fact that their existence affects and is affected by things outside of their embodied experience. Bataille's theory of subjectivity is nonanthropocentric in that he frames human existence in the context of a wide array of natural forces on a variety of scales: atoms, single-celled organisms, plants, animals, the biosphere, the universe. Human subjectivity is not exceptional for Bataille, and he cautions in *Erotism* that we should not discount the interiority of even single-celled organisms: 'I do warn you … against the habit of seeing these tiny creatures from the outside only, of seeing them as things which do not exist inside themselves. You and I exist inside ourselves. But so does a dog, and in that case so do insects and creatures smaller still.'[2] Further, the interiority of all beings, including humans, is fragile and susceptible to outside influence: 'What one calls a "being" is never perfectly simple, and if it has a single enduring unity, it only possesses it imperfectly: it is undermined by its profound inner division, it remains poorly closed and, at certain points, open to attack from the outside.'[3] Bataille's nonanthropocentric approach to human subjectivity provides a framework for understanding how cinema can negotiate between multiple subject positions (characters, camera, spectators) and might question or even reformulate the complex interplay between human subjects and the outside world.

Two recent films self-consciously address issues of interiority and selfhood in relation to nature: Lars von Trier's *Nymphomaniac (Vol I & II)* (2013) and Jonathan Glazer's *Under the Skin* (2013). I will focus in particular on the ways that both films represent the inner experiences of their protagonists through representations of obscure and irrational natural landscapes. Bringing these two theoretical poles – ecology and subjectivity – into conversation will allow me to explore how subjectivity is constituted through excess; *Under the Skin* and *Nymphomaniac* are useful in that they articulate an unstable and ecologically oriented version of cinematic subjectivity. The two films do this in slightly different ways: *Under the Skin* exemplifies ipseity primarily on the level of representation, through abstract imagery that destabilizes the spectator's grasp on filmic reality, while *Under the Skin* explores subjectivization through form, as it undermines its own internal logic in interpreting the experiences of its protagonist.

Subjectivity and excess

In *The Universe of Things*, Steven Shaviro considers that, broadly speaking, we can conceive of objects in terms of either substance or relations. He argues further that, since both conclusions can be drawn from experience, deciding between these theoretical approaches is an aesthetic matter rather than an ontological one: 'It is finally a matter of *taste* and is not subject to conceptual adjudication.'[4] Shaviro turns to Alfred North Whitehead as a thinker concerned with *both* the privacy and relationality of all objects; Bataille similarly views things in terms of a tension between isolation and interconnectivity, but he is less certain that we can acquire knowledge about objects in the face of this contradiction. Bataille's thought is an attempt to theorize what inevitably resists theorization, and the messiness of his writings – which address a wide variety of subjects, from microbiology to economics to astronomy to anthropology, through a range of writing styles, including poetry, philosophy and pornographic prose – reflects an excessive reality that does not fit into the ordered systems of thought and language.

Bataille's philosophical aims are self-defeating and impossible. He laments in *Inner Experience* that to remain true to the object of his thought, he really ought to remain silent, though his compulsion towards knowledge continuously drives him to theorize the unknowable: '*The word silence is still a sound*, to speak is in itself to imagine knowing, and to no longer know, it would be necessary to no longer speak.'[5] Bataille likens his philosophy to religious mysticism in that it is governed by negativity and nonknowledge: 'It brings to a world dominated by thought connected with our experience of physical objects (and by the knowledge developed from this experience) an element which finds no place in our intellectual architecture except negatively as a limiting factor.'[6] It is impossible to access this unknown element through subjective experience – we are closed off from it because it exists apart from the relationality through which we ordinarily perceive the world of physical objects.

Despite Bataille's epistemological doubt about reality outside of thought, he discusses subjectivity in a strikingly materialist way. For readers acquainted only with Bataille's reputation for transgression, his long discussions of natural phenomena are likely to be surprising. He begins *The Accursed Share*, his two-volume work on political economy, with a description of the movement of energy in the biosphere;[7] *Erotism*, his work on human sexuality, starts with a lengthy analysis of the reproduction of plants, animals and simple organisms.[8] Bataille is intensely attuned to the isolated experience of human existence, which is an aspect of his writing very apparent in his graphic accounts of sex and violence; however, he simultaneously upholds that we cannot be considered independently from each other or the natural world. Although Bataille is a correlationist in that he believes we cannot conceive a reality outside of subjective impressions, he does not give the human subject ontological priority, and he resists the anthropocentrism that speculative realists argue characterizes post-Kantian philosophy by insisting on excess as an originary principle. A system, he argues, is always conditioned by what is outside of itself rather than its own self-constitution. This motivates Bataille's thinking on a wide variety of topics: *The Accursed Share*, for example, outlines why economies are better understood by what they waste or squander than what they productively consume, while in *Erotism* he argues that social laws are best understood by their exceptions, what they make taboo. Individual human subjects are no different for Bataille. Though we conceive of ourselves as discrete and discontinuous, our existence is nevertheless predicated on a continuous world that remains obscure until we die and our subjective boundaries are erased. To return to the definition of inner experience I outlined in the introduction, Bataille draws from atomic theory to explain the paradox of individual selfhood, or *ipseity*:

> Man can enclose being in a simple, indivisible element. But there is no being without 'ipseity.' *Without 'ipseity,' a simple element (an electron) encloses nothing.* The atom, despite its name, is a composite, but only possesses an elementary complexity: the atom itself, because of its relative simplicity, can only be determined through 'ipseity.' Thus the number of particles that compose a being intervenes in the constitution of its 'ipseity': if the knife of which one successively replaces the handle then the blade loses the shadow of its ipseity, it is not the same as a machine, in which would have disappeared, replaced piece by piece, each of the *numerous* elements that made it new: still less a man whose constituent parts die incessantly (such that nothing of these elements that we *were* subsists after a certain number of years). I can, if necessary, admit that from an extreme complexity, being imposes upon reflection *more* than an elusive appearance, but complexity, raised degree by degree, is for this *more* a labyrinth in which it wanders endlessly, loses itself once and for all.[9]

We experience ourselves as unified beings discrete from one another, but when we attempt to trace our limits, we discover that this unity is more mysterious than it first appears; we turn out to be composite beings with unstable boundaries. Despite the instability of these boundaries, however, we find ourselves unable to transcend them, because doing so would erase what differentiates us from the world – what constitutes us as subjects in the first place.

Joseph Libertson reads Bataille's ipseity as nonanthropocentric because although correlationism is inherent to the economy of thought, it does not

Eco-Consciousness in *Under the Skin and* Nymphomaniac   107

exhaust this economy, and there is always something that 'escapes the power of comprehension, on the basis of its power to escape this power'.[10] This alterity is passive, negative and entirely apart from the restricted economy of relations acting on and through the subject, which is why the subject's constitution through alterity is non-relational – relation is a power, a positive force, while alterity is 'a passivity or susceptibility'.[11] Cary Wolfe makes a similar point when he discusses human thought in terms of autopoiesis, or 'openness from closure';[12] while an autopoietic system cannot conceive of anything except in terms of its own frames of reference, it nevertheless remains prone to influence from the outside and adapts itself to accommodate new information and flows of energy from its environment. That subjectivity can only understand and relate to the world through the restricted economy of thought and language does not imply that there is no general economy that operates entirely outside these terms, or that this outside exists independently; for Libertson, alterity 'collaborates' and contaminates.[13] Subjectivity is therefore less like a fortress impermeable to invasion and more like wounded skin.

Human subjectivity is therefore differentiated through closure, meaning that it is susceptible to but closed off from the outside world; however, there is no Cartesian sphere of self-constitution and certainty, because interiority is also *invaginated*. Invagination, an embryological term imported to the humanities through Maurice Merleau-Ponty's theory of flesh and later adopted by other French thinkers like Jacques Derrida and Jean-Luc Nancy,[14] occurs in embryological development when a spherical collection of cells (called a blastomere) indents to form a cavity that will eventually become the gut. Invagination marks the moment when an organism differentiates between its inside and outside by developing distinct germ layers. Crucially, the 'inside' of the organism does not develop because its surface is punctured or penetrated from the outside, but rather because it folds in on itself. Nancy uses the term often in describing embodied experience as a constant enfolding in an effort to find an ever-elusive self:

> The body is nothing but the outside: skin exposed, a network of sentient receivers and transmitters. All outside and nothing like 'me' that would be held inside that wrapping. There is no ghost in the machine, no dimensionless point where 'I' feel or feel myself feeling. The inside of the envelope is yet another outside, developed (or de-enveloped) otherwise, full of folds, turns, convolutions, and adhesions. Full of invaginations, small heaps, and conglomerations.[15]

The term 'invagination' suggests a feminine understanding of embodied experience through the allusion to vaginal folds and the analogy to penetrative heterosexual sex: just as a man does not access a woman's interiority through said sex act, a subject cannot access any 'inner truth' through lived experience, which is always immanent, external and enfolded. For Nancy, interiority is inaccessible in much the same way as the real, and our own subjectivity can only be read externally, on the surface.

It is worth reflecting on the gendered connotations of Nancy's terminology here because they illuminate similar conceptual tangles in Bataille's ontology. Nancy's use of the term 'invagination' in some ways reinforces heteronormative understandings of sexuality or experience by evoking gendered binaries: penetrated/penetrative, active/passive, male/female. However, by framing the concept in terms of a generative biological process more primordial than sexual difference – germ layer differentiation – Nancy suggests that invagination refers to embodied experience more generally, rather than an experience particular to female subject formation. Men are equally invaginated, even if culture does not recognize them as such, and although we necessarily understand differentiation according to the heteronormative logic of the dominant ideology, Nancy's philosophy also suggests ways that embodiment is in excess of that logic.

Similarly, Bataille's ideas about gender do not escape patriarchal heteronormativity, and in fact frequently reinforce it. Sean Connolly, for example, observes 'the (sexist) centrality of male narrators and their contrasting female counterparts, like *Madame Edwarda*, Simone in *Story of the Eye*, or Pierre's mother in *My Mother*. Men seek women, and women seduce men into sex, violence, and transgression.'[16] However, heteronormativity in Bataille is a restricted economy that cannot contain the excesses of sexual desire. Sex acts in Bataille are often penetrative but seldom procreative: in *Story of the Eye*, Simone pleasures herself not only with the male narrator but also with female partners, as well as with eggs, bull testicles and eyeballs inserted both vaginally and anally. Bataille's thought does not align with progressive ideas about sexuality and gender because, crucially, sex is not an affirmation of identity; instead, as Connolly argues, Bataille's ontology 'necessarily implies a challenge to all categories of personal identity, including those that pertain to gender and sex'.[17] Instead of subverting heteronormativity through any kind of positive alternative, Bataille's excessive logic 'liberates sexuality' from productivity through a 'general economy of desire'.[18] Although Bataille frequently favours non-procreative sex (anal sex, masturbation, necrophilia), all sexuality partakes in this general economy and therefore any sex act, no matter how seemingly heteronormative, exceeds any normative logic we might impose upon it.

This logic – excessive rather than progressive – also informs Nancy's view of embodied experience, in which all subjects, no matter how seemingly masculine and potent, are invaginated and vulnerable to external reality. This view of subjectivity as folded inside out is not merely metaphorical, but is instead a physical condition of embodied experience: when a zygote invaginates, it folds inwards to form a channel so that the 'outside' passes through without penetrating the cell layers on either side. Nancy uses this as a way of explaining our interiority as a play of surfaces that never accesses an internal essence or truth, since our efforts to penetrate the inner core of our being can only result in creating more folds. Nancy's excessive logic of subjectivity cannot affirm any positive determination of self, but instead frustrates stable categories of identity, just like sexual experience in Bataille. 'Inside' and 'outside' should therefore not be understood in simple spatial terms, as a sphere within which I exist, and beyond which we can locate the real. Rather, subjectivity is a complex process that constantly enfolds inside and outside, and that shifts in relation to a complex environment containing myriad other constantly enfolding beings. Understood in this way, subjectivity and self-knowledge become a play of surfaces that never penetrate into an inner truth or an outer reality. Correspondingly, *Nymphomaniac* and *Under the Skin* both articulate subjectivity in terms of a play of surfaces and a turning inside out.

Interiority and inner experience

Under the Skin begins with a black frame and a frantic score of scurrying strings rising on the soundtrack. A blue light glows in the distance, and a jump cut brings us closer to the source before cutting again to reveal a series of circular shapes floating in a line away from the light. The shapes are vague and nearly abstract, but they call to mind the opening images of *2001: A Space Odyssey* (Stanley Kubrick, 1968) of the Earth lit from behind by the sun; the reference suggests that the shapes we first see in *Under the Skin* might be a spaceship, or some other kind of celestial object. The shapes 'eventually resolve themselves to be the focusing shutter of a camera,'[19] before the image is suddenly illuminated and the artificial, circular lines become a bright hazel human eye. This sudden reversal across a huge spatial range – from cosmic to personal, mediated through a camera – provides an initial visual example of the way that *Under the Skin* deals with questions of human subjectivity. The film's title already evokes its concern with interiority, which it investigates through a series of ambiguous spaces and images that subvert our expectations. Though *Under the Skin* is a film about interiority, we are precluded from the thoughts of characters, as there is no voice-over and very little dialogue. The spectator is therefore encouraged to read things 'on the surface', though, as in the opening scene, this surface is constantly flipping, reversing and turning inside out.

In the following scene, a motorcyclist takes the lifeless body of a woman into the back of a van. The van seems to contain a featureless white void, where a naked woman (Scarlett Johansson) removes the dead woman's clothes and puts them on herself. It is unclear whether the space inside the van is real or metaphorical, and the scene can be read in a number of ways. Ara Osterweil, for example, reads the scene as the alien donning the dead woman's skin;[20] this takes an interpretive leap, however, since the dead woman is clearly not Scarlett Johansson and only her clothes are removed. The scene might take place in a real, physical place – another dimension, maybe, or a gate to the alien's home world – or it might depict a psychic process, of the alien acquiring a human persona. This indeterminacy of inner and outer spaces is a central aesthetic feature of *Under the Skin*, which poses a number of metaphysical questions about interiority and embodiment while also quite literally turning people inside out: the narrative follows the alien as she seduces men around Glasgow and takes them to an inky black pool where they are skinned and their organs harvested.

The alien's impenetrable expression as she drives around Glasgow searching for victims gives the sense of her outer appearance as a persona or mask, an impression emphasized by her bright lipstick and dark eye make-up. An early scene establishes her lack of empathy, as she watches a mother and father drown and leaves their baby crying on the beach. However, as the narrative progresses, she seems to gradually develop an emotive inner life, a process tied to her gradual awareness of her human body as more than just an external skin. She is first surprised by her body when a man hands her a rose at a traffic stop and she recoils at the sight of blood on her hands. As she drives away, she sees the flower seller bandaging his hands, but her shock initiates a sense of uncertainty about her body. Later in the film, she flees the city and heads to the Highlands, where she stops at a café and tries to eat a slice of cake. She abruptly coughs it back up, but her failed attempt at eating suggests a curiosity about her inner self

Eco-Consciousness in Under the Skin *and* Nymphomaniac   111

that turns out to be a dead end; her attempt at ingestion results in revulsion, a blockage. In Nancy's terms, this preclusion from interiority is characteristic of embodiment: we search for our inner selves, a place to locate the 'I', only to find that 'I remain a null point of spirit nowhere to be found in this entanglement smeared with pulp, tissues, and fluids.'[21]

The alien's inability to penetrate her exterior surface leads to a preoccupation with the holes – or lack thereof – in her skin. In the Highlands, the alien goes home with a man she meets on a bus. After he goes to bed, she examines her body in a full-length mirror: dimly lit by the red glow of an electric heater, she bends her knees and twists her body to examine the effects on her reflection. Later, the man and the alien attempt to have sex. She stops him suddenly, shocked and leaps into the corner to shine a lamp on the place where her genitals should be. It is unclear whether she is disturbed by the presence of an opening or the absence of one (though the earlier, failed attempt at eating suggests the latter), but the man's attempt to penetrate her apparently calls the integrity of her body into question. The alien's investigations into the holes in herself – her invaginations, the places where the body's boundaries break down or fold in on themselves – amount to little positive knowledge. These holes do not open onto a legible inner self, nor do they block out harm or outside influence, and her human skin, which is meant to be a protective shield over her alien body, proves to be simultaneously fragile and impenetrable. Reading her 'on the surface', the spectator cannot breach her boundaries to find answers about her subjective position, and once her alien body is exposed in the final sequence – shiny, black, featureless – this too becomes just another surface, one even more inscrutable and opaque than her outer human skin. The alien's gradual self-awareness is associated with a surface-level exploration of her body's boundaries; *Under the Skin* suggests that being human means having a self contained in a human skin, a self that cannot transcend its body but which nevertheless opens onto a wider reality through convolutions and invaginations that render its boundaries unstable.

If *Under the Skin* is about someone trying to determine the limits of their own existence – their ipseity, as determined by their physical body – then *Nymphomaniac* is about the negotiation of subjectivity through a multitude of perspectives. *Nymphomaniac* is composed of a series of chapters, through which self-proclaimed nymphomaniac Joe recounts her life story to Seligman (Stellan Skarsgård). The story is intended to prove that she is a 'bad human being', deserving of the beating that left her bloodied in the alley where Seligman found her. Though the narrative is more or less linear – or rather, circular, beginning with Joe bloodied in the alley and ending by explaining how she arrived there – it is diverted through a number of interruptions and explanations from Seligman. In the first chapter of Joe's story ('The Compleat Angler'), she recounts her first sexual experiences: masturbating as a child, losing her virginity, competing with a friend to see how many men they could seduce on a train trip. Seligman, who later identifies himself as asexual and who professes to spend most of his time reading, relates her experiences to his own frames of knowledge, often through analogies about natural phenomena. In 'The Compleat Angler', Seligman relates Joe's behaviours to those of a fish, inspired by his passion for fly-fishing. He interrupts Joe's story about trawling for men on a train – she narrates as the events are shown onscreen – to compare their actions to 'reading a river' for fish. The image literally rewinds to account for Seligman's analysis, and the footage of the two young girls looking into the compartments repeats, this time superimposed with images of reeds floating in a river current as Seligman explains how the behaviour of fish is determined by river topography.

Joe, too, uses nature analogies to explain her own experiences. She tells Seligman that her only sin is 'demanding more of the sunset', and a sunset appears as she describes her longing for more spectacular colours. She describes a childhood masturbatory activity called 'playing frogs', which involved sliding on her belly on a flooded floor; the froglike movements of the two young girls shown in flashback are preceded by a close-up of a green frog jumping into water. In a later chapter, Joe describes feeling like a 'potted plant' during a sado-masochistic relationship with a man named K (Jamie Bell): she describes him constantly checking her 'cunt juice' the way old ladies check if their plants need watering, and the descriptions of both actions are paired with corresponding images. While *Under the Skin* has formal restraint in that it shows far more than it tells, and does not even show enough to ensure a straightforward reading, *Nymphomaniac* is characterized by narrative excess: it both tells and shows far more than it needs to, with images corroborating seemingly insignificant details and analogies that do not in the end amount to a definite reading. The indexical relationship between words and images does not give the sense of a single underlying reality, but rather enhances the feeling of slippage between perspectives as Joe's story proliferates into a multitude of metonymic images.

Because the narrative takes place as a dialogue, the spectator is called upon to navigate these excesses of information to determine their own interpretation of Joe's life story. The conversations between Joe and Seligman touch on a number

Eco-Consciousness in *Under the Skin and* Nymphomaniac

of controversial issues – religion, race, abortion – certain to provoke strong reactions. Seligman is initially characterized as a 'proper' liberal humanist: he is a well-read atheist who believes in women's rights and often chides Joe for making politically insensitive statements. Joe, on the other hand, reveals a number of problematic opinions: she rejects the label of sex addict by identifying as a nymphomaniac and asserts that her nymphomania makes her immoral in some absolute sense; she insists on calling the black men with whom she engages in a threesome 'negroes' and tells Seligman that 'any woman who tells you negroes don't turn her on is lying'; during a lengthy sequence in the director's cut when she recounts her (incredibly graphic and brutal) experience of performing an abortion on herself, she insists on describing the process in detail and rebukes Seligman for suggesting that a woman's right to choose overrides the infliction of trauma on the foetus. The presumably liberal, culturally literate spectator, uncomfortable with Joe's position, is likely to align him or herself with Seligman, at least until the final sequence.

After Joe has told her story, and insisted that she behaved immorally by wilfully disregarding the feelings of others in order to achieve her own sexual satisfaction, Seligman replies that she was 'simply a woman demanding her right', and that her story would not seem as subversive – would even be banal – had she been a man. His passionate feminist sermon is enhanced by flashbacks of all of the film's relevant events, granting his reading of them a sense of finality and certainty. After he finishes, Joe tells him she is too tired to argue and declares him to be her first true friend. This seemingly happy ending to Joe's tale provides a satisfying final reading that neatly ties up loose ends. However, after Joe has fallen asleep, Seligman creeps back into her room in only a pyjama top; he climbs into bed with her, stroking his flaccid penis and grabbing her buttocks. She wakes up in surprise and the screen goes black before we hear him protest, 'But you've fucked thousands of men.' A gunshot is heard, followed by fleeing footsteps, and the credits roll. Seligman's act of sexual assault contradicts his previous characterization as a kind-hearted feminist asexual and impels a reconsideration of his readings of Joe's narrative. It also implicates the spectator by demanding that they re-evaluate the degree to which they have been complicit in Seligman's position, which in the end is revealed to be based in violence and misogyny. The ending emphasizes that the narrative has not merely been a negotiation between two perspectives (Seligman's and Joe's) but rather a dialogue between two people self-consciously staged for a third – the spectator. Read in light of Seligman's final act, his determination to read Joe's life against her own interpretation is recast not as generous and encouraging (as his 'feminist' diatribes would seem to suggest) but violent and appropriative. The point is not that Joe is 'right': *Nymphomaniac* does not result in a positive affirmation of her un-PC excesses. Nor does the emphasis on a third term in the equation – the position of the spectator – result in a dialectical solution or higher-order truth. Rather, as Lynne Huffer argues, *Nymphomaniac* ends with a more troubling negativity that unsettles the entire narrative structure.[22] This ending, as well as being narratively excessive in that it adds on to a story that had already reached a satisfying conclusion, is also excessive in the sense that it goes beyond the hermeneutic logic it itself had established, which the ending reveals to have been founded in masculine aggression and power. The film's critique is levied not merely at Seligman but also at his frames of knowledge, drawn from a broad tradition of Western thought referenced throughout the narrative.

Nymphomaniac's critique of liberal humanism is characteristic of von Trier's cinema, which often makes the spectator unexpectedly complicit in acts of violence or degradation.[23] *Nymphomaniac* is most explicit about this critical project, however, as evidenced by the sheer range of topics covered, including race, religion, abortion and women's sexual autonomy. This exaggerated emphasis on von Trier's preoccupation with the flaws in Western thought is associated with an abundance of natural imagery: just as new readers of Bataille might be surprised by his frequent allusions to the natural sciences and use of biological examples, viewers drawn in by *Nymphomaniac*'s titillating title and provocative advertising campaign – which included a series of fourteen posters, each featuring one of the actors in the apparent throes of an orgasm – would probably be frustrated by the film's frequent detours and analogies. The association between sex and nature, if read in Bataillean terms, provides a form of resistance to the film's narrative logic: to recall Bataille's argument, sex is a means for communing with the sacred natural world, which Bataille sees not as a transcendent 'other realm' but rather a reality in excess of structuring forces like language, law, consciousness or reason. Sex is heavily regulated in human societies through taboos and institutions such as marriage because of its transgressive power: there is something excessive in the sexual experience that cannot be harnessed for useful purposes, and that often works against our better judgements or makes us behave irrationally. Because sex has the potential to work against the profane world of work and reason, it is associated with the sacred – another word for alterity, or the outside of human thought. The importance of nature in *Nymphomaniac* can therefore be read as part of its critique of Western liberal humanism: like the missing 'inner

Eco-Consciousness in Under the Skin *and* Nymphomaniac   115

truth' of Joe's personal narrative (to which I will return shortly), the natural images cannot entirely be put to work in the service of narrative.

There is something in *Nymphomaniac's* natural images that remains extraneous or excessive, and that resists Seligman's attempts to appropriate them into a signifying discourse. What does an image of frogs leaping add to the phrase 'playing frogs'? How is an image of a sunset enhanced by the simultaneous description of its spectacular colours? The doubling of these representations – through both words and images – indicates a gulf between language and reality, further destabilizing the truth claims offered by the narrative. There are even further levels of mediation, of course, because the images are cinematic representations of natural phenomena rather than the phenomena themselves, and the cinematic image, as we saw in the last chapter, is already implicated in human ways of seeing; the images are also mediated through the perceptual and cognitive systems of particular spectators. These refractions do not expose an 'inner truth' of representation, nor do they suggest that truth is merely interpretation, since the film's final moments calls the entire practice of hermeneutics into question. Rather, *Nymphomaniac* ends with an implosive negativity that exposes the limits of its own mediated representations. While *Nymphomaniac's* narrative is ostensibly an attempt to figure out the truth about Joe, she becomes lost in the film's excessive play of images and interpretations.[24] Like the alien in *Under the Skin*, Joe can only be read on the surface, one that is constantly shifting and evading straightforward signification. My point is not that the truth becomes lost in a postmodern slippage of signs, nor that it is revealed to be relational or non-existent, but rather that this slippage opens onto a different order of truth – one that belongs not to reason but to alterity. *Nymphomaniac's* narrative structure is based in a negotiation of perspectives, but rather than resolving them it ends in a Bataillean negation that does not serve the discursive system by being synthesized into a higher-order truth; instead, it points to an excessive remainder that violates the systems of narrative and meaning.

Mete Ulaş Aksoy, commenting on Bataille's reworking of G. W. F. Hegel, explains that 'transgression, if being worthy of its name for Bataille, should put the system in jeopardy, managing to dodge the dialectical movement'.[25] Bataillean negation is not antithetical, as it does not constitute a complete reversal or contradiction of a claim or point of view. Rather, it is a point of access onto something beyond or lacking a point of view. This kind of negativity is frustrating because it doesn't even allow for the satisfaction of complete annihilation: Shaviro argues that Bataille's 'obsessive meditations concern – and participate in – a catastrophe all the more obscure and unsettling in that it refuses apocalyptic closure'.[26] The troubling excesses of Bataille's work are not quite nothing, but not quite something either; they are something *else*, something 'out there' and exterior that also turns out to be disturbingly intimate because, as Libertson suggests, alterity is not independent from subjectivity but instead conditions and contaminates it.[27] Instead of choosing between perspectives, *Nymphomaniac* opts for this 'something else': it reinforces the gulf between perspectives that is not quite their negation, a gulf also alluded to by the film's excessive natural imagery.

Sex and transgression

Both *Nymphomaniac* and *Under the Skin* use sexuality as a way of representing the limits of subjectivity. In Bataillean fashion, both films link sex with death: Bataille writes that eroticism 'is assenting to life up to the point of death',[28] meaning that the erotic provides a way of approaching the limits of consciousness, the places where we border onto another world or another person. This is paradoxical because the erotic both affirms the subject's finitude – its inescapable enclosure – and also requires a desire to move beyond these subjective boundaries. It is not quite an impulse for self-destruction, because although it desires the erasure of differentiation between self and world, it also requires that these boundaries are reinforced, or else there would be no subject to desire its own erasure. The subject that confronts its own limits through an erotic experience flirts with death but in the end resists it, therefore 'assenting to life' despite considering the possibility of its own annihilation. While sex and death seem like opposing forces, since one begets life and the other ends it, for Bataille they are inexorably connected.

Bataille argues in *The Accursed Share* that, counterintuitively, death is a luxury: it is wasteful because it involves the loss of energy without return – specifically, the loss of all the energy required to grow and maintain the organism over the course of its life. Death allows for sexual reproduction, which makes possible the discontinuity of the subject from its environment. He contrasts this with asexual reproduction, which involves the continuity between one generation and the next so that we cannot determine where the parent ends and the offspring begins:

> As we know, death is not necessary. The simplest forms of life are immortal: The birth of an organism reproduced through scissiparity is lost in the mists of time. Indeed, it cannot be said to have parents. Take for example the doubles of *A'* and *A'*, resulting from the splitting in two of *A: A* has not ceased living with the coming into being of *A'*.[29]

More complex – or what he calls 'burdensome'[30] – forms of life delay the disappearance of the parent through death until long after the reproductive process, thereby squandering an excess of energy (since neither life nor death are necessary for Bataille) into the production of discontinuous offspring. Death and waste are therefore the conditions for subjectivity, which can only be achieved through sexual reproduction: the ipseity of an individual subject results from its discontinuity from its parents and other organisms of its kind.

This squandering of resources fits into Bataille's broader ontology of excess, which sees life as a 'wild exuberance' that continuously wastes energy without return. Sexual reproduction is one way of squandering energy; Bataille lists meat-eating as another: 'If one cultivates potatoes or wheat, the land's yield in consumable calories is much greater than that of livestock in milk and meat for an equivalent acreage of pasture.'[31] *Under the Skin* similarly associates sexuality with meat-eating, though less explicitly than its source material: while Michael Faber's novel describes in detail the industrial practices through which human meat is harvested,[32] in the film these processes are more abstract. In the first of these sequences, the alien seduces a man and brings him to a tenement flat; she turns the key in the door and he follows her into the darkness, after which there is a cut to a black, non-descript space. The man undresses and leaves a trail of clothing on the black floor, which is only differentiated from the rest of the space through reflections in its glassy surface. Drums plod on the soundtrack as strings rise up in a pace that matches the walking movements of the two figures. Naked, he walks towards her as she walks backwards; he gradually sinks into the glassy surface of the floor, which now appears to be made of a thick black liquid. The camera tracks forwards past his sinking body and the alien stops and turns around. The music fades from the soundtrack as the alien silently picks up the discarded articles of clothing, her body reflected in the undisturbed black surface of the pool. The man is nowhere to be seen. As with the prior sequence in the white van, it is unclear whether the scene is actually occurring or is meant as a metaphorical representation of the man's demise. The spatial discontinuity across the cut between the outside of the flat and the inside void is reinforced by the movements of the two figures, who cross more ground than could possibly be contained by the building; because there are no distinguishing features of the environment, close-ups on the man make his movements appear unnatural, as though he is walking in place. The man and the alien never touch, but the sequence is explicitly sexual: the man has an erection as he sinks into the pool, and Scarlett Johansson's body is on display as the driving force leading the victim, seemingly unaware of his surroundings, to his death.

This first sequence establishes the pattern for the alien's seductions, and each subsequent 'sex' scene reveals slightly more information. She meets the next man in a club, where they dance together; his movements carry across a cut back to the void, as he dances in place to the same percussive rhythm from the last such scene. A long shot reveals the alien to be walking backwards on the surface of the pool while the man, now naked, gradually sinks into the inky pool. She walks back over the surface before a cut to the man below, floating in liquid and illuminated by blue light. He encounters what appears to be another man (presumably the first) floating in an unearthly way; he touches the man's wrinkled skin, which appears to grasp him back before it screams and retreats back into the darkness. The whole skin then wrinkles and folds in on itself, rippling for a moment like a sail in the void. In the next shot, a trough filled with sanguine liquid flows towards a red, illuminated opening. The liquid disappears into the hole before a transition to a series of abstract red shapes, then a red line, then a light that could be a star. The implication is maybe that the man's insides are sent 'elsewhere', and that the abstract images somehow represent the process through which this occurs. The shapes also look something like blood under a microscope, suggesting that the abstract images are not on a cosmic scale but rather a molecular one – a closer look at what is 'under the skin'. This echoes the indeterminacy between inner and outer spaces in the opening sequence and enhances the sense of disorientation that pervades the void scenes. The question posed by the film's title therefore continually proves difficult to answer because the film slips between spaces at various scales rather than probing under the surface to expose a previously hidden truth.

By relating this process of 'turning inside out' to sex, *Under the Skin* emphasizes what is at stake in the erotic; namely, the exposure of self to the outside. The men are not consumed by the alien, but instead by the space around her, and rather than penetrating the flesh of the other, the sexual act in *Under the Skin* involves a penetration of self by the outside. When the men sink into this outside, they are turned inside out. In Bataillean terms, these 'sex' scenes visualize what is risked in the erotic – namely, differentiation, the limits between self and other. Bataille writes that there is an inexorable gap between us:

> You and I are *discontinuous* beings. But I cannot refer to this gulf which separates us without feeling that this is not the whole truth of the matter. It is a deep gulf, and I do not see how it can be done away with. None the less, we can experience its dizziness together. It can hypnotise us. The gulf is death in one sense, and death is vertiginous, death is hypnotising.[33]

Because for Bataille the ipseity of the other is impenetrable – 'no communication between us can abolish our fundamental difference' since 'if you die, it is not my death'[34] – we can only relate to each other in virtue of the gulf between us, and these relations are limited to experiencing its 'dizziness' together. Intersubjectivity for Bataille is therefore fundamentally irrational: it is predicated not on the commonalities in our capacity for reason, but rather *on the limits* of these capacities. While a subject might wish to penetrate or be penetrated by another person[35] – the object of desire, whose ipseity is discontinuous and wholly other – the sexual encounter cannot breach the gulf that disconnects us. Intersubjectivity involves mutually exposing ourselves to alterity, to the unknowable outside of thought. However, this relationship is more complex than merely 'me' versus 'you', an 'inside' in here versus an 'outside' out there: as with the ambiguous spaces in *Under the Skin*, the distinctions marking these differences are often obscure and unstable.

The void sequences also question the ethics of meat-eating by exploring the relationship between matter and subjectivity. The alien's gradual development of empathy works against her ability to hunt her victims, eventually resulting in her inability to follow through with killing her last victim, credited as The Deformed Man (Adam Pearson), whom she finds walking to Tesco alone. The man is obviously unaccustomed to the alien's seductive strategies: she flatters him, telling him he has beautiful hands and probes him about his relationships with other people (he has none). The scene plays with the idea of seeing beyond appearances – of being interested in someone for more than just their looks – but turns it into something risky and menacing. A close-up shows the man pinching himself, suggesting that he is at least willing to entertain his own good luck in encountering a beautiful woman who wants to take him home. The spectator, however, is aware that the alien's interest in the man's inner self is more literal than he realizes: the cliché that 'we're all the same underneath the skin' is true in a brute, material sense, since the man's disfigured face hides the same mass of blood and organs harvested in earlier scenes.

The alien brings the man to the black void as usual, but on her way out of the building, the alien pauses to look at herself in a mirror. She had previously been shot observing herself, fragmented, in various mirrors – her lips in a hand mirror as she put on lipstick, her eyes in the rear view of the van – but the sight of her full face in this mirror makes her pause. Osterweil reads this is an initial moment of subjectivization: 'As in Jacques Lacan's theory of the mirror stage, the birth of the self emerges here from the simultaneous recognition of, and estrangement from, her own reflected image.'[36] This contradiction between recognition and estrangement occurs through the alien's recognition of self *as other*, seen from the outside as a body wrapped in skin. This process of identification is profoundly alienating because of the gap between experiencing oneself from the inside while simultaneously observing it from the outside, as extended matter. Nancy writes about embodiment as a mutual intrusion: 'the body's the intruder that, without breaking in, can't penetrate the self-present point that the spirit is.'[37] The body remains foreign to a spirit that Nancy defines as pure negativity, since 'the body keeps its secret, this nothing, this spirit that isn't lodged in it but spread out, expanded, extended all across it, so much so that the secret has no hiding place, no intimate fold where it might some day be discovered.'[38] We are nothing in excess of our meat, but this nothingness is ontologically significant rather than being reducible to our brute materiality. The alien's reflection on herself in the mirror seemingly leads to an awareness that she is nothing more than meat, and that consequently her victim – whom she had previously seen as mere meat – must also be a self. She lets him go, an act of mercy resulting from an awareness of self as other (and vice versa), which occurs not because of some deep inner connection but rather a recognition on the surface, at the level of skin. This scene also suggests the possibility of empathetic connection across species lines, as the alien and her human victim share similar experiences of interiority. The alien's empathy with her victim occurs not because they are the same underneath – they are not, as the final sequence reveals – but because they share an alienation from their outer appearances: they both feel differently on the inside from what they are on the outside.

Nancy writes that truth occurs on the level of skin, since it marks the unstable division between inside and outside: 'the truth is skin. Truth is in the skin, it makes skin: an authentic extension exposed, entirely turned outside while also enveloping the inside, a sack crammed with rumblings and musty odors.'[39]

Eco-Consciousness in Under the Skin *and* Nymphomaniac   121

The truth revealed is disappointingly material – that we are living meat, a sack containing nothing but noise and organs – but also gestures towards excess and alterity, that we are not all. This exposure to the outside that constitutes our relationship to ourselves and to others is also what is at stake in the sexual experience: 'the body is related to the body of the other sex. In this relation, its corporeality is involved insofar as it touches through sex on its limit: it delights, meaning that the body is shaken outside itself.'[40] Sex is a way of experiencing the body at its limit, a limit that can only be transcended through death, and *Under the Skin* interrogates these processes by externalizing erotic and intersubjective relationships and making them into something that truly risks turning the subject inside out.

Sex in *Nymphomaniac* is similarly transgressive in that it not only pushes the boundaries of morality but also interrogates the limit between society and nature. Bataille, like Nancy, argues that sex is ontologically excessive, more than just being morally so. *Nymphomaniac* exemplifies this idea in a number of ways, since its sex scenes are excessive in both an aesthetic sense – they are 'too much,' unnecessary – and a practical one, since they involved a large amount of labour despite the fact that the most explicit scenes were cut from the theatrical version. The director's cut contains a number of scenes featuring un-simulated sex using body doubles, and a great deal of impressive CGI is used to make it look as though the actors are really having sex. The director's cut is not widely available, nor was it widely screened, and its extra eighty-four minutes add little to the narrative. An immense amount of labour was required to film each sex scene twice: the negotiation of two sets of contracts (Gainsbourg and Martin have both said in interviews that the limits of their roles had to be very clearly defined[41]), the meticulous blocking of two scenes with two separate sets of actors, the use of prosthetics for the main actors, the post-production CGI to unify the two scenes seamlessly, the editing and re-editing required for the release of two separate versions. The result is arguably a disappointing and inferior film, and reviews for the director's cut are more tepid than for the theatrical release. *IndieWire* reviewer James Berclaz-Lewis, who defends the theatrical version as superior, summarizes the difference between cuts as simple addition:

> That's not to say that the longer version doesn't offer its fair share of surplus sex. But it's a case of slight extensions rather than wholesale scenes ... In fact, most of Joe's sexual encounters are afforded a couple of extra frames, along with a few generous close-ups. Sprinkle a few more bodily juices and you've essentially

covered the extent of the alleged 'controversial' bonus content offered by the director's cut.[42]

Berclaz-Lewis's criticism suggests that these additional sequences do not 'add up' to anything, whether in terms of narrative understanding or aesthetic value; they are superfluous, excessive – sacrificial in the Bataillean sense since they are literally wasted labour. Though this description of the extra scenes as mere addition, along with reports that audiences surveyed after watching both versions had trouble accounting for the increased running time of *Vol. I* (the extra scenes *Vol. II* are more obvious),[43] might be dismissed as artistic failure, they also add an extra-textual dimension to the film's concern with mathematics.

Nymphomaniac describes sex in numerical terms, generally through addition. When Joe tells Seligman about her loss of virginity to Jerôme (Shia LaBoeuf), she recounts that he 'humped me three times' – numbers appear counting upwards with his thrusts as the event is shown in flashback – and then turned her over and 'humped me five times in the ass', at which point a plus-sign appears, followed again by the count upwards to five. Seligman explains that 3 and 5 are Fibonacci numbers, but Joe brushes off his attempt to rationalize her experience by telling him, 'that may be, but in any case, it hurt like hell'. Seligman's comment that Joe's sexual experience is somehow connected to a mysterious order of the universe, especially the golden ratio visible in structures in nature, is given credence by the appearance of the numbers onscreen. It is also reinforced by Joe's seemingly intuitive mechanical skill: on her way out of Jerôme's apartment, she casually repairs the moped that he had been struggling to start before their sexual encounter. During a later scene, Jerôme fails to parallel park his car, and Joe

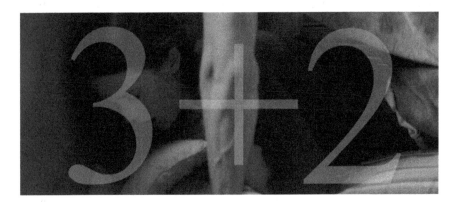

Figure 11 Numbers and sex in *Nymphomaniac Vol. I* (Lars Von Trier, 2013).

Eco-Consciousness in Under the Skin *and* Nymphomaniac 123

insists on giving it a try. To his frustration, she parks it perfectly, an action shown in an overhead shot superimposed with diagrams demonstrating the physics of her manoeuvre. Joe's knowledge of how things work is not reasoned, nor does she seem to direct it towards any employable skill (until the final chapter, she seems to float through dead-end desk jobs). Rather, it seems to connect her with an obscure order of things, a mathematizable structure to existence that she knows not through reason but simply by nature.

Seligman's interpretations constantly try to grant meaning to these events, but in the end his interpretations, like the extra scenes in the director's cut, amount to nothing, or even to loss. During the last chapter in *Vol. I*, 'The Little Organ School', Joe recounts her experiences with three lovers, inspired by a taped recording of Bach and Seligman's explanation of polyphony ('the idea that every voice has its own melody, but together in harmony'). Seligman explains that Bach's music is based on a 'rather incomprehensible mystique concerning numbers', and numbers once again appear on screen as he explains that the Fibonacci numbers have been used throughout history to try and find a divine methodology in art and architecture, a statement supported by images of illustrative diagrams and classical artistic references – the Last Supper, the Parthenon. Seligman relates this to Bach's polyphony, which forms a melody on the organ called 'Cantus Firmus' with a base voice, the left hand and the right hand. Joe uses this to jump into a story about the harmony between her various lovers, whom she explains add up to a complete sexual experience. This harmony is composed of three lovers: a reliable base voice called F (Nicolas Bro), an unpredictable left hand called G (Christine Gade Bjerrum) and Jerôme, who completes the harmony when she falls in love with him.

When Joe finishes telling Seligman about her lovers, the screen is divided in three, with each third looping various details of their relationships as the Bach tape plays in the background. The addition of the three sequences through the split screen suggests a sense of completeness – arithmetic leading to a whole number – that matches Bach's harmony. But while Joe explicitly introduces the story as a way of providing a complete account of her sexual history, in the end it amounts to a loss; specifically, the loss of her orgasm, an event that abruptly marks the end of *Vol. I*. Joe's desire for plenitude and fulfilment, indicated by her plea a few moments earlier for Jerôme to 'fill all her holes', results in a total loss of the pleasure she sought through sex. The complicated stylistic methods that *Nymphomaniac* uses to make sense of these events (diagrams, metaphorical images, intercutting, repetition) give the impression of coherence, as though the images should amount to a clear revelation, related to Seligman's descriptions of divine methodology. However, this mathematization of sexuality amounts to simple addition that refuses to suggest a totality.

The loss of Joe's sexual pleasure critiques the idea of reason and specifically mathematics supporting a higher-order truth about the universe; instead, what results is a pure and simple loss, as the three lovers add up to the negation of Joe's sexual satisfaction. *Nymphomaniac* visualizes Joe's sexual experiences through a mathematical formula, and Joe anticipates that the three lovers will work together to form a harmony, resulting in sexual completion; however, the film refuses to complete the formula, so that one + one + one = nothing. Mathematics, ostensibly the most objective and least objectionable form of rational and cosmological inquiry, cannot account for Joe's experience and instead leads to the loss of what she values most. This critique of mathematics as a way of understanding the universe can be brought to bear on thinkers like Meillassoux and Ray Brassier; though Brassier and Meillassoux attempt to disengage from any theological foundations for mathematics, they argue that mathematics is the means by which reason can comprehend the world outside of thought.[44] *Nymphomaniac*, like Bataille, provides a different view of alterity by revealing that Seligman's attempts to mathematize Joe's reality are founded in an appropriative masculine logic rather than any kind of objective understanding. *Nymphomaniac* refuses to allow the numbers to suggest a whole, and the film's self-destructive gestures – in *Vol. I* with the loss of Joe's orgasm and in *Vol. II* with the unseen death of Seligman – suggest that alterity is not something known. If we can experience it at all, it is felt rather than reasoned, the way that Joe experiences her orgasms or intuits the workings of mopeds and automobiles.

Death and discontinuity

Nymphomaniac suggests that by losing her orgasm, Joe also loses her point of access to the sacred. At the beginning of *Vol. II*, Joe describes her first, spontaneous orgasm at the age of 12. In the director's cut, the scene is preceded by an extended black screen that echoes the beginning and ending of the film. Bird songs rise slowly on the soundtrack for a few moments before the image appears: a flashback of Joe as a child lying in the grass on a hillside. She looks around, and there is a cut to a series of shots of natural scenes – grasses in the wind, a bee in a flower, a waterfall – before Joe begins to shudder and rise up

Eco-Consciousness in Under the Skin *and* Nymphomaniac   125

into the air. A long shot from below her feet shows her suspended above ground, flanked by two ghostly apparitions: one woman dressed in gold riding a bull, and another in Roman clothes holding a baby. Seligman, incredulous, tells Joe that her vision is like a 'blasphemous retelling of Jesus's transfiguration on the mount', with the figures of Moses and Elijah replaced by the Whore of Babylon and Veleria Messalina, 'the most notorious nymphomaniac in history'. Joe seems unfazed by Seligman's incredulity and uninterested in his reading, telling him that she is as innocent to the religious as he is to sex. Seligman had also linked her story to blasphemy in an earlier scene in which she describes the workings of an organization called the 'Little Flock,' which encouraged young women to engage freely in sexual behaviour while rejecting society's emphasis on romantic love; at their meetings they had played a theme on the piano, which Seligman explains is called 'the Devil's interval' and was banned in the Middle Ages.

Nymphomaniac is Bataillean in its way of using religious themes in order to evoke their blasphemous undersides. For Bataille, our relationship to the sacred is double-sided and includes both religious mysticism and Dionysian excess. Sexual obscenity is a way of relating to the sacred because it calls our subjectivity into question: 'obscenity is our name for the uneasiness which upsets the physical state associated with self-possession, with the possession of a recognised and stable individuality'.[45] Seen in this way, the film challenges the spectator to view Joe's sexuality as genuinely transgressive, rather than bringing it in line with social codes either by condemning it or domesticating it within the PC rhetoric that Seligman uses to such nefarious ends. Joe is both a nymphomaniac and a bad person: she is immoral because she positions herself outside, or at least at the margins of morality, and she is a nymphomaniac because her sexuality has the potential to upset social norms. Joe's sexuality is therefore blasphemous in that it aligns her with a reality that exceeds the frameworks imposed upon it.

While Seligman's analogies posit nature as knowable, the film itself disrupts the spectator's knowledge at key points in the narrative. The film opens with a black screen that runs for several moments to the sounds of water falling and metal creaking. These sounds are immersive, aligning with Timothy Morton's 'ambient poetics': 'ambience denotes a sense of a circumambient, or surrounding, *world*. It suggests something both material and physical, though somewhat intangible, as if space itself had a material aspect'.[46] Morton traces the etymology of ambience to 'the Latin *ambo*, "on both sides" ',[47] and argues that ambient sounds destabilize boundaries between subject and object, inside and outside. While the cinematic image, as argued in the last chapter, gives

126   *Limit Cinema*

the impression of objectivity through representational devices such as single-point perspective, ambient sound collapses the distance between spectator and screen: Morton writes that acousmatic sound 'comes "from nowhere," or it is inextricably bound up with the space in which it is heard'.[48] By disconnecting these initial sounds from their sources, *Nymphomaniac* initially refuses to posit the diegesis as something 'out there', in a world of a different order from the space inhabited by the spectator. This sense of ambiguity is recuperated into a more conventional representational framework when the image appears, as the sounds are retroactively tied to their sources: water flows through drainage pipes and over a shed with a tin roof and rain trickles down the walls and of a metal fan creaking in the wind. Eventually the camera settles on Joe lying prostrate in the alley, implying a new interpretation for the sounds: they might have been from Joe's perspective as she listened to the sounds of the alley with her eyes closed. But before the image appears, the ambient sounds create a sense of situatedness without identification and are therefore neither subjective nor objective. They are too particular to provide a sense of context or mastery at the same time as they are too indeterminate to suggest a specific subject position.

The spectator's inability to see in the opening scene relates to a broader trope of blindness in von Trier's cinema. Cary Wolfe argues that von Trier's *Dancer in the Dark* critiques the 'humanist schema of visuality'[49] through its thematic concern with blindness: 'the film uses the "pathological" fact of Selma's blindness and the compensatory strategies it generates to disclose a radically deconstructed notion of the visual'.[50] Bataille similarly uses the notion of visuality against itself, an idea summarized by Benjamin Noys:

> Vision is possible only through the original violence of the aperture that opens the eye, an aperture which is also a blind spot. The blind spot is the part of the eye which makes vision possible and the part which makes that vision incomplete or impossible. It is the aperture which opens the possibility of vision but which vision cannot comprehend visually.[51]

Bataille relates this to the relationship between knowledge and nonknowledge and argues that the former is only possible through the latter: knowledge is conditional on its own incompleteness, just as vision is made possible through a constitutive blind spot. For Bataille, this blind spot is associated with death, and he repeatedly refers to punctured and mutilated eyeballs to evoke horror at the loss of the visual – a theme also prevalent in *Dancer in the Dark*, in which Selma's (Björk) blindness leads to her unjust execution. Eyes for Bataille are unsettling

Eco-Consciousness in Under the Skin *and* Nymphomaniac   127

because either they can denote the interiority of the other, as 'windows to the soul', or else they can indicate its loss, as in the staring eyes of a corpse. The opening sequence of *Nymphomaniac* similarly evokes a sense of blindness that precludes complete or totalizable knowledge; by emphasizing the space around the screen through ambient sound, the screen itself is exposed as limited, partial. This self-reflexive gesture towards the limitations of the medium can only be temporary, because once the image appears *Nymphomaniac* falls into a more conventional cinematic pattern. However, the gap in knowledge suggested by the opening scene is re-opened at crucial moments in the film: at the beginning of *Vol. II* in the director's cut when Joe experiences her first orgasm, and at the end when Joe shoots Seligman.

Blindness is therefore associated with sexuality on the one hand and death on the other, aligning with the duality of the Bataillean sacred: the film articulates sex and death as things that cannot be seen despite being crucial structuring forces. As Huffer argues, what dies in *Nymphomaniac*'s final moments is not only Seligman but also his world view and its effects on the film's narrative structure. The suicidal gesture of the film calls his epistemological strategies into question, strategies based in a tradition of Western thought that separates subjects and objects and mobilizes this distinction in order to maintain systems of oppression. Seligman's act of sexual violence therefore does not work against his prior characterization as a proper liberal humanist, but is rather symptomatic of it. His death destabilizes these structures without offering a new alternative: as Huffer explains it, '*Nymphomaniac*'s final shot refuses resolution. Reinforced by the film's consistent blurring of its own diegetic borders, the final shot risks an opening into an unknown … future.'[52] Seligman's death is therefore sacrificial in Bataillean terms, in that it serves nothing and breaks down systems of meaning. The black screen during Seligman's death evokes this world of the sacred where distinctions between subjects and objects begin to blur, a world that is inaccessible to us – we cannot see it because our modes of perception are implicated in subject/object distinctions, but we can trace the effects of these lacunae on our modes of representation. Death according to Bataille opens onto the continuous world that exceeds subjective limits, and although *Nymphomaniac* offers no alternative to the profane distinction between subject and object that constitutes the discontinuous human world (doing so would only recuperate the radical negativity of the final sequence into the structures of meaning established by the narrative), it works against what Wolfe calls 'the humanist desire for holism, unity and coherence'.[53] The blind spots that punctuate the film therefore structure subjectivity in a thoroughly posthuman way, as a system that differentiates itself from a broader reality through a constitutive gap or absence that will always remain unseen and unknown. In contrast to the humanist desire for completeness, *Nymphomaniac* calls attention to the impossibility of totalized knowledge, since knowledge itself is predicated on its own violent and irrecuperable negation.

The ending of *Under the Skin* bears striking similarities to *Nymphomaniac*. Both films conclude with attempted rape and murder and with images of falling snow: Joe ends her story where it began, with her lying bloodied in the snowy alleyway, while at the end of *Under the Skin* the alien is sexually assaulted and murdered as blustering snowflakes fall over a Highland forest. Before she is murdered, the alien meets a logger on a trail who cheerfully asks her if she is new to the area and whether she is alone, recalling her earlier probing questions of her victims. She carries on down the trail before finding refuge in a bothy, where she is awakened by the logger standing over her. Like the film's opening, the final scene plays with inside/outside distinctions: while the alien sleeps, there is a shot of her sleeping form superimposed onto the forest outside, suggesting either a dream (internal) or an association between her (external) body and the landscape. After she is awakened by the logger and he chases her outside, he rips a hole in her back, and the wound leaks a black substance onto his hand; she unpeels her human skin and reveals a black shape underneath. This blackness has the same glassy texture and appearance as the

Figure 12 Sleeping in the highlands in *Under the Skin* (Jonathan Glazer, 2013).

Eco-Consciousness in Under the Skin *and* Nymphomaniac   129

pool where she skinned her victims, associating the alien's internal form with an exterior space. A number of subsequent shots/countershots further trouble internal/external distinctions. When she is first wrestled to the ground, there is a shot of her terrified expression before a POV shot looking upwards towards the sky at falling snow; after the alien unpeels her human skin, she holds the mask in her hands and it blinks, wearing the same terrified expression as in the previous shot. The logger then douses her in gasoline and lights a match, and she runs into a clearing where she eventually falls and emits a thick black cloud of smoke. We watch the alien's smouldering body for a moment before the camera tilts upwards to track the smoke rising towards the sky. Eventually the camera settles in an upward-facing position with the snow falling softly on the lens, echoing the earlier POV shot from the alien's perspective but from a mysterious, unclaimed perspective.

Nancy writes that photographic images are like death masks: 'the photograph *itself* as a death mask, the instantaneous and always rebegun image as the casting of a presence in contact with light, the casting of a presence fleeing into absence'.[54] Death masks provide a surface for something surfaceless and a gaze for something sightless; their underside reveals nothing, the same way that turning a photograph around only shows us a blank reverse side rather than a deeper ontological truth. Nancy connects photographs and other images to the sacred, which he describes as 'inseparable from a hidden surface, from which it cannot, as it were, be peeled away: the dark side of the picture, its underside or backside'.[55] The reverse side of the alien's human skin, when peeled away from her body, is as black as the void; like Nancy's image, the thin exterior of her blinking human face covers over a depthless darkness. The alien's gaze at her discarded human face is an echo of the earlier scene in the mirror in that they both suggest the alien's simultaneous identification with and alienation from her outer appearance. The alien witnesses herself *as other* at the moment of her death, at the same time as the spectator is made aware of her true form. Because her alien body is visually associated with the exterior space of the void, her gaze at her human face is an impossible perspective – the outside looking in. This is the perspective of the death mask, which has no look: 'the *Geist* or face of the dead man forms a face-to-face that is blind'.[56] As with *Nymphomaniac*, blindness once again evokes a world without sight, inevitably hidden from our limited structures of representation.

Death for Bataille is the impossible moment of transgression between inside and outside. It is impossible because it erases the subjective boundaries that

130   *Limit Cinema*

determine the difference in the first place; like the experience depicted in the *ling-chi* photograph I discussed in the introduction, it can only consist of a 'not yet' experienced subjectively until experience is no longer possible. Radical exteriority, which Bataille associates with the continuous natural world, is only possible at the expense of subjectivity. However, *Under the Skin*'s evocation of death in this final sequence – of transgression across a limit – is finally counteracted by the snowflakes on the lens. This gesture towards the camera implicates the spectator and once again flips the order of things inside out; the image of exteriority that concludes the film is revealed to be staged subjectively, for the spectator as witness. These continuous reversals suggest that the sacred can never be accessed or appropriated because the limit does not conceal some inner truth: once we approach the outside, we inevitably discover that we have turned back inwards, invaginated and folded into an immanent cinematic universe.

Conclusion

I have argued that Bataillean notions of ipseity and transgression are relevant for film ecocriticism. Although Bataille is a correlationist in that he thinks we cannot have knowledge of reality outside of human thought, his philosophy attempts to discern how a theory of nonknowledge might help us approach what is in excess of our ability to understand. Through a close reading of the shifting perspectives in *Nymphomaniac* and *Under the Skin*, I have explored how a theory of cinematic subjectivity might attune itself to the unknowable outside of thought. Bataille provides a way of avoiding the anthropocentrism inherent to theories such as psychoanalysis or phenomenology that posit everything in relation to a human subject, while also recognizing that the boundaries between subjects and objects are not easily breached. Remember that for Bataille alterity is not relational: subjectivity does not actively relate to the outside of thought but is instead contaminated with it through a passive process of differentiation. Like psychoanalysis and phenomenology, Bataille's ontology requires an investigation of human subjectivity, but for Bataille the human is constituted by alterity rather than the other way around. Rather than attempting to see beyond the limits between inside and outside, I have attempted to trace the limit itself; cinema provides a useful terrain for doing so, since it constantly negotiates between various subject positions. Tracing the movements of cinematic subjectivity reveals subjective limits to be fragile, unstable and constantly turning inside out. The cinema screen, like Nancy's photograph, does not conceal a deeper truth; but if, as Nancy argues, truth is at the level of the skin, then the play of surfaces across a film screen can be useful in understanding how human subjectivity touches the limits of objective reality. Though this chapter has provided a way of reading cinematic subjectivity in relation to an environment that exceeds it, questions remain about what we could or should do in response. The ecological crisis demands action, and the next chapter will explore what films might be able to teach us about forging a new kind of relationship with the environment. If our relationship with nature has to do with affect and nonknowledge, then what kind of affective response is appropriate? Or, phrased another way: how might cinema teach us to love nature, and what could this love imply for our future?

Notes

1 Meillassoux, *After Finitude*, 7.
2 Bataille, *Erotism*, 14–15.
3 Ibid., 96.
4 Shaviro, *The Universe of Things*, 41.
5 Bataille, *Inner Experience*, 20 (emphasis original).
6 Bataille, *Erotism*, 23.
7 Bataille, *The Accursed Share: Vol. I*, 19–22.
8 Bataille, *Erotism*, 13–17.
9 Bataille, *Inner Experience*, 86.
10 Libertson, *Proximity*, 1.
11 Ibid., 12.
12 Wolfe, *What Is Posthumanism?*, 15.
13 Libertson, *Proximity*, 12.
14 There are also similarities with Deleuze's concept of the fold: Simon O'Sullivan explains that the fold allows Deleuze to rethink subjectivity in that 'it announces that the inside is nothing more than a fold of the outside' (Simon O'Sullivan, 'The Fold', in *The Deleuze* Dictionary, ed. Alan Parr (Edinburgh: Edinburgh University Press, 2010), 107) . As I mentioned in the introduction, however, there are differences in the ways that Deleuze and Bataille conceive of the relation between inside and outside; further, Deleuze's fold, influenced by Gottfried Wilhelm Leibniz and Alfred North Whitehead, emerges from a somewhat different genealogy of ideas than Nancy's invagination, and so I hesitate to conflate the two notions

132   *Limit Cinema*

here. See Gilles Deleuze, *Foucault*, trans. Sean Hand (Minneapolis: University of Minnesota Press, 1986); Gilles Deleuze, *The Fold: Leibniz and the Baroque*, trans. Tom Conley (London: Athalone, 1993) .

15   Jean-Luc Nancy, 'Inside Out', *Philosophical Salon*, 4 April 2015, http// thephilosophicalsalon.com/inside-out. Accessed 21 October 2019.

16   Sean P. Connolly, 'Georges Bataille, Gender, and Sacrificial Excess', *The Comparatist* 38 (2014), 110.

17   Ibid., 113.

18   Ibid., footnote 1. Connolly is paraphrasing Shannon Winnubst, 'Bataille's Queer Pleasures: The Universe as Spider or Spit', in *Reading Bataille Now*, ed. Shannon Winnubst (Bloomington: Indiana University Press, 2007), 75–93. Winnubst's volume provides an excellent survey of Bataille's relevance for contemporary thought and politics, and her essay is particularly insightful in its exploration of the queer implications of Bataille's work. See also: Zeynap Direk, 'Erotic Experience and Sexual Difference in Bataille', in *Reading Bataille Now*, 94–115. Because Bataille's general economy of sexuality does not oppose heteronormativity but instead simultaneously challenges and supports it, queer and feminist scholars also frequently condemn Bataille's work: see especially Andrea Dworkin's scathing critique in *Pornography: Men Possessing Women* (New York: Putnam, 1981), 175–6.

19   Sheryl Vint, 'Skin Deep: Alienation in *Under the Skin*', *Extrapolation* 56, no. 1 (2015), 4.

20   Ara Osterweil, '*Under the Skin*: The Perils of Becoming Female', *Film Quarterly* 67, no. 4 (2014), 45.

21   Nancy, 'Inside Out'.

22   Lynne Huffer, 'The Nymph Shoots Back: Agamben, *Nymphomaniac*, and the Feel of the Agon', *Theory & Event* 18, no. 2 (2015).

23   See Caroline Bainbridge, *The Cinema of Lars von Trier: Authenticity and Artifice* (New York: Columbia University Press, 2007); Alyda Faber, 'Redeeming Sexual Violence? A Feminist Reading of *Breaking the Waves*', *Literature and Theology* 17, no. 1 (2003), 59–75; Mette Hjort, 'The Problem with Provocation: On Lars von Trier, L'Enfant Terrible of Danish Art Film', *Kinema*, Fall (2011); Lori Marso, 'Must We Burn Lars von Trier? Simone de Beauvoir's Body Politics in *Antichrist*', *Theory & Event* 18, no. 2 (2015); Scott Loren and Jörg Metelmann, 'Lars von Trier and Woman's Films: Misogyny or Feminism?' in *Irritation of Life: The Subversive Melodrama of Michael Haneke, David Lynch, and Lars von Trier* (Marburg: Schüren Velag 2013), 141–72; Magdalena Zolkos, 'Violent Affects: Nature and the Feminine in Lars von Trier's *Antichrist*', *Parrhesia* 13 (2011), 177–89; Rosalind Galt, 'The

Suffering Spectator? Perversion and Complicity in *Antichrist* and *Nymphomaniac*', *Theory & Event* 18, no. 2 (2015).

24   I owe this argument to Christine Evans, who makes a similar point in her upcoming monograph *Slavoj Žižek: A Cinematic Ontology* (London: Bloomsbury, 2022).

25   Mele Ulas Aksoy, 'Hegel and George Bataille's Concept of Sovereignty', *Ege Academic Review* 11, no. 2 (2011), 217.

26   Shaviro, *Passion & Excess*, 37.

27   Libertson, *Proximity*, 12.

28   Bataille, *Erotism*, 11.

29   Bataille, *The Accursed Share: Vol. I*, 32.

30   Ibid., 33.

31   Ibid.

32   Michael Faber, *Under the Skin* (San Diego: Harcourt, 2000).

33   Bataille, *Erotism*, 12–13.

34   Ibid., 12.

35   While this model is seemingly heteronormative in its privileging of penetrative sex, Bataille's general economy of desire and Nancy's concept of invagination exceed the narrow logic of dominant ideological ideas about sexual identity. Heterosexuality is conditioned by the general economy of desire, and so Nancian/Bataillean ideas about sexuality do not necessarily overturn heteronormativity; however, invagination exceeds male/female relations and so penetration does not always occur within the bounds of heterosexual sex. All bodies are vulnerable, all bodies capable of penetration. Accordingly, a number of scholars link Bataille's view of sexuality to queer theory: Lisa Downing and Robert Gillet, for example, use a genealogical approach to trace the affinities and incompatabilities between Bataille's thought and contemporary queer theory (Lisa Downing and Robert Gillet, 'Georges Bataille and the Avant-Garde of Queer Theory?: Transgression, Perversion and the Death Drive', *Nottingham French Studies* 50, no. 3 (2011), 88–102). See also: Shannon Winnubst, *Queering Freedom* (Bloomington: Indiana University Press, 2006), which uses Bataille and Foucault to explore queer notions of freedom; Dave Holmes, Stuart J. Murray and Thomas Foth (eds), *Radical Sex Between Men: Assembling Desiring-Machines* (London: Routledge, 2018), which uses opening quotes from Bataille, Foucault and Derrida to frame its engagement with sexuality and draws from Bataille in essays throughout; and Eric Robertson, 'Wasted Sex, Wasteful Bodies: Queer Ecology and the Future of Energy Use', *English Language Notes* 55, nos. 1–2 (2017), 33–40, which reads Bataillean notions of waste in relation to both ecology and queer sexuality.

36   Osterweil, '*Under the Skin*', 49.

37 Jean-Luc Nancy, *Corpus*, trans. Richard A. Rand (New York: Fordham University Press, 2008), 154.

38 Ibid., 156.

39 Ibid., 159.

40 Ibid., 160. In discussing sex in terms of sexual difference, Nancy again prioritizes heterosexual experience here. However, since Nancy's philosophical project in general uses deconstruction to destabilize the foundations of Western culture (Christianity, subjectivity, freedom, morality, etc.), his writing rejects essentialism and therefore leaves room for alternative understandings of sex and gender. In other words, although Nancy's writing views heterosexuality and sexual difference as normal and foundational to Western culture, his entire ontology destabilizes the very notions of 'normal' and 'foundational' while also recognizing their power on our lives and interactions.

41 Oliver Lunn, 'Talking to Stacy Martin about Her Fake Sex with Shia LaBoeuf', *Vice*, 26 February 2014, https://www.vice.com/en_ca/article/7b78dz/the-inner-workings-of-lars-von-triers-fake-sex-scenes. Accessed 26 April 2021; Boyd van Hoeij, 'Charlotte Gainsbourg on Being Lars von Trier's "Nymphomaniac": "I Was Disturbed, Embarrassed, and a Little Humiliated,"' *IndieWire*, 25 March 2014, http://www.indiewire.com/2014/03/charlotte-gainsbourg-on-being-lars-von-triers-nymphomaniac-i-was-disturbed-embarrassed-and-a-little-humiliated-28659/. Accessed 21 October 2019.

42 James Berclaz-Lewis, 'Berlin Review: Why the Shorter Version of "Nymphomaniac Volume I" Is Better Than Lars von Trier's Director's Cut', *IndieWire*, 9 February 2014, http://www.indiewire.com/2014/02/berlin-review-why-the-shorter-version-ofnymphomaniac-volume-i-is-better-than-lars-von-triers-directors-cut-30180/. Accessed 21 October 2019.

43 Leslie Felperin, 'Bigger, Longer, Uncut: A Critic's Take on the Director's Cut of *Nymphomaniac*', *Hollywood Reporter*, 10 February 2014, http://www.hollywoodreporter.com/news/nymphomaniac-directors-cut-a-critics-678792. Accessed 19 October 2019.

44 Meillassoux, *After Finitude*; Brassier, *Nihil Unbound*.

45 Bataille, *Erotism*, 17–18.

46 Timothy Morton, *Ecology without* Nature, 33.

47 Ibid., 34.

48 Ibid., 41.

49 Wolfe, *What Is Posthumanism?*, 169.

50 Ibid., 189.

51 Benjamin Noys, *Georges Bataille: A Critical Introduction* (London: Pluto, 2000), 30.

52 Huffer, 'The Nymph Shoots Back'.

53 Wolfe, *What Is Posthumanism?*, 173.
54 Nancy, *The Ground of the Image*, 99.
55 Ibid., 2.
56 Ibid., 82.

4

Limits of love in *Grizzly Man* and *Konelīne: Our Land Beautiful*

Introduction

The ecological crisis compels us to form a positive relationship with nonhuman reality. As previous chapters have made clear, however, forming positive knowledge about reality beyond our conceptual frameworks poses great difficulties. Drawing from Bataille, my argument to this point has tended towards a largely negative and potentially pessimistic reading of our relationship with nature. I have thus far questioned our ability to know nonhuman nature at all and have used cinema and film theory in order to argue against the position of thinkers like the speculative realists who assert that reasoning about a thought-independent reality is possible (see Chapter 3). Through Bataille's concepts of transgression, sacrifice and inner experience, I have also argued that reason is not always the best way of thinking about the relationship between humans and nature, and that the aesthetic excesses of cinema can evoke other kinds of relations to nature – in terms of, for example, the sacred versus the profane (see Chapter 2) or erotic experience (see Chapter 4). Because I take a post-theological approach, I have maintained that there is no God or system of meaning that can help us maintain a positive relationship with reality outside of thought. While this might suggest a sense of nihilism about humanity's relationship with nonhuman reality, however, I have simultaneously asserted that the ecological crisis demands that we try and relate to a reality that we can never fully understand. This chapter will more fully explore the 'impossible imperative', to which I have alluded previously, and will argue that love can provide a way of meeting the demand to engage with the unknowable. Two films, Werner Herzog's *Grizzly Man* (2005) and Nettie Wild's *Konelīne: Our Land Beautiful* (2016), demonstrate that love for nature will always be imperfect because it inevitably involves subjective desire and projection. Despite these difficulties, however, I argue that love is an integral part of our engagement with the environment and should therefore not be discounted in any ethics of the nonhuman.

Love for the real

Love might seem like an unusual place to start in thinking about how to relate to the environment, since it seems incorrigibly subjective and anthropocentric. Love is prone to over-sentimentalizing that mischaracterizes its object on the one hand, and fits of jealousy, possessiveness or even violence on the other. Despite these imperfections, however, scholars from a range of disciplines – theology, anthropology, philosophy and film studies – have recently begun to examine love as a way of engaging with nature. Michel O'Gorman, for example, argues that speculative realism's turn towards objects is less a radically new form of realism than a posthumanist form of romanticism.[1] He writes that posthumanism's turn towards objects, exemplified especially by speculative realism but also by other forms of new materialism, is motivated by

> (a) a desire to connect with the nonhuman world in ways that ignore the lessons of poststructuralism; and (b) a romantic wonder about the infinite world of things acting in the universe. For indeed, romance is what drives this attraction to the cyborg, the animal, and more recently, the inorganic thing. And by 'romance' I mean not only the literary genre – I am unabashedly talking about love.[2]

O'Gorman argues that speculative realism's claim that it seeks knowledge about objects in-themselves rather than as they appear for us is betrayed by rhetorical devices that make evident their authors' subjective desires. The long lists of objects of various scales, from microscopic to cosmic, that frequent the texts of Graham Harman, Ian Bogost, Jane Bennet and Bruno Latour are evidence of their love, 'at once an indicator of finitude (here's what I have) and infinity (here's what I desire). Just as importantly, [the list] is an indicator of possession (this is what I own, this is what I know)'.[3] Rather than removing the author's subjectivity from the equation, then, speculative realism unwittingly makes evident a psychological truth rather than an ontological one. O'Gorman writes that the desire for objects expressed by speculative realism is often erotic, even pornographic, such as Bogost's descriptions of objects 'rubbing shoulders' in a process that 'happens fast and hot, the universes of things bumping against one another in succession'.[4] These erotic attachments to objects are, O'Gorman argues, in some sense 'unrigorous',[5] even naïve, because love itself is a difficult and messy concept. He argues that by denying its own desires in claiming to move beyond the structures of human subjectivity, speculative realism ignores poststructuralism's warnings against cohesion and unity in order to echo romantic ideas of nature as harmonious and amenable to our identification. Despite these difficulties, however, O'Gorman wants to claim something positive in what speculative realism denies, and he suggests that posthumanist love for objects has radical potential for thinking of the relationship between humans and nonhumans.

If love for objects cannot be avoided – if philosophies of the nonhuman are in some sense doomed to betray our desire – then perhaps we ought to account for love in our environmental ethics. O'Gorman traces ideas of love backwards from speculative realism to the romantics to the New Testament to Plato, a genealogy that supports his characterization of love as an unrigorous concept that is difficult to pin down or define in a systematic way. Poststructuralists often characterize love in terms of impossibility or paradox, from Lacan's famous maxim that love is giving what one does not have to someone who does not want it, to Jean-Luc Nancy's descriptions of love as giving presence to something that is absent.[6] There is a post-theological dimension to these theories of love, since they all refer back to or deconstruct the ways that Christian notions of love have helped to shape Western thought.[7] In this regard, Kierkegaard is an important precursor, and his *Works of Love* tackles what he sees as a paradox at the heart of Christian love.

Kierkegaard sees a contradiction in the biblical injunction to love all people equally (*agape*, divine or neighbour love) and the preferential loves we hold for some people above the rest (erotic love for one's spouse, filial love for friends and family). Although Kierkegaard argues that *agape* is the only true form of love, Sharon Krishek argues that he has difficulty disentangling from particular human expressions of love in order to theorize love on a universal scale.[8] Kierkegaard associates neighbour love with self-denial, since it requires unselfishly wishing the best for the other even at the expense of one's own desires; preferential love, on the other hand, is always selfish to some degree since we make the choice of one person at the exclusion of others according to our subjective desires and inclinations. Krishek writes that although Kierkegaard favours non-preferential love, 'he definitely does not want to ignore or deny our corporeal, worldly existence',[9] and that *Works of Love* is therefore plagued with a problem of preferential love that Kierkegaard cannot quite square with the injunction to love the neighbour.[10] These ambivalences suggest that conceptual difficulties with love might be related to the problem of parsing out distinctions between the subjective and objective – the issue at the heart of this book. O'Gorman's point that speculative realism mistakes subjective desires for objective truths is symptomatic of this problem, suggesting that the age-old question of what constitutes love might still be relevant for twenty-first-century philosophies of the nonhuman.

This question of how to love nature has also recently taken root in the burgeoning field of Christian environmentalism,[11] which works against the resistance of some Christians (the mainstream of the American religious right, for example) to global warming and other environmental problems by pointing out places where the Bible encourages stewardship rather than domination over nature. Susan Bratton explicitly links Christian environmentalism to the conflict between neighbour and preferential love, revising Kierkegaard's problem to question whether our love for nature ought to take the form of *eros* or *agape*.[12] Bratton notes that Christian ethics are based in love and makes the argument that ethical engagement with nature should be founded in *agape*, or self-sacrificing spiritual love, rather than *eros*, which she defines as 'love of beauty or natural love with the desire to possess'.[13] She argues that while a surprising number of theologians have posited *eros* as the proper form of Christian love for the environment,[14] *agape* allows for a more ethical form of engagement with nature because it does not require reciprocity. Bratton argues that *eros* should not be written off entirely, since our appreciation for nature and desire to possess knowledge about it are integral components of our experience; however, erotic love is always founded on the sensible and is therefore too subjective and selective in its preferences. She writes:

> Aesthetic eros can also create environmental difficulties (overcollection of rare species, for example), and can easily produce ethical models that incorrectly value nature or are selfishly human-centered. Aesthetic eros can be nonconsumptive and appreciative of nature, for example, when one admires mountain scenery or observes wild birds in flight ... however, it is subject to self-concern and acquisitiveness, and therefore ... needs to be transformed.[15]

Bratton explains that *agape* is generally conceived as a transformative element that can correct the selfish tendencies of *eros*, and she applies this line of thinking to love for nature to argue that *agape* – modelled on God's self-giving and non-preferential love for creation – can help mitigate the dangers posed by over-attachment to earthly human sensory experience.

Bratton's argument that we should love nature non-preferentially, without the need for reciprocity or the expectation it will love us back, initially seems convincing given that more possessive kinds of love for nature have led to measurable harm. Further, *agape* seems at first to be less anthropocentric in that it seeks to disentangle us from the particularities of human desires and inclinations in favour of a more objective, selfless form of love. However, because the framework of this book is post-theological, we cannot follow Bratton in assuming the existence of a God whose divine love can serve as a model for human interactions with nature. Without God there is no way of firmly adjudicating the difference between subjective impressions and objective influence; the limits between these poles are too unstable. Our love is therefore simply too imperfect to be held to Bratton's standards for *agape*. While I am suspicious of Bratton's faith in the transformative powers of divine love, however, post-theology asserts the importance of religious frameworks on our thinking, and it is therefore worth taking seriously how this conflict between *eros* and *agape* might contribute to a post-theological environmental ethics.

Both Bratton and Kierkegaard draw the distinction between *eros* and *agape* in terms of self-affirmation/selfishness and self-effacement/sacrifice. This suggests that erotic love moves from the subject outwards, towards the sacred, while *agape* moves in the other direction. But because these movements are not easily distinguished, a post-theological understanding of love views the relationship between subject and object in love less determinately. Bataille is useful here because the conflict between self-affirmation and self-denial that Krishek locates in *Works of Love* is similar to the Bataillean erotic, which is characterized as an undecidable movement of self-containment and self-erasure. Like Bratton and Kierkegaard, Bataille makes use of theological ideas to theorize erotic love and sacrifice. However, while the former two suggest that erotic love does nothing to call the integrity of the self into question because it only reinforces subjective desires and preferences, for Bataille the erotic is exactly what puts the subject at risk: 'eroticism always entails a breaking down of established patterns, the patterns ... of the regulated social order basic to our discontinuous mode of existence as defined and separate individuals'.[16] Because Bataille defines the erotic as 'assenting to life up to the point of death',[17] the erotic entails both self-affirmation and self-sacrifice in a movement that tests but ultimately reinforces subjective limits.[18] The subject can only experience this movement from the inside outwards, since subjectivity is defined through the limits of ipseity; however, Bataille's ontology insists on forces outside of experience that impress themselves on our structures of perception and meaning. The impossible structure of love identified by Kierkegaard, Bataille, Lacan and Nancy is therefore analogous to the paradox of inner experience in that both are structured by a contradictory movement across the limit between subjectivity and the sacred.

Love is inherently anthropocentric in that it cannot break from subjective limits; however, it is also by definition a susceptibility to something outside of ourselves. Matthew Abbott writes about love in Nancy, observing that 'thinking love requires generosity, receptivity, and openness to something in excess of the thinker – which is to say, it requires love'.[19] Because 'thought does not master its object'[20] – because thought cannot appropriate what it thinks – its relationship to its object is a dynamic process that can never complete itself: 'this "being put to the test" is crucial to it [love], and persists with it at all times; there is no way of proving it once and for all, and so the task it sets is continual'.[21] This dynamic process is inevitably anthropocentric because it is bound with human finitude. However, as I have discussed throughout this book, finitude is not closed off from alterity but is instead constituted by it: Libertson argues that Bataille provides a 'communicational definition of closure',[22] wherein differentiation and finitude are the products of communication rather than their originators. As a result, Nancy and Bataille's evocations of love as susceptibility to alterity open more optimistic possibilities than the critiques against *eros* outlined above. Love that does not model itself on the divine is not necessarily limited to a selfish desire to possess or appropriate the other (though Nancy admits that love is ambivalent and always holds the possibility for violence and harm[23]). If we think love for the nonhuman in these terms, then we can only love from the inside, as ourselves, and, as with our love for another person, we can never be sure we are doing it right. This uncertainty requires that we keep working and testing our approach based on feedback from the beloved; love is therefore an autopoietic process of constant readjustment rather than a stable entity.

Kay Milton, who advocates love for nature in a secular context, argues not only that love ought to be central to environmental ethics but also that it already is, because any rational debate about how to fight to preserve nature already presupposes a level of care and emotional investment.[24] Milton contends that affect is an integral part of the way that we process and respond to information from our environments, whether they be social or natural, and she resists rationalist/humanist frameworks that oppose reason and emotion. Like the Christian environmentalists, Milton does not want to discount the ways that supposedly non-rational modes of engagement with nature can motivate our behaviour in positive ways. If affect drives us to form value judgements about things – and can, as Milton argues, inspire us to hold nature as sacred[25] – then film can use emotional engagement to influence our thinking about the environment in ethically significant ways. Even rhetorical environmentalist documentaries reinforce their claims by appealing emotionally to the spectator: Al Gore's personal anecdotes in *An Inconvenient Truth* (2016) relay how he came to care about global warming, while images of animal suffering in pro-vegan documentaries like *Earthlings* (2005) or *Cowspiracy* (2015) appeal to audience empathy. Films that are less explicitly about environmental issues can also affectively engage viewers in relation to natural spaces or phenomena: as Adrian Ivakhiv argues, while films are 'limited in their capacity to convey knowledge about socio-ecological issues … they can bring attention to those issues, or, more subtly, they can affectively orient viewers to such issues or to the images, representations, and arguments in which those issues are registered and conveyed'.[26] The remainder of this chapter will investigate how *Grizzly Man* and *Koneline* 'affectively orient viewers' towards the environment through love: they represent human relationships with the environment as fraught and contradictory, and exploring these contradictions will help us trace the possibilities and problems of love for nature.

The two films are similar in a number of ways: they are both documentaries set in North America's Pacific Northwest (*Grizzly Man* in Alaska, *Koneline* in British Columbia), and they both explore a number of conflicting opinions on how best to engage with the region's rugged wilderness. There are some important differences between the films, however. Love in *Grizzly Man* primarily appears on the level of content: we know that the film's central character, Timothy Treadwell, loves nature because he tells us so repeatedly. This love is contested both within the film text – Herzog's voice-over and a number of talking head interviews with the film disagree overtly with Treadwell – and in the academic commentary on the film, which often engages with this dialectic to favour one side over the other. I am using *Grizzly Man* as a case study for nature love because the film has been discussed extensively and has become something of a litmus test about audience feelings towards nature; I frequently see this in my own students, who have strong reactions to Treadwell's interactions with the bears that are difficult to unpack because they are so immediate and visceral. The bulk of this chapter will therefore be spent engaging in the Treadwell versus Herzog debate in order to draw out its implications for nature love. Though nature in *Grizzly Man* is largely

144   *Limit Cinema*

characterized in pessimistic or negative terms, I will argue that love in the film finally exceeds the dialectic established between Herzog and Treadwell. This excess will be used to transition to *Koneline*, which holds more optimistic possibilities for loving nature. Love in *Koneline* operates more on the level of form, as an aesthetic mode of being in relation to nature; its aesthetic *eros* encourages a love that recognizes, yet exceeds differences.

'Warring simplifications' in *Grizzly Man*

Grizzly Man is a documentary about the life and death of Timothy Treadwell, who lived among wild Alaskan grizzlies for thirteen summers before he was killed and eaten by one, along with his girlfriend Amie Huguenard. Herzog's film draws from the 100-plus hours of footage that Treadwell shot over the course of his time in Alaska, intercutting this found footage with talking head interviews. The film's central conflict is between two opposing views on nature: Herzog's more nihilistic view of nature as predicated on 'chaos, hostility, and murder' versus Treadwell's more sentimental view of nature as harmonious and reciprocal. As the extensive critical discourse surrounding the film suggests, however, these two positions are overdetermined by the film itself, and the excesses and ambiguities in *Grizzly Man*'s representation of nature are used to make a multitude of sometimes complementary, sometimes conflicting arguments about love for nature. This section will work through the various readings of the film to examine their various contradictions; in the next two sections I will build from these analyses in order to trace the paradoxical movements of love within the film itself.

Ned Schantz argues that *Grizzly Man*'s apparently 'warring simplifications' result in a paradoxical excess of information so that 'it takes several analytical passes to render anything like a complete account of their main events'.[27] The film's excesses of signification that burst out from an apparently simple conflict – nature as good versus cruel or violent – might account for not only the differences of opinion expressed in the film but also the debates and controversies that surround it. To varying degrees, and against the general thrust of the film, ecocritical readings tend to side more with Treadwell as at least 'an approach rooted in love' and a 'small step in the right direction':[28] while they tend to agree that Treadwell made some flawed assumptions in his interactions with the grizzlies, ecocritics often applaud his willingness to blur the boundaries between the human and the animal and his capacity for empathy with nature.[29] On the other side of the Treadwell/Herzog debate are those that approach *Grizzly Man* from an auteurist perspective, and therefore situate the film in Herzog's larger concerns with themes of madness and humanity against nature: Laurie Ruth Johnson, for example, interprets Herzog through 'forgotten' ideas in German romanticism about nature being sick, baneful or cruel,[30] while Brad Prager views Herzog as an anti-romantic who rejects the anthromorphization of nature.[31] Still others argue that, rather than being diametrically opposed, Herzog and Treadwell are two sides of the same coin:[32] Julie Schutten exemplifies this view by framing both Herzog and Treadwell as narcissists who project their own respective views on nature.[33] In addition to the range of interpretations and ethical claims about Treadwell and Herzog, there are still more disagreements about the appropriate theoretical conclusions to be drawn from the film. Herzog is discussed variously as a romantic,[34] an anti-romantic[35] and a modernist[36] – descriptions that all work against Herzog's own description of his work as emulating the 'heroic and tragic ideals of classical antiquity',[37] not to mention his general distaste for academic approaches to his work in general.[38] Further, *Grizzly Man* has been seen as exemplifying Gilles Deleuze and Félix Guattari's becoming-animal,[39] as well as failing to exemplify it.[40] It has been read as negotiating Agamben's notion of the 'anthropological machine' in order to maintain the distinction between human and animal,[41] or else raising the possibility of blurring these boundaries in a posthuman way.[42] While there are a number of possible interpretations for every film, the wide range of critical responses to *Grizzly Man* suggests that the film is especially overdetermined or excessive. Most of the above scholars write explicitly about *Grizzly Man* in terms of love, and the conversation can be seen as a broad debate about whether and how it is appropriate to love nature. Since love is characterized by impossibility and contradiction, the intense polemics surrounding the film might be attributed to the methodological difficulties in dealing with the idea of love. Rather than attempting to overcome these difficulties, the following sections will trace some of them within the film by taking a closer look at the conflicts between Treadwell and Herzog, and relating these conflicts to the distinctions between *eros* and *agape*. My own reading of the film keeps open the various contradictions raised by *Grizzly Man*'s love for nature by theorizing the film in terms of Bataillean eroticism.

The bears don't love you, Timothy (or do they?)

Grizzly Man begins with a long shot of two grizzlies grazing in a lush green field with snow-topped mountains in the distance. The title appears and Treadwell enters the frame, explaining the behaviours of the two bears, 'Ed' and 'Rowdy'. The sudden appearance of Treadwell within the space occupied by wild grizzlies is shocking because it immediately breaks with the conventions of wildlife documentaries. Anat Pick observes that for wildlife documentaries like *Planet Earth*, 'not only the voice-of-god but also the eye-of-god is typical':[43] David Attenborough's voice-over narration along with spectacular shots created through long lenses and high-definition cinematography contributes to a sense of an objective gaze. *Planet Earth*'s making-of featurettes further emphasize this technological mediation by exposing the long and often tedious processes behind the series' dramatic footage, and they reveal that camera operators were often a great distance from the action and generally had to wait for long stretches of time to capture brief moments of activity. *Grizzly Man*, by contrast, collapses the distance between film-maker and filmed subject, and Treadwell's appearance among the grizzlies in the opening shot of the film blurs the human/animal distinction that is usually held sacred by wildlife documentarians. The dangers posed by this blurring of boundaries are immediately made apparent when the timeline for Treadwell's life (1957–2003) appears underneath his name. There is an immediate connection between death and love: Treadwell blows a kiss towards a bear in the background, saying 'I love you Rowdy', before he exits the frame and makes the unsettling announcement: 'I can smell death all over my fingers.'

Treadwell's presence among the grizzlies is explicitly framed (by Herzog) as an attempt to 'leave the confinements of his humanness'. Read in Bataillean terms, this desire is transgressive because it both affirms and risks the erasure of Treadwell's subjective boundaries, thereby destabilizing differentiation between self and world. As Schutten argues,

> the dissonance felt by viewers of the film surrounds a disconfirmation of human faith in the nature/culture binary, and that Treadwell's death is troubling because the predator/prey relationship makes humans 'pieces of meat' and, as such, objects rather than subjects. This interruption forcibly moves humans to the nature side of the dualism, thereby questioning the superiority of the culture side of the binary by exposing human vulnerability.[44]

This blurring of boundaries is not merely abstract or representational, but, most importantly, material, in that Treadwell's body quite literally became part of the grizzly and had to be exhumed from it. Treadwell's love for the grizzlies makes explicit what is always at stake in the Bataillean erotic; namely, death, or the complete dissolution of self.

Eroticism is a mode of communication with alterity, and Treadwell frequently seeks to directly communicate with bears and other animals. Early in the film, Treadwell introduces us to a bear named The Grinch, who ambles across a stream towards Treadwell. As she approaches, he attempts to calm her by saying 'Hi, Grinch, how are you' in a relaxed, high-pitched voice. She continues towards him and he begins to assume an offensive stance, his voice switching registers as he gestures towards her and intones, 'Don't you do that!' As she retreats, he switches again, apologizing to the bear and telling her that he loves her. While it is tempting to read this scene as a naïve projection of sentimental feelings that result in a near miss, Hediger suggests that Treadwell's repeated pronouncements of love are more complex than it seems:

> The phrase signifies in a radically different fashion for human viewers in the cinema than it does for the bears who are its immediate audience, so it functions at once as animal vocalization and as speech. For the bears, its sing-song nature may well have helped Treadwell communicate his ostensibly peaceable intentions, as he believed. But that very same attribute – the sing-song sound – combined with the semantics of the phrase, lead many cinema viewers to think him simply foolish or crazy.[45]

The reading that Hediger attributes to the cinema audience, of Treadwell as 'foolish or crazy', would suggest that *Grizzly Man* is about a unidirectional and ultimately failed relationship: Treadwell's unwise attachments to the bears are met with indifference and finally hostility. However, Hediger's posthumanist reading argues that the film's pathways of communication are more complex and multi-directional – especially due to the multiple layers of mediation through Treadwell's and then Herzog's footage, a point to which I will return – and that consequently *Grizzly Man* 'demonstrates compelling cross-species communication'.[46] Hediger's reading looks past the conflict between Herzog and Treadwell to consider the multiple perspectives and ambiguities negotiated through the cinematic medium; this opens up at least the possibility of reciprocation, even if it cannot be verified or exactly determined.

148   *Limit Cinema*

We see these possibilities for reciprocation especially when Treadwell interacts with wild foxes. While the grizzlies generally seem indifferent, are occasionally tolerant and sometimes seem curious or aggressive towards Treadwell, the foxes actively seek him out for play and physical affection. In one scene, Treadwell shoots upwards towards the roof of his tent as a fox walks overhead; Treadwell touches one of the paws and the fox seems to touch him back. Treadwell exits the tent and runs as the fox chases him across the grass. It is difficult to read this scene as anything but a genuine, mutual encounter between a human and a wild animal, and even Herzog's voice-over praises Treadwell 'as a filmmaker' for capturing such beautiful unscripted moments. While interactions like these may raise ethical concerns – as scientists and ecologists mention throughout the film, Treadwell's presence in the park was generally harmful in that it accustomed the wildlife to his presence and taught them not to fear humans – they also indicate that Treadwell's engagements with wild nature were not as unidirectional as Herzog's voice-over might suggest.

The risk of Treadwell's encounters, however, is that they are irrevocably tainted by projection and sentimentality. In a sequence about midway through the film, Treadwell explains his motivation for leaving civilization in a series of monologues. He confesses to Iris the fox that he had problems with drugs and alcohol and that his connection with the bears was key to his recovery: 'So I promised the bears, that if I would look over them, then would they please

Figure 13 Reciprocal interaction with fox in *Grizzly Man* (Werner Herzog, 2005).

Limits of Love in Grizzly Man *and* Koneline   149

help me.' Treadwell's imagined contract with the bears exemplifies the kind of preferential love derided by Kierkegaard and Bratton in that it is conditional on reciprocation and the cooperation of the other rather than 'a completely self-giving engagement with the world'.[47] Treadwell loves the bears because of what they can do for him, and he fantasizes about his ability to provide for them in turn (throughout the film, Herzog and others undercut this fantasy, since Treadwell was 'protecting' the bears in a national park). Therefore, while Treadwell's love for nature might have resulted in genuine cross-species communication, these encounters are not neutral or unclouded by sentimentality. Further, his preferential love for bears and foxes occasionally leads him to neglect or misunderstand other aspects of the Alaskan wilderness. In one scene he mourns the death of a baby fox who has been eaten by wolves; he angrily swats away flies that swarm around the carcass, telling them to 'have some respect'. He similarly laments the deaths of bear cubs, killed by male grizzlies or eaten by their mothers to stave off hunger. Scenes like these indicate that Treadwell does not love the bears or foxes as they are, but rather as he desires them to be, and this kind of preferential love often inhibits a more holistic understanding of their position in a broader ecology.

As Treadwell's confessions imply that his love for nature originates with his own troubled psyche, it is tempting to psychoanalyse him. Just after Treadwell's talk with Iris, he delivers an extended soliloquy about his failed relationships with women[48] and laments that 'it would have been a lot easier' if he were gay and could solicit sex whenever he wanted without dealing with the mysteries of female subjectivity. Dominic Pettman argues that 'the evidence accumulates that the guardian of the grizzlies "doth protest too much"' and that 'one can't help but wonder if an attraction to men, and a revulsion of this attraction, led Treadwell to flee his family in Long Island, change his name, abuse alcohol and other drugs, and ultimately seek spiritual solace in the wilderness'.[49] Such speculations are anthropocentric in their insistence on human subjectivity as their hermeneutic centre, looking to Treadwell's psychological structure rather than his external relationships to determine the 'truth' of his relationship with the grizzlies. However, Carman argues that queer interpretations of Treadwell's relationship with the bears open up radical possibilities for ecological thinking. Though he does not go so far as to agree with Pettman that Treadwell must have been gay, Carman posits that Treadwell's love for the grizzlies is queer in that it disrupts identification according to natural/unnatural binaries: 'the fact that Treadwell viewed the physiology of animal sex with fascination and excitement, coupled with his nonessentialist aim of going animal, suggests that his own pleasures (dead-set as they were on animal objects) escaped heteronormative control'.[50] For Carman, Treadwell does indeed project his desires onto the bears, but this does not eliminate the possibility of an encounter across the animal/human border because Treadwell's queer desire for the bears unsettles this very distinction. In this reading, Treadwell's erotic attachment to animals does not make his relationship with them disingenuous, but rather interrupts anthropocentric attachments to nature/culture binaries.

As Michel Foucault argues, Bataillean transgression does not reinforce binaries but rather mobilizes and unsettles them: 'Transgression, then, is not related to the limit as black to white, the prohibited to the lawful, the outside to the inside, or as the open area of a building to its enclosed spaces. Rather, their relationship takes the form of a spiral which no simple infraction can exhaust'.[51] Because transgression is related to finitude in that it measures 'the excessive distance that it opens at the heart of the limit' and thereby 'affirms limited being',[52] it cannot be totalizing or impartial; instead, transgression exposes the limits of knowledge and subjectivity, beyond which nothing can be known. Treadwell's love for the bears therefore affectively engages the spectator with the possibility of not knowing, and with death as one part of the circumvoluted process of transgression. We see another part of this process in a scene in which he expresses his delight upon encountering the fresh excrement of Wendy, one of his favourite bears: 'It was inside her!' he exclaims, touching it to feel its warmth. Bataille associates excrement, along with sexuality and other acts of expenditure and abjection, with the excessive realm of general economy, and this act of seeking to understand Wendy based on what she has expelled therefore aligns with Treadwell's generally transgressive relationship with the bears: his love for them consistently troubles but can never eradicate the distinctions between human and nonhuman, subjective and objective.

Herzog's romantic nihilism

Herzog's attitude towards nature, though more nihilistic than Treadwell's, is no less romantic in that it betrays a sentimentality that exceeds his attempts at rationalization. Numerous readings of the film position Herzog in relation to German romanticism, which views nature in terms of binaries such as 'beneficent' and 'baneful', 'reason and passion, civilization and wild nature,

Limits of Love in Grizzly Man *and* Koneline   151

and knowledge and belief'.[53] Johnson argues that 'Herzog is simultaneously an exponent and critic of romanticism' in that he 'develops and reinterprets several of [its] most progressive and skeptical features', including 'an ironic exploration of the limits of Enlightenment thinking about nature, individual consciousness, and community'.[54] Prager makes a similar claim, though like Johnson he cautions against the 'assertion that Herzog is a Romantic in the traditional sense';[55] rather, Prager argues that Herzog's stance is more critical in that it echoes ideas from 'the best Romantic works [that] are meant to call into question our ideas concerning the limits or the boundaries on perception'.[56] For Prager and Johnson, Herzog aligns with versions of romanticism that posit an irreparable fissure between humans and nature, rather than more sentimental notions of nature as authentic, beautiful or idyllic.

Herzog's relationship with romanticism leads to questions about whether his view of nature in *Grizzly Man* is more 'truthful' than Treadwell's, or whether it too involves projection. By discussing Herzog's perspective, I do not mean to speculate about his intentions; rather, I am concerned with his presence in the film as both a character, seen in his voice-over commentary and interactions with interview subjects, and narrative voice, seen in, for example, the stylistic interventions on Treadwell's footage, such as editing decisions or music. 'Herzog' within *Grizzly Man* is therefore a discursive pattern that relates to Treadwell's position in various ways, generally through conflict, but also sometimes through convergence. While Treadwell is concerned with the crossing of boundaries – of blurring the lines between human and animal – Herzog insists on reinforcing them, and his voice-over frequently expresses scepticism about our ability to see past certain limits. In his first voice-over, Herzog tells us that Treadwell crossed an 'invisible borderline', a comment that plays over hand-held footage of a bear investigating Treadwell's presence. Treadwell reaches out to touch the bear, before the bear suddenly gets too close and Treadwell threatens it to dissuade its aggressive advance. This sudden shift in tone, from curiosity to aggression, is highlighted by an abrupt stop in the music, a stylistic intervention that reinforces Herzog's moralizing about Treadwell's transgressions. Herzog's scepticism about the possibility of knowledge about nature is also seen in the way that he repeatedly turns the focus away from questions about external reality and towards questions about inner life: for Herzog, Treadwell's is a story about 'human ecstasies and darkest inner turmoil' rather than a positive connection with wild nature. In line with this assertion, he often psychologizes the Alaskan landscape, and at one point he says over spectacular helicopter shots of glaciers: 'it seems to me that this landscape in turmoil is a metaphor of his [Treadwell's] soul'. This refusal to read the landscape as itself, instead insisting that it can only reveal subjective human truths, suggests that meaning for Herzog remains restricted to the realm of the human, though his characterization of nature as founded on 'chaos, hostility, and murder' implies that human claims to significance can be violently disrupted by an unknowable external reality.

Like Treadwell, Herzog projects his own vision onto the landscape, but he does so in a way that is arguably more self-aware in its recognition of the limits of that vision and its impotence in the face of a larger, indifferent reality. Herzog uses Treadwell's death as a case in point about the indifference of nature, since it violently undercuts Treadwell's attempts to find meaning with the bears. Herzog can only appropriate the footage in Treadwell's absence, resulting in a representational fissure that hangs over the entire film: Treadwell's death throughout *Grizzly Man* is referred to obliquely through language or symbolism, but is never directly shown. This seems to be the result of deliberate omission rather than lack of information, because Herzog refers several times to photographs of Huguenard's and Treadwell's corpses in the coroner's office. Further, in the much-discussed scene in which Herzog listens to an audio recording of their deaths, there are multiple layers of mediation that occlude audience knowledge.[57] Herzog explains in voice-over that Treadwell's camera was on during the event, though he was not able to remove the lens cap, and at first the spectator cannot see Herzog's reactions but only Treadwell's friend Jewel Palovak's responses to them. The camera tracks to watch her expressions for a moment before panning to settle on the side of Herzog's face, hidden from us by a hand raised to his furrowed brow; he tells Palovak to turn it off and insists that she destroy the recording. These multiple refractions of the event – first through the audio recording, then Herzog's descriptions, Palovak's expressions and the camera shooting the scene – disrupt the apparently indexical relationship between the recording and the real event, and the interdiction on the direct representation of Treadwell's death establishes the event as the film's invisible, traumatic centre.

This trauma is represented simultaneously through lack and excess, as the absence of more direct representations leads to overdetermined interpretations of the event that can never quite appropriate it. Treadwell's death is described as a tragedy, as well as a case of him 'getting what he deserved', in the words of pilot Sam Egli; some suggest that his death was an inevitable or unsurprising consequence of his interactions with the grizzlies, while others claim that it was only a series of uncharacteristic mistakes in his last summer that led to the attack. These conflicts between lack and excess – between the absence and overdetermination of meaning – are related to the structure of desire, which, as Stefan Herbrechter and Ivan Callus argue, 'is at once blind and uncontrollable. It is an essential aspect of the human but at the same time it is a threat because it does not distinguish in its object between human and inhuman.'[58] Neil Badmington makes a similar point when he argues that 'desire is unruly, troubling, ongoing. It never falls under the control of the subject of humanism. It mocks mastery.'[59] Though desire is anthropocentric in that it structures human subjectivity, it also continuously undermines the subject's position through lack: desire longs for its impossible completion in the other and therefore undermines the human subject's mastery over extraneous nature.

Because desire for the other is based in our own lack, it is unsurprising that Herzog's position in *Grizzly Man*, which continually emphasizes the limits of human perception, betrays a desire that exceeds his authorial control. Herzog establishes himself as a voice of reason within the text, aligning himself with various experts, such as bear biologist Larry Van Daele and Alutiiq museum director Sven Haakanson Jr, that denounce Treadwell's attitude towards the bears as dangerous, over-sentimental and irrational. This would seem to suggest that Herzog's feelings about nature are more akin to the environmentalist *agape* advocated by Bratton than Treadwell's erotic attachments to the bears. While Herzog is obviously in awe of nature, the relationship he espouses is not predicated on reciprocity or empathy; Herzog feels towards nature without expecting it to feel or respond back. However, by viewing nature as uniformly chaotic, hostile or indifferent, Herzog's position is also selective in its interpretation, and his scepticism causes him to overlook the possibilities for genuine cross-species communication that I discussed in the previous section. As the romantic interpretations of his work suggest, Herzog's awe in the face of nature's overwhelming indifference is no less a projection than Treadwell's belief in the bears' friendliness. Gellkman sees a complicity in their positions, since the 'vehemence of Herzog's rebuttal bespeaks an identification with his protagonist, for the ... sentiment of indifference presupposes an irreducible demand for empathy'.[60] While Herzog's characterization of nature is different from Treadwell's, he similarly desires something from nature that it cannot provide: it is neither totally empathetic nor antipathetic, and therefore exceeds the dialectic staged between *Grizzly Man*'s two central perspectives.

154 *Limit Cinema*

This excess is Bataillean in that it does not result in a positive meaning – the synthesis that completes the Hegelian dialectic – but rather in an abstract negativity linked to the real of Treadwell's death. Lisa Trahair describes the difference between the productive negativity of the Hegelian dialectic and the abstract negativity of Bataillean general economy, both of which result from an encounter with the other: while the Hegelian dialectic is related to the struggle 'to the death' between the master and slave, Trahair explains that Bataille makes a mockery of this by pointing out that 'if a real death were to result from the duel between two consciousnesses, there would be no meaning'.[61] This is because death is not the 'sublative negativity' of the dialectic that can be systematized into a higher order truth – an antithesis that can be synthesized into a positive meaning – but is rather 'abstract negativity, death pure and simple, mute and non-productive death, meaningless within the system and losing meaning in any effort to make it meaningful'.[62] So while we might see a dialectic functioning between the perspectives of Treadwell and Herzog in the film (the conflict between Treadwell's beatific view of nature and Herzog's more nihilistic one might be synthesized into a view that sees nature as somewhere in between or, as mentioned earlier in the chapter, that sees Treadwell and Herzog as two sides of the same coin), Treadwell's death complicates the process. The representational gap in *Grizzly Man* surrounding the real of Treadwell's death is in part a recognition of death as abstract negativity, as something that resists incorporation within a system. This negativity intrudes on the dialectic between Treadwell and Herzog's views of nature because Treadwell's death exposes the limits of both perspectives and their inability to come to terms with nature as abstract negativity. Both Treadwell and Herzog impose meaning on nature according to their respective desires, but *Grizzly Man*'s representational gaps prevent these from being synthesized into a coherent, objective whole. The multiple mediations of Treadwell's death do not replace or cover over the event, but rather gesture towards it as an excess of representation, an abstract negativity that unsettles any sense of stable, self-contained subjectivity.

Despite *Grizzly Man*'s representational interdictions and Herzog's insistence on the indifferent brutality of nature, however, Herzog nevertheless cannot keep from attempting to find meaning in Treadwell's death. Rather than finding meaning in Treadwell's relationship with the bears, he locates it in the medium of cinema: he praises Treadwell as a film-maker who was able to, often despite himself, shoot scenes with 'a strange secret beauty'. In one such scene, Treadwell repeatedly runs in and out of frame, leaving the camera to capture the wind

Limits of Love in Grizzly Man *and* Konelīne   155

rustling through leaves and tall grass. Herzog muses that 'sometimes images themselves develop their own life, their own secret stardom'; his allusions to the magic of cinema, rather than of nature itself, make it clear that these representations are still inevitably tethered to the camera and its construction of reality. Herzog's sentimentality for the cinematic image aligns him with a theoretical tradition that views cinema as a form of love for the real, or in other words a desire to obtain from reality something that it cannot quite provide. This position is most evident in a much-quoted passage from André Bazin's *What Is Cinema?*:

> The aesthetic qualities of photography are to be sought in its power to lay bare the realities. It is not for me to separate off, in the complex fabric of the objective world, here a reflection on a damp sidewalk, there the gesture of a child. Only the impassive lens, stripping its object of all those ways of seeing it, those piled-up preconceptions, that spiritual dust and grime with which my eyes have covered it, is able to present it in all its virginal purity to my attention and consequently to my love.[63]

The relationship between the photographic/cinematic image and the real is related to our desire to see the world objectively, unfettered by 'piled up preconceptions'. This desire, like all desire, is impossible to fully satisfy, and Bazin's myth of total cinema, which he describes as the driving impulse of the medium to provide a perfect and objective reproduction of reality, is therefore an unobtainable goal. Just as O'Gorman argues that speculative realism evinces a fantasy of objectivity – an erotic longing for the real – rather than a grasp on objectivity itself, for Bazin cinema is based on the desire to access reality in its 'virginal purity' rather than any actual possibility of doing so. Crucially, this does not preclude a relation to the real, but is rather the very condition of it: Bazin's famous claim that realism can only be achieved through artifice (as also discussed in Chapter 3) is a recognition that our access to the real is limited by and mediated through perception. Herzog's love for the cinematic image in *Grizzly Man* is therefore a desire that is inevitably frustrated but that nevertheless persists as a condition for our relation to nature.

However, there is a more obvious way that Herzog expresses sentimentality in the film. Malacaster Bell points out that the ending of *Grizzly Man* is undeniably sentimental, despite Herzog's frequent diatribes against Treadwell's sentimentality in his voice-over narration:[64] after Herzog tells us that Treadwell's story gives us insight into our inner nature, ultimately granting meaning to his life and death, we see Treadwell walking up a sunlit stream with two grizzlies following close behind him. The 'scene is in soft focus and is without a trace of menace or danger – it really is as if Treadwell and the bears have bonded … as children of the universe',[65] and Bell uses this scene as evidence that even Herzog cannot quite rid himself of sentimental attachments. Sentimentality for Bell involves overlooking the complexity of the object of affection in order to align it with some symbolic virtue: often innocence, as with children, or moral purity, as with Treadwell's refusal to see the bears as anything other than totally good.[66] Bell argues that our relationships with animals are particularly prone to sentimentality because the extent of our ability to know them is uncertain, and that often we 'get so caught up in valuing the target as a symbol for some value that we neglect the real interests of the target or fail to respond properly to its value'.[67] Therefore, while Bell argues that a convincing case can be made that Treadwell did 'at least have partial knowledge' of the Alaskan bears,[68] as evidenced by his ability to peacefully coexist with them for many years, his sentimentality eventually became problematic and resulted in harm to both parties.

However, sentimentality for Bell is an ambivalent rather than wholly negative aspect of our loving relationships, because although it poses problems in its selective appreciation of the other, it can also provide us with the reassurance we need to overcome solipsistic attachment to our own species or subject positions: 'It is natural to experience anxiety and frustration as we attempt to gain knowledge of another. Sentimental affection is valuable because it allows us to continue to love in the face of anxiety'.[69] Sentimentality allows for this because it simplifies the overwhelming complexity of the other and reduces it to terms that we can understand and align with our own emotional attachments. Although Bell warns that sentimentality should not be our sole mode of engagement with nonhuman animals, he insists that it is unavoidable – as Herzog's surprisingly sentimental ending demonstrates – and can have positive effects.

Sentimental attitudes are important for my purposes because, as a way of dealing with anxiety over uncertainty about the other, sentimentality provides a means of responding to the impossible imperative (which, to recall, is my term for our responsibility to engage with alterity despite our inability to do so). Bell's argument suggests that while complete knowledge of the nonhuman other's complex existence is impossible, the oversimplification of sentimentality can encourage enough positive affect that we might at least keep trying, rather than retreating into solipsistic doubt about the existence of nonhuman minds.[70]

Grizzly Man's concluding tone of sentimental, positive affect, which occurs despite the doubts raised through the narrative about our ability to know nonhuman minds, has implications beyond the Treadwell/Herzog dialectic: while I have been discussing love for nature in terms of representation, as something that *Grizzly Man* explores on the level of content, the final sequence also turns sentimentality towards the spectator. I never fail to find this sequence incredibly moving, and inevitably finish the film by feeling Treadwell's death as a tragic but meaningful loss despite my complicated and frequently negative attitudes towards him over the course of the film. Against the better judgement of its own authorial voice, *Grizzly Man's* final scene encourages an affect in the spectator that the film itself has often deemed irrational. This final emphasis on irrational sentimentality is the most radical aspect of *Grizzly Man's* treatment of nature love: it provokes an affect in excess of reason and asks the spectator to love despite an abundance of arguments against it.

Our mind/our land beautiful

Though *Grizzly Man's* sentimental ending hints at optimistic possibilities for human–animal relationships, the actual results of these interactions within the film are hardly reassuring. I have been arguing that love is a necessary and desirable part of our ethical engagement with nature, but I do not wish to suggest that we all risk death by plunging into the wilderness in the vain hope of forging an uncertain connection with dangerous animals. While the textual density of *Grizzly Man* makes it an apt object for teasing out some of the implications and contradictions of human love for nature, this section will look at a somewhat more hopeful example of what this love might look like. *Koneline* offers an example of love for nature on a formal level in that its mode of representation operates through aesthetic *eros* by encouraging sensory engagement with the landscape. Similar to *Grizzly Man*, *Koneline* negotiates between a number of perspectives on the relationship between humans and the landscape they inhabit. The description on the film's website reads: 'Some hunt on the land. Some mind it. They all love it. Set deep in the traditional territory of the Tahltan First Nation, *Koneline* captures beauty and complexity as one of Canada's vast wildernesses undergoes irrevocable change.'[71] The film centres on the controversial Red Chris mine in north-western British Columbia, and though it does not avoid the intense polemics surrounding the construction, it exceeds them through what I will describe as a loving aesthetic.

Konelīne's interview subjects are all residents or visitors to the region affected by the Red Chris mine: Wild interviews a number of Tahltan – both those opposed to the mine for environmental reasons and those who rely on it for economic ones – as well as local business owners and workers who exhibit a range of opinions. Interviews are intercut with spectacular sequences of natural, social and industrial activities, which are enhanced through a percussive score and vibrant, slow-motion cinematography. There are a number of striking helicopter shots of forests and rivers; electrical towers are installed; fish are harvested, moose and stone sheep are hunted; the owner of a hunting expedition company uses a boat to bring her team of horses across a rushing river; Tahltan community members participate in an energetic gambling tournament; a blockade is established against mining and government officials. *Konelīne* does not distinguish aesthetically between 'natural' and 'unnatural' elements of the environment, as industrial equipment/labour and scenes of natural splendour are shot with the same spectacular cinematography and similarly enhanced with stylistic techniques such as slow motion (in this it is similar to *Tectonics* – see Chapter 3). The result is an emphatically beautiful film that aestheticizes all aspects of the landscape, from trees and rivers to power lines and quad bikes to the fresh blood of salmon and moose.

The film won awards at a number of Canadian film festivals and received a warm reception from both left- and right-leaning Canadian newspapers, perhaps because of its refusal to draw binaries and its emphasis instead on spectacle and

Figure 14 Moose hunt in *Konelīne: Our Land Beautiful* (Nettie Wild, 2016).

positive affect: Chris Knight for the conservative *National Post* gives the film three and a half stars out of four and praises it for its 'moral ambiguity' and 'fantastic visuals';[72] Kate Taylor and Linda Barnard, writing for centre-left-oriented papers (*The Globe and Mail* and *Toronto Star* respectively) lauded the film for being 'subtle and remarkably even-handed'[73] and applauded Wild for her 'restraint in stepping out of the way to let people from tribal elders to a wilderness hunting guide and miners tell their stories without passing judgment'.[74] The praise garnered by the film suggests that it ruffled few feathers despite its potentially controversial subject matter (the conflicts between environmental and economic interests are particularly heated in Canada, which relies heavily on primary sector industries such as mining and oil and gas extraction that face frequent resistance from environmentalist and Indigenous groups). Though its poetic approach might be viewed as a failure to mobilize environmental sentiments for political change, *Konelīne* also holds potential for encouraging an ecological awareness of the landscape by negotiating its various perspectives and tensions without implying that they can finally be solved. Given that I have been defining love as an ever-unfinished and uncertain response to something outside of ourselves, we might read *Konelīne* as using beautiful aesthetics to express and evoke love – in all its indeterminacy – for nature.

Konelīne begins with a spectacular helicopter shot of dense green pine forest and water mirroring a bright blue sky as a man says in voice-over, 'There is no word in our language, there is no word for wild. How can you have an up if you don't have a down, right?' This breakdown of the binary between natural and cultural spaces foreshadows the film's holistic view of the changing landscape. The film is not an argument for or against the mine, somewhat of a departure from Wild's previous documentaries: *FIX: Story of an Addicted City* (2002), for example, chronicles the establishment of the first North American safe injection site in Vancouver, while *A Place Called Chiapas* (1998) looks at the Zapatista Indigenous uprising in Mexico, and ticket sales were used to help raise funds for the group. While *Konelīne* does not shy away from social and environmental issues, it also does not moralize or take a position among the various perspectives examined in the film. Instead, *Konelīne* situates its characters and events in a broader ecology, viewing them all as part of a changing landscape.

Konelīne's central subjects are Oscar Dennis (the man in the voice-over from the beginning) and his family. Dennis works to record and preserve the Tahltan language, while his mother leads a blockade against the mine. The white proprietor of a local eatery also opposes construction, because it disrupts the breeding ground of the local stone sheep; she tells us this as she strokes a stuffed specimen of the species, one of many that decorate the walls and corners of her establishment. Her position is complicated somewhat by the mixed patronage of her restaurant: she talks about educating tourists and hunters as Tahltan children tell us the names of the stuffed animals in their language, but we also see workers on break, identifiable through their high-visibility vests and boots. That these workers are probably connected to the mine, either directly or indirectly through the power companies that supply its electricity, highlights the complexity of negotiating economic and environmental concerns in the area. Wild also interviews a number of workers at the mine, some of whom seem to have uncomplicated and positive views of the construction – one man explains that being outdoors is much better than sitting in an office – while others are more ambivalent. A Tahltan worker describes his reticence to talk freely either to his family or his company, but concedes that the mine provides a roof over his head and food for his children. The young president of the Tahltan nation is willing to hear out the representatives from the mine and the B.C. government because of the economic opportunities the project could offer the community, while some elders express their discontent with the lack of transparency in the process. Dennis, who fiercely opposes the construction, in the end concedes that the community needs the mine for economic reasons, though he bitterly expresses his desire to leave the area before it turns into an industrial wasteland.

The film's refusal to draw the conflict in terms of strict binaries (wilderness/ civilization, white settler/Tahltan) is part of the reason for its reception as 'remarkably even-handed', despite the fact that the film's focus is on Tahltan and local workers rather than government officials or company executives; there are no extended interviews with the latter.[75] However, nor are there overt attempts to discredit or undermine these individuals or their institutions, somewhat of a departure from the Griersonian tradition of Canadian documentary that seeks to persuade the public to take sides in social issues.[76] This tactic is familiar from other important Canadian documentaries about Indigenous blockades, such as Alanis Obamsawin's *Kanehsatake: 270 Years of Resistance* (1993), which explicitly seeks an alternative to the dominant white settler narrative by giving voice to the Mohawk struggle during the Oka Crisis.[77] *Koneline*, which is far less polemical, gives voice to a variety of perspectives all connected by the land without trying to resolve their differences or reduce them to familiar binaries. The film's paralleled hunting sequences are a case in point here: the film intercuts between two Tahltan men hunting moose with high-powered rifles and two white hunters using bows and arrows to hunt stone sheep. Both pairs explicitly associate the activity with a connection to their ancestors and the landscape, and though there is an ironic joke here – the Tahltan hunters efficiently kill and butcher a moose cow while one of the white hunters explains that he has been hunting since 1975 without ever killing anything with a bow and arrow – the film itself does not pass judgement in either case.

Koneline allows all inhabitants and visitors to north-western British Columbia to connect with the landscape, and these connections are primarily framed in terms of affect. Often, the film asks its audience to consider aspects of the environment that would normally be considered ugly in a new way, the strikingly beautiful moose hunting sequence being a case in point: bright red blood drips and foams on the green grass; skin and white strips of fat are cut from the carcass; muscles are exposed, twitching in the gleaming sunlight. There is no sense of horror to the slaughter (though squeamish spectators may be horrified regardless), nor does the event seem trivial or wasteful, and one of the men laments that the act is hard to do as he commemorates the kill by carving a notch into his knife handle. Milton draws from anthropologist Tim Ingold to argue that hunting is linked to heightened identification with animals because 'subsistence hunters know a great deal about what animals do and why, and so have a particularly strong sense of their personhood"[78] Hunting in *Koneline* is similarly represented as a means of connecting with animals: one of the white hunters explains that it allows him to get as close to the stone sheep as a natural predator would and implies that this 'closeness' goes beyond mere geographic proximity. However, *Koneline* also suggests that this knowledge of nonhuman animals is useful in other contexts and does not always lead to death or harm; the film's fishing and hunting sequences are paralleled with a scene in which the community bands together to help fish move upstream to spawn after a rockslide blocks the river. Children run with wriggling fish and toss them in a tank; salmon are transported by helicopter in big metal canisters, a woman kisses a salmon gently before submerging it. Death is represented as merely part of an ecological process: the Tahltan help the salmon to spawn so that they will have fish to catch and eat in a few years' time, part of a cycle in which the Tahltan have been participating, as a woman tells us in voice-over, for 8,000 years. Dying may mark the limit of the human subject, but *Koneline* gestures towards the part it plays in an irreducibly complex ecology that expands far beyond our finite frameworks and timescales. In Bataillean terms, the film acknowledges that

162   *Limit Cinema*

the restricted economy of the human is related to the general economy of its ecological relations.

But while the idyllic fishing and fish-saving sequences might suggest a naïve endorsement of a return to nature or a problematic romanticization of Indigenous relationships with the land, *Konelīne*'s industrial sequences suggest that there is no difference between natural and artificial relationships with nature. Van Royko's cinematography does not distinguish between shots of Tahltan fishing as they have for millennia and workers putting up electrical towers to provide power to the new mine, suggesting a parallel in how these actions affect and are affected by the environment. This is not to say that the film endorses both activities equally; the refusal to moralize suggests instead that *Konelīne* recognizes that humans are irrecoverably part of the north-western B.C. ecology, and that nature/culture binaries falsely distance us from our points of connection with the natural world. A particularly spectacular sequence observes a group of workers erecting an electrical tower: a helicopter flies the tower through a mountain pass as the men crouch in anticipation; percussive sounds and chimes rise on the soundtrack as we see wind from the propellers blow dust around the men. The helicopter dangles the tower and the men grab hold, grappling with the wind and the weight of the large steel object in spectacular slow motion for a few minutes before they lock the tower into a pole on the ground. Shaviro, summarizing Whitehead, 'defines beauty as a matter of differences that are conciliated, adapted to one another', which means that 'beauty is appropriate to a world of relations, in which entities continually affect and touch and interpenetrate one another'.[79] If beauty is relational, then the helicopter sequence's beauty is in the dynamic encounter it evokes between wind, steel, workers, soil, camera and spectator. *Konelīne*'s aestheticization of the north-western B.C. landscape draws on these relational aspects of beauty with its dynamic images of encounters between various elements of the environment, natural as well as human-made. The film's beauty is therefore ecological in its representation of multifaceted elements of the British Columbia landscape, and in representing both natural and artificial changes through the same aesthetic lens it neither privileges nor discounts the human.

Shaviro (following Harman) advocates aesthetics as first philosophy, because our aesthetic relationships with things precede all other modes of encounter: 'When objects encounter one another, the basic mode of their relation is neither theoretical nor practical and neither epistemological nor ethical.

Limits of Love in Grizzly Man and Koneline   163

Figure 15 Aestheticizing industry in *Koneline: Our Land Beautiful* (Nettie Wild, 2016).

Rather, before either of these, every relation among objects is an aesthetic one.'[80] He continues that

> Aesthetics is about the *singularity* and *supplementarity* of things: it has to do with things insofar as they cannot be cognized or subordinated to concepts and also insofar as they cannot be utilized, or normatively regulated, or defined according to rules. No matter how deeply I comprehend a thing, and no matter how pragmatically or instrumentally I make use of it, something of it still escapes my categorizations.[81]

Shaviro links aesthetics explicitly to affect, in that an aesthetic experience involves feeling this excess in the object. He avoids anthropocentrism by asserting that all objects participate in aesthetic experiences because they all feel something of other things, in their own ways: the men feel the wind from the helicopter that hovers above in the air and dangles the electrical tower so that its movements are swayed by a push and pull of multiple physical forces. Crucially, for Shaviro this emphasis on aesthetics does not eliminate the need to theorize the subject, despite his insistence on undermining anthropocentrism. He explains later in the chapter that 'aesthetic experience is always asymmetrical; it needs to be posed in terms of a subject, as well as an object'.[82] Relations are not homogeneous and equal, so that subjects and objects can no longer be differentiated; rather, these differences are established only from particular, situated perspectives that change when they come into contact with each other. Like Shaviro, *Koneline* implies that affective relationships to the landscape come prior to ethics or political debate, and

164   *Limit Cinema*

its dynamic aesthetics encourages the spectator to feel before coming to any conclusions. Because *Konelīne* mediates these experiences through cinema, it must represent them for the human subject that is inevitably implied by the apparatus. But this ostensible anthropocentrism, read through Shaviro's aesthetics, also calls attention to the ways that the human subject is situated in the film's perceptual ecology and is alerted to the excess of representation that Shaviro argues characterizes every aesthetic experience.

Konelīne's emphasis on aesthetics does not preclude political debate, but rather evokes the relation between particular and general economy. Like *Konelīne*, Bataille links human economic interests to ecology, and a passage from *The Accursed Share* is worth quoting at length here:

> The human mind reduces operations, in science as in life, to an entity based on typical *particular* systems (organisms or enterprises). Economic activity, considered as a whole, is conceived in terms of particular operations with limited ends. The mind generalizes by composing the aggregate of these operations. Economic science merely generalizes the isolated situation; it restricts its object to operations carried out with a view to a limited end, that of economic man. It does not take into consideration a play of energy that no particular end limits: the play of *living matter in general*, involved in the movement of light of which it is the result. On the surface of the globe, for *living matter in general*, energy is always in excess; the question is always posed in terms of its extravagance. The choice is limited to how the wealth is to be squandered. It is to the *particular* living being, or to limited populations of living beings, that the problem of necessity presents itself. But man[83] is not just the separate being that contends with the living world and with other men for his share of resources.[84]

The realm of general economy – of 'living matter in general' – is associated with death, eating, sex and waste, which Bataille argues are all related to unproductive expenditure that cannot be subsumed into the particular requirements of restricted economies (whether it be a single human subject or an entire culture). While we might read these activities through restricted frameworks of meaning – as I am doing here, for example, by discussing them through language – something always exceeds these efforts and is therefore wasted rather than serving the aims of a system.

I have been arguing throughout this book that although these excesses cannot be appropriated by language, they can be gestured towards through cinema. The beauty of *Konelīne* exceeds the rational frameworks of polemic and politics by insisting on affective engagement over argumentation. This is not the naïve

Limits of Love in Grizzly Man *and* Konelīne   165

holism of someone like Timothy Treadwell, who projects onto nature and believes in the fundamental interconnection of all things; nor is it the problematic back-to-nature rhetoric that romanticizes Indigenous cultures as the answer to global capitalism, thereby relying on problematic us/them dualisms. Rather, *Konelīne's* is the holism of general economy, one that recognizes a world of irreducible difference and complexity. This world is not disconnected from human politics and economics, as the film's central conflicts make clear, but rather exceeds them, is affected by and affects them. The film's loving aesthetic positions the spectator in relation to these processes, and although *Konelīne* cannot escape the trappings of the apparatus – representation remains irrevocably for us – the film's excesses alert us to differences that cannot be reconciled or explained away. The film does not adjudicate between environmental and economic concerns, but rather explores their interrelations and/or contaminations; it draws parallels between different people and processes (white settler/Tahltan, natural/industrial activities) without collapsing them into a reductive argument or restricted economy of sameness. *Konelīne's* aesthetics affirms Shaviro's points that aesthetics precedes ethics or politics, and that reality is experienced before it is judged or carved up by language. That the camera inevitably represents these experiences in relation to a human spectator does not undermine the film's ecological message but rather reinforces that humans are involved in the ecology of the represented landscape.

Towards the end of *Konelīne*, Oscar Dennis explains the use of pronouns in the Tahltan language to describe something as beautiful: the 'k' in 'konelīne' is a personal pronoun for the landscape, so that it means something like 'our land beautiful'. He continues that the pronoun can also refer to a mental landscape, so that one can use the same word to say, 'my cognitive landscape is beautiful'. The word indicates a turning inside out of the subject in a way that resonates with Bataillean *eros* the relation between the restricted economy of a human subject and the general economy that exceeds subjective limits. That the word *konelīne* draws this parallel through beauty speaks to the relationship between aesthetics and love; Bratton refers to this relationship as aesthetic *eros*. But while Bratton argues that aesthetic *eros* can be overly subjective, selective or self-centred, *konelīne* suggests that the ambiguities and ambivalences inherent in love for nature ought not to be corrected but embraced. The absence of an adjudicating God or coherent, totalizable notion of objectivity makes it difficult to determine how to escape the subjective trappings of aesthetic *eros*, such as projection or sentimentality; but recognizing that we can only love nature as ourselves, and not in a God-like, holistic or totalizing way does not imply that we resign ourselves to solipsism. Though aesthetic *eros* carries risks (as do all forms of love), it also holds the potential to disrupt anthropocentrism by exposing the subject to alterity. The beautiful aesthetics of *Konelīne* evokes a world of differences beyond subjective limits; these differences are not opposed or reconciled but placed in dynamic relation, represented for a spectator who is encouraged to feel and, hopefully, to love.

Conclusion

Though it would be too much to say that love provides a solution to the fraught and difficult relationship that humans have forged with nonhuman reality over the modern era, I have argued that it is an important part of the way that we relate to nature and therefore cannot be left out of environmental ethics. Cinema, which often centres on themes of love, can help us to trace the paradoxical movements of various kinds of love for nature. *Grizzly Man* enacts a dialogue between various perspectives on nature, and its excesses of representation spiral around the limit between human and nonhuman realities. The film's multiple layers of mediation – through Herzog's appropriation of Treadwell's footage – do not refract or cover over the real of nature, but rather touch on it from several different directions by pointing out the limits of various subjective viewpoints. I attributed the contradictions and ambiguities of *Grizzly Man* to the ways that it mobilizes different forms of love, since Treadwell's erotic fixation on the bears is negotiated by and against Herzog's conflicting awe at the sublimity of nature. While in *Grizzly Man* these differences are often staged through violence and conflict – between Treadwell and Herzog, and between Treadwell and the bears – *Konelīne* offers a more optimistic view of what love for nature might look like. *Konelīne*'s beautiful aesthetics exceeds the polemics surrounding the Red Chris mine, and the film explores various perspectives without attempting to reconcile their differences, emphasizing instead a kind of affective engagement that I described as aesthetic *eros*.

Erotic attachments to nature are inevitably subjective and therefore anthropocentric, but they also bring the subject to its limit and expose us to the not-self, the not-human. This does not constitute a 'solution' to the ethical problems posed by ecological crisis, but theorizing our response through love implies that there can never be a solution. There is only a process, which we must keep on adjusting based on responses from the beloved. Humanity's love for the nonhuman is an asymmetrical non-relation with no knowledge and no guarantees; however, though love cannot breach subject/object boundaries, it is necessitated by communication with alterity and therefore takes us to the limits of our subjective frameworks. These communications with nature are inevitably fettered by subjective desires and projections, but this does not mean that we are imprisoned within our perceptual spheres; in fact, the restricted economy of subjectivity is always contaminated with and constituted through the general economy of nonhuman reality. This general economy is beyond comprehension, and as Bell points out, we frequently attempt to domesticate it through sentimental attachments. Sentimentality is often a response to our contact with the outside, a way of bringing the unknowable within the boundaries of what we can know and cope with. This inevitably results in oversimplification but, because we are finite after all, the question is not how to avoid these reductive conclusions but rather how they might contribute to better engagements with the world.

Notes

1 Michel O'Gorman, 'Speculative Realism in Chains: A Love Story', *Angelaki* 18, no. 1 (2014), 31–43.
2 Ibid., 31–2.
3 Ibid., 33.
4 Quoted in O'Gorman, 'Speculative Realism', 33.
5 Ibid., 35.
6 Catherine Kellogg explains Nancy's reading of the phrase 'I love you' in this way: 'Signs literally take the place of missing referents, and in this sense signification, while naming a "presence", is always already pointing beyond itself towards what is not and cannot be present.' Lacan refers to love as giving what one does not have in several seminars, starting with *Seminar V*; Slavoj Žižek frequently refers to this definition in exploring the difficulties of neighbour love. He writes that

> finding oneself in the position of the beloved is so violent, traumatic event: being loved makes me feel directly the gap between what I am as a determinate being and the unfathomable X in me which causes love. Lacan's definition of love ('Love is giving something one doesn't have') has to be supplemented with: 'to someone who doesn't want it'. Is this not confirmed by our most elementary experience when somebody unexpectedly declares passionate love to us? The

first reaction, preceding the possible positive reply, is that something obscene, intrusive, is being forced upon us.

Catherine Kellogg, 'Love', in *The Nancy Dictionary*, ed. Peter Gratton and Marie-Eve Morin (Edinburgh: Edinburgh University Press, 2016), 152; Jacques Lacan, *The Seminar of Jacques Lacan: Book V Formations of the Unconscious, 1957–1958*, ed. Jacques-Alain Miller, trans. Russell Grigg (Hoboken, NJ: Wiley, 2017); Slavoj Žižek, 'From *Che Vuoi?* To Fantasy', *Lacan.com*, 7 April 2009a, http://www.lacan.com/essays/?p=146. Accessed 30 October 2019.

7   See especially Jean-Nancy, *Dis-enclosure: The Deconstruction of Christianity*, trans. Bettina Bergo, Gabriel Malenfant and Michael B. Smith (New York: Fordham University Press, 2008); Jean-Luc Nancy, *Adoration: The Deconstruction of Christianity II*, trans. John McKeane (New York: Forham, 2012).

8   Sharon Krishek, 'Two Forms of Love: The Problem of Preferential Love in Kierkegaard's *Works of Love*', *Journal of Religious Ethics* 36, no. 4 (2008), 595–617.

9   Ibid., 599.

10 Though Krishek argues that *Works of Love* cannot account for this problem, she locates a solution in another Kierkegaard text, *Fear and Trembling*, through the paradox of faith. There, as Krishek points out, 'the paradox of faith refers to the ability to sustain simultaneously the two movements of faith, which seem to contradict each other'; she writes that

> Rather than understanding it [love] as structured in the shape of self-denial alone, as Kierkegaard seems to be doing in *Works of Love* ('Christian love is self-denial's love'), I suggest that we understand it in terms of the double movement of faith. In other words, I suggest that we understand *Kjerlighed* (the one true love) as structured in the shape of self-denial (resignation) and unqualified self-affirmation (repetition) tied paradoxically together.

This 'solution' affirms rather than overcomes the paradox. Krishek, 'Two Forms', 613, 615.

11 See Kathryn Blanchard and Kevin O'Brien, *An Introduction of Christian Environmentalism* (Waco, TX: Baylor University Press, 2014) ; Dieter Hessel and Rosemary Ruether, eds, *Christianity and Ecology* (Cambridge, MA: Harvard University Press, 2000).

12 Susan Bratton, 'Loving Nature: Eros or Agape?' *Environmental Ethics* 14, no. 1 (1992), 3–25.

13 Ibid., 4.

14 See Richard Cartwright Austin, *Beauty of the Lord: Awakening the Senses* (Atlanta, GA: John Knox, 1988); and Jay McDaniel, *Of God and Pelicans: A Theology of Reverence for Life* (Louisville, KY: John Knox, 1989).

15 Bratton, 'Loving Nature', 14.

16 Bataille, *Erotism*, 18.

17 Ibid., 11.

18 This is similar to Kierkegaard's paradox of faith; see Krishek, 'Two Forms'.

19 Matthew Abbott, 'On Not Loving Everyone: Comments on Jean-Luc Nancy's "L'amour en éclats" ["Shattered Love"]', *Glossator* 5 (2011), 143.

20 Ibid., 142.

21 Ibid., 140.

22 Libertson, *Proximity*, 12.

23 Nancy refers to the risks posed by love frequently but perhaps most succinctly in a lecture for children on love:

> There are risks involved in all this, great risks. We can be mistaken, and we can confuse the image of the other person that we have in us, the other person such as we see him or her, with the real person, who is necessarily different from the image. Every practice of love consists in a back and forth between the real person and the powerful image I have of him or her. None of this is simple, and it can easily backfire.

Jean-Luc Nancy, *God, Justice, Love, Beauty: Four Little Dialogues*, trans. Sarah Clift (New York: Fordham University Press), 75–6.

24 Kay Milton, *Loving Nature: Towards an Ecology of Emotion* (London: Routledge, 2002).

25 Ibid., 92–109.

26 Adrian Ivakhiv, *Ecologies of the Moving Image* (Waterloo, ON: Wilfrid Laurier University Press, 2013), 299–300.

27 Ned Schantz, 'Melodramatic Reenactment and the Ghosts of *Grizzly Man*', *Criticism* 55, no. 4 (2013), 597.

28 Jennifer Ladino, 'For the Love of Nature: Documenting Life, Death, and Animality in *Grizzly Man* and *March of the Penguins*', *ISLE* 16, no. 1 (2008), 82.

29 See: Colin Carman, 'Grizzly Love: The Queer Ecology of Timothy Treadwell', *GLQ* 18, no. 4 (2012), 501–28; Ryan Hediger, 'Timothy Treadwell's Grizzly Love as Freak Show: The Uses of Animals, Science, and Film', *ISLE* 19, no. 1 (2012), 82–100; Ivakhiv, *Ecologies of the Moving Image*; Jeong and Andrew, 'Grizzly Ghost'; Ladino, 'For the Love of Nature'.

30 Laurie Ruth Johnson, *Forgotten Dreams: Revisiting Romanticism in the Cinema of Werner Herzog* (Rochester: Camden House, 2016).

31 Brad Prager, *The Cinema of Werner Herzog: Aesthetic Ecstasy and Truth* (New York: Wallflower, 2007). See also Benjamin Noys, 'Antiphusis: Werner Herzog's *Grizzly Man*', *Film-Philosophy* 11, no. 3 (2007), 38–51.

32   See OlegGelikman, ' "Cold Pastoral": Werner Herzog's Version of Epson', *MLN* 123, no. 5 (2012), 1141–62; Elizabeth Henry, 'The Screaming Silence: Constructions of Nature in Werner Herzog's *Grizzly Man*', in *Framing the World: Explorations of Ecocriticism and Film*, ed. Paula Willoquet-Maricondi (Charlottesville: University of Virginia Press, 2010), 123–33; David Lulka, 'Consuming Timothy Treadwell: Redefining Nonhuman Agency in Light of Herzog's *Grizzly Man*', in *Animals and Agency: An Interdisciplinary Exploration*, ed. Sarah McFarland and Ryan Hediger (Leiden: Brill, 2009), 67–88

33   Julie Schutten, 'Chewing on the Grizzly Man: Getting to the Meat of the Matter', *Environmental Communication* 2, no. 2 (2008), 193–211.

34   Gelikman, 'Cold Pastoral'; Hediger, 'Freak Show'; Johnson, *Forgotten Dreams*.

35   Prager, *Werner Herzog*; Noys, 'Antiphusis'.

36   Lulka, 'Consuming Timothy'.

37   Johnson, *Forgotten Dreams*, 3.

38   In an interview with Paul Cronin, Herzog opines that 'academia is the death of cinema'. Paul Cronin, ed. *Herzog on Herzog* (London: Faber and Faber, 2002), 15.

39   Ivakhiv, *Ecologies of the Moving Image*; Jeong and Andrew, 'Grizzly Ghost'.

40   Lulka, 'Consuming Timothy'.

41   Stefan Mattessich, 'An Anguished Self-Subjection: Man and Animal in Werner Herzog's *Grizzly Man*', *English Studies in Canada* 39, no. 1 (2013), 51–70; Dominic Pettman, '*Grizzly Man*: Werner Herzog's Anthropological Machine', *Theory & Event* 12, no. 2 (2009).

42   Carman, 'Grizzly Love'; Hediger, 'Freak Show'; Henry, *Forgotten Dreams*; Ivakhiv, *Ecologies of the Moving Image*; Jeong and Andrew, 'Grizzly Ghost'; Schutten, 'Chewing'.

43   Anat Pick, 'Three Worlds: Dwelling and Worldhood on Screen', in *Screening Nature: Cinema Beyond the Human*, ed. Anat Pick and Guinevere Narraway (New York: Berghahn, 2013), 23.

44   Schutten, 'Chewing', 195.

45   Hediger, 'Freak Show', 90.

46   Ibid., 83.

47   Bratton, 'Loving Nature', 92.

48   His confession here seems at odds with the obvious love for him that his ex-girlfriend Jewel Palovak and friend Kathleen Parker display in interviews, not to mention the fact that Treadwell was accompanied by women on a number of his Alaskan summers. Herzog points out that his footage avoids shooting these women because they contradict his vision of himself as a lone adventurer.

49   Pettman, 'Grizzly Man', 39.

50   Carman, 'Grizzly Love', 509.

51 Foucault, 'A Preface to Transgression', 35.

52 Ibid., 36.

53 Johnson, *Forgotten Dreams*, 2.

54 Ibid., 3.

55 Prager, *Werner Herzog*, 12.

56 Ibid.

57 Jewel Palovak reveals in a Reddit interview that it was she rather than Herzog who insisted that the audio would not be included. Palovak owns the rights to Treadwell's estate, including his footage, and she explains:

> When we started production everyone involved, except for myself, wanted to use at lest [sic] a bit of the audio tape in the movie, but contractually it was off the table. I agreed to let Werner hear it because I felt as the director it was important to his perception. Once he listened he knew that it didn't belong in the movie.

https://www.reddit.com/r/IAmA/comments/25gw7r/hello_reddit_i_am_jewel_palovak_confidante_and/. Accessed 1 November 2019.

58 Stefan Herbrechter and Ivan Callus, 'What Is a Posthumanist Reading?' *Angelaki* 13, no. 1 (2008), 101.

59 Badmington, *Alien* Chic, 139.

60 Gelikman, 'Cold Pastoral', 1159.

61 Lisa Trahair, *The Comedy of Philosophy: Sense and Nonsense in Early Cinematic Slapstick* (Albany, NY: SUNY, 2007), 8.

62 Ibid.

63 Bazin, *What Is Cinema?*, 1:15.

64 Malacaster Bell, '*Grizzly Man*, Sentimentality, and Our Relationships with Other Animals', in *Understanding Love: Philosophy, Film, and Fiction*, ed. Susan Wolf and Christopher Grau (Oxford: Oxford University Press, 2014), 15–36.

65 Ibid., 23.

66 Ibid., 29.

67 Ibid.

68 Ibid., 33.

69 Ibid., 35.

70 Ibid., 34–6.

71 https://www.canadawildproductions.com/film/koneline/. Accessed 1 November 2019.

72 Chris Knight, '*Konelīne: Our Land Beautiful* Serves Moral Ambiguity and Beautiful British Columbia Visuals', *National Post*, 9 June 2016, http://news.nationalpost.com/arts/movies/koneline-our-land-beautiful-serves-moralambiguity-and-beautiful-british-columbia-visuals. Accessed 1 November 2019.

73 Kate Taylor, '*Into the Forest* and *Konelīne* are Two Women-Driven Stories of Survival', *Globe and Mail*, 3 June 2016, http://www.theglobeandmail.com/arts/film/film-reviews/koneline-and-into-theforest-are-two-women-driven-stories-of-survival/article30249533/. Accessed 1 November 2019.

74 Linda Barnard, 'Reel Brief: Mini Reviews of *Maggie's Plan, Khoya, Koneline*, and *45 Years*, and *10 Cloverfield Lane* on DVD', *Toronto Star*, 9 June 2016, https://www.thestar.com/entertainment/movies/2016/06/09/reel-brief-mini-reviewsof-maggies-plan-khoya-koneline-and-45-years-and-10-cloverfield-lane-ondvd.html. Accessed 1 November 2019.

75 This was not for lack of trying: Wild remarks that getting inside access to the radical militia for *A Rustling of Leaves: Inside the Philippine Revolution* (1988) was easier than trying to get interviews with mining executives. Conversation with Nettie Wild, at 'Our Land Beautiful: An Evening with Nettie Wild and Betsy Carson', Congress 2019, Vancouver British Columbia, 3 June 2019.

76 John Grierson, the Scottish film-maker and theorist famous for coining the term 'documentary', was also the first Canadian film commissioner. He founded the National Film Commission in 1939, which later became the National Film Board of Canada. The NFB has long been associated with the kinds of persuasive, socially conscious documentaries advocated by Grierson, who believed that documentaries could serve an important social role in persuading the public. See *Grierson*, Roger Blais's 1973 NFB documentary available at http://www.nfb.ca/film/grierson/. Accessed 1 November 2019.

77 The Oka Crisis was a 1990 land dispute between the Mohawk community of Kanehsatake, Quebec, and the town of Oka over the proposed construction of a golf course. The situation escalated to an armed stand-off, and Obamsawin's documentary chronicles the military siege tactics used against the Mohawk protesters. Though *Kanehsatake* was produced by the NFB and won a number of awards, it was rejected by the CBC in Canada and premiered instead in Britain on Channel Four. *Kanehsatake* is available at https://www.nfb.ca/film/kanehsatake_270_years_of_resistance/. Accessed 1 November 2019.

78 Milton, *Loving Nature*, 50.

79 Steven Shaviro, *The Universe of Thing: On Speculative Realism* (Minneapolis: University of Minnesota Press, 2014), 42.

80 Ibid., 52–3.

81 Ibid., 53.

82 Ibid., 63.

83 Bataille is of course following the conventions of his day when he uses 'man' (*l'homme*) to refer to humankind in general, and throughout this book I have used more inclusive terminology (humankind, the human) to refer to the same

Limits of Love in Grizzly Man *and* Konelīne   173

object. However, there is a sense in which the figure to whom Bataille refers actually is masculine – specifically, the active, self-constituted male subject of the Enlightenment that Bataille's ontology calls into question.

84   Bataille, *The Accursed Share: Vol. I*, 23.

Conclusion

This book has proposed a Bataillean film-philosophy for the Anthropocene. My point of departure for a Bataillean reading of twenty-first-century cinema was the end of the world: I connected the stakes of my argument to Timothy Morton's assertion that hyperobjects such as climate change are calling anthropocentrism into question through the risk of annihilation. I have proposed limit cinema as a category of films that destabilize humanist assumptions while simultaneously bearing witness to human finitude and fallibility. Bataille's philosophy provides a useful method for theorizing this tension because transgression emphasizes the contradictions at the limit between self and world rather than overstepping this limit or attempting to reconcile its differences. Because cinema negotiates tensions between subjectivity and objectivity – between its indexical mode of representation and its basis in human subjectivity – it is integral to the philosophical questions at the heart of this book. My analysis has focused primarily on aesthetics and metaphysics by theorizing the relationship between cinematic representation and the unrepresentable outside of thought; I have also asserted, however, that the stakes of my claims are ethical, driven by the urgency of the ecological crisis. In this conclusion, I will explore some of the broader implications of my argument, especially as they relate to an ethics of the Anthropocene. This book has asserted the impossibility of seeing beyond subjective limits while simultaneously endorsing a confrontation with those limits; accordingly, this conclusion is also something of a personal reflection, an attempt to articulate my thought processes and confront my limitations, hopefully in order to open my thinking to new possibilities and future directions.

Throughout this book, I have argued for a middle road between the sometimes-myopic humanism of twentieth-century thought and the decentred ontologies of the nonhuman turn, a negotiation driven by the observation that striving towards objectivity sometimes leads us to overlook places where our thinking is incorrigibly subjective. The negotiation of subjective and objective forces in the contemporary art films discussed in this book provides useful examples of this kind of dynamic, middle-ground thinking that remains at the limits of thought rather than trying to fall on one side or the other. I proposed Bataille as a thinker that allows us to theorize the fraught territory between self and world, and argued that limit cinema articulates this territory through a Bataillean logic of transgression. The films discussed herein evince a desire to overcome subjective limits while also bearing witness to the impossibility of doing so. While Bataille provides the framework, cinema gives us a way of tracing the limit itself: because cinema is founded in subjective modes of perception, it can help us push against the boundaries of our human ways of apprehending the world. The ontological question at issue in the nonhuman turn – how do we think beyond ourselves? – becomes an aesthetic question in the films I have categorized as limit cinema, because they all use the qualities of the medium in order to rethink cinematic representation. Limit cinema is therefore defined through its way of articulating the contamination of representation by the unrepresentable, and although I have remained sceptical about our ability to access the latter, I have argued that the tension between these two concepts is a productive area for philosophical inquiry. This is not a new question, of course; Cary Wolfe argues in *What Is Posthumanism?* that art's privileged relationship to alterity relies on the way that it dislocates perception and communication, a point that resonates with Fred Botting's summary of the Bataillean real as 'an impossible, inexpressible, ineffable and undifferentiated space outside language'.[1] However, while the discussion has frequently touched on the real – in the sense of alterity, the outside of thought or, as Quentin Meillassoux calls it, the absolute – the real itself is not my object of analysis. Rather, limit cinema exposes the place where we touch on the real but do not cross over into it; like the absent interiority in Nancy's invaginated concept of the body, the real remains forever on the other side of a twisting and convoluted skin. Theorizing the real through transgression means that it is not a static entity – a monolithic void at the edge of reason – but rather operates in dynamic relation to the autopoietic system of subjectivity. Though we cannot see it 'in itself', this book has been an effort to trace its effects on the cinematic medium, from within the boundaries of human thought and perception.

Part 1, on Objectivity, looked at different ways of characterizing and relating to the outside of thought through cinema. In Chapter 1, I described objectivity in terms of the Bataillean sacred, and I interpreted the films of Ben Wheatley and Apichatpong Weerasethakul as evincing two kinds of relationships to the sacred natural world. Wheatley uses generic structures against themselves though a logic of sacrifice: not only is sacrifice a recurring narrative trope, it also inheres in the formal structure of his cinema. The aesthetics in Apichatpong, on the other hand, operate through eroticism, framing the relationship between humans and nature in terms of ambiguous sensual encounters. While Wheatley operates in a Western and specifically British context, Apichatpong combines Western influences (especially Surrealism) with Thai politics and religion: in Wheatley, the sacred is associated with pre-Christian Paganism, but in Apichatpong it emerges from the animist traditions of the Isaan region, in contrast with mainstream Thai Buddhism. The divide between humans and nature in Apichatpong is therefore related to a number of other complicated distinctions, including East/West and animism/Buddhism.

I was careful to situate Apichatpong's cinema in context and have tried as much as possible to derive my conclusions throughout from the films themselves rather than a forced or rigid application of my theory, with the inevitable caveat that the perspective from which these conclusions emerge is my own, inflected with my interests, preconceptions and limited frames of knowledge. Questions remain, however, about the ethics of applying my admittedly Eurocentric methodology to non-Western cinemas. I argued in the introduction that my motivation for selecting films from a variety of national and cultural contexts is tied to the global stakes of the ecological crisis: phenomena such as global warming transcend national boundaries, and my analysis of the ecological implications of cinematic representation has attempted to follow suit. My ability to do so was limited by the scope of this project, in that I opted for depth over breadth in my selection of examples; other limitations and blind spots also result from this choice, for example, in the relative dearth of female film-makers (Nettie Wild and collaborators like Amy Jump notwithstanding, as well as the influence of my own queer and feminine subject position). The films discussed herein were chosen because they articulate the relationship between humans and nature as complex and contradictory, a dynamic process that is best theorized through Bataille's ideas of transgression and inner experience. Apichatpong's Surrealist influences make his films amenable to Bataillean analysis, though they also push against Bataille's thought in a number of interesting ways; as mentioned in Chapter 1, the transgressions of his films are much quieter than those of film-makers like Wheatley that exploit the shock value of explicit violence. If my methodology is to prove useful, however, its reach will have to be expanded to include a wider range of films from a variety of cultural contexts. My methodology is not intended as static or hermetically sealed, but ought rather to change in response to new objects of inquiry; though pursuing this through a 'world of cinemas'[2] carries risks (reading films out of context, mischaracterizing or misunderstanding unfamiliar references and histories), I would rather confront these risks through careful research than avoid engaging with films that may not align with my point of view. I hope that the reader has been convinced that Bataille's philosophy, which is open to difference, contradiction and change over time, opens new possibilities for reading the relationship between global cinema and the nonhuman.

While Chapter 1 largely focused on representation by engaging in close textual analysis, Chapter 2 raised questions about the cinematic medium and its ability to represent nonhuman reality. I argued that although films are able to call attention to perspectives beyond the human, their ability to break with anthropocentric modes of perception is ultimately limited by the apparatus. There is therefore a conflict between form and content when films attempt to break with human perspectives, a conflict that I argue is productively interrogated in Lisandro Alonso's *Jauja* and Peter Bo Rappmund's *Tectonics*. An ecocritical reading of both films therefore requires analysis on two levels: close textual analysis reveals elements of content and style that undermine anthropocentrism, while considerations about the medium itself reveal ways that these films remain implicated in human ways of seeing. I argue that both *Jauja* and *Tectonics* self-consciously make use of this conflict in order to undermine the sense of objective mastery implied by the apparatus. My reading of *Tectonics* and *Jauja* draws an analogy between the need to push against the limits of the human – the ethical project necessitated by the ecological crisis – and the need to push against the limits of the cinematic medium. This ties ethical responsibility to aesthetic inquiry in that the need for a more holistic world view is tied to an understanding of the relationship between representation and reality. While films are no more able to transcend their modes of representation than humans are able to break with their modes of perception, they can undermine the sense of objective mastery implied by the apparatus from within. These methods for rupturing totalizable knowledge are useful in considering how we humans might make room for the nonhuman in our ethics and ontologies.

Undermining anthropocentrism – acknowledging that we are not everything, and that our perspectives are not the only ones that matter – requires us to recognize our limits and avoid mistaking particular points of view for objective truth. Chapter 2 is only a starting point in this regard, and it raises a number of questions about how cinema and media theory might contribute to the task of

Conclusion

deconstructing anthropocentric notions of objectivity. How do other forms of media articulate the relationship between human perception and extrahuman reality? What changes when technologies are not based in Renaissance principles of perspective (for instance, in the case of motion capture[3])? While these questions raise exciting possibilities for future research, I would caution against assuming that other media might somehow be 'better' at attaining any kind of objective or nonhuman perspective. All modes of representation are finite in their ability to express or communicate reality, and a central aim of this book has been to assert the importance of paying attention to these limits.

Part 2, on Subjectivity, conceded that if we cannot escape human subjectivity, we might as well rethink it, prompted by the urgency of the ecological crisis. Chapter 3 argued that film ecocriticism needs a new way of thinking subjectivity and spectatorship, one that recognizes the limitations of the human perspective while also acknowledging its implication in cinematic representation. I proposed a new way of thinking cinematic subjectivity through Bataille's notion of inner experience; to avoid reading the Bataillean subject as a stable or consistent entity (it is not the self-contained and self-evident interiority of the Cartesian *cogito*), I also referred to Nancy's notion of invagination. For Nancy, subjectivity can only be read on the surface, which is constantly folding and reversing across the limit that distinguishes self and world. I traced these movements in two films that explicitly represent human subjectivity in relation to nature: Lars von Trier's *Nymphomaniac* and Jonathan Glazer's *Under the Skin*. Both films understand subjectivity as an unstable surface, a thin membrane that always pushes what it cannot contain to the other side. This 'other side' is unknowable and unreachable, but I suggested that we can gesture towards it through self-reflexive representational lacunae. Both *Under the Skin* and *Nymphomaniac* construct these lacunae through sex and violence: like Bataille, they associate eroticism and death with nature and unknowable alterity. My reading of Bataillean transgression throughout this book has tended to look elsewhere from its more traditional associations with cultural taboos about sex and violence, reading it instead as a crossing of the boundary between the human subject and nonhuman reality. Chapter 3, however, suggests points of connection between my largely metaphysical interpretation of transgression and more conventional interpretations of the concept,[4] a connection that could potentially form pathways to new areas of research. I mentioned in the introduction that my motivation for selecting art films and experimental documentaries was that their excessive stylistic elements more clearly reflected the ambiguities of transgression. However, I do not think that my Bataillean methodology applies only to art cinema, and exploring transgression and the nonhuman in genre cinemas would be a productive area of future research, especially considering the proliferation of environmental themes in big-budget films aimed at international audiences, from *Avatar* (James Cameron 2009) to *Avengers: Endgame* (Anthony Russo and Joe Russo 2019).

In Chapter 4, I looked for a response to ecological crisis through love. I have asserted throughout this book that the ecological crisis makes an ethical demand that is impossible to meet because it encourages us to respond to a reality that we can never fully understand. Love is a way of exceeding our subjective limits and is therefore theoretically impossible: as Marcel O'Gorman points out, love is a notoriously troublesome and messy concept, and it is difficult to constrain it within the confines of reason. This impossibility at the heart of love is analogous to the impossible demand posed by the Anthropocene. *Konelīne* and *Grizzly Man* both encourage a love for nature that exceeds rational argumentation: the sentimental ending of *Grizzly Man* suggests a sympathetic reading of Treadwell's relationship with nature, in contradiction to the position expressed by Herzog's authorial voice; *Konelīne* operates through an aesthetics of love that explores different perspectives without reconciling their differences. The ethics of the latter inheres in an emphasis on affect before argumentation, and aesthetic *eros* provides a way of exceeding polemics and of viewing the landscape as beautiful and worthy of protection despite the abundant political and environmental challenges it faces. I wanted to end this book on an optimistic note and to suggest a way forward despite our limited ability to think about and respond to the ecological crisis. If hyperobjects like climate change are so irreducibly complex that they exceed our frames of thought and extend farther into the future than we are capable of imagining, then reason alone is insufficient for confronting the problem. I have offered love as an alternative because love is an impossible relationship with alterity; it recognizes differences without needing to constrain them to a rational framework. Jean-Luc Nancy argues that writing about love is a way of expressing it, so that love is deployed by our attempts to understand it rather than 'being something we can extricate and contemplate at a distance'.[5] I therefore offer this book as an act of love – love for this fragile, imperfect and overwhelmingly complex world and for all of the plants, people and creatures that inhabit it with us. I hope the reader has been encouraged to share in this love with me.

Notes

1 Botting, 'Reflections of the Real', 24.
2 David Martin-Jones, 'Introduction: Film-Philosophy and a World of Cinemas', *Film-Philosophy* 20, no. 1 (2016a), 6–23.
3 Philippe Bédard, 'The Protean Camera', *Synoptique* 5, no. 2 (2017), 15–36.
4 It also forms a bridge between this book and my earlier published works, which focused on the transgressive sex and violence in European new extremist cinema. See especially Chelsea Birks, 'Body Problems: New Extremism, Descartes and Jean-Luc Nancy', *New Review of Film and Television Studies* 13, no. 2 (2015), 131–48.
5 Nancy, *The Inoperative Community*, 83.

Bibliography

Abbott, Matthew. 2011. 'On Not Loving Everyone: Comments on Jean-Luc Nancy's "L'amour en éclats" ["Shattered Love"]'. *Glossator* 5: 139–62.

Adelaar, Samuel. 2017. 'A World in the Making: Contingency and Time in James Benning's BNSF'. *Film-Philosophy* 21 (1): 60–77.

Aksoy, Mele Ulas. 2011. 'Hegel and George Bataille's Concept of Sovereignty'. *Ege Academic Review* 11 (2): 217–27.

Andermann, Jens. 2014. 'Exhausted Landscapes: Reframing the Rural in Recent Argentine and Brazilian Films'. *Cinema Journal* 53 (2): 50–70.

Andrew, Dudley. 2010. *What Cinema Is!* Oxford: Wiley Blackwell.

Andrew, Dudley, and Hervé Laurencin, eds. 2011. *Opening Bazin: Postwar Film Theory and Its Afterlife*. Oxford: Oxford University Press.

Andrew, Dudley, and Seung-hoon Jeong. 2008. 'Grizzly Ghost: Herzog, Bazin and the Cinematic Animal'. *Screen* 49 (1): 1–12.

Andrews, Nigel. 2010. 'Nigel Andrews Talks to Thai Filmmaker Apichatpong Weerasethakul'. *Financial Times*, 12 November.

Austin, Richard Cartwright. 1988. *Beauty of the Lord: Awakening the Senses*. Atlanta, GA: John Knox.

Badmington, Neil. 2004. *Alien Chic: Posthumanism and the Other Within*. London: Routledge.

Bainbridge, Caroline. 2007. *The Cinema of Lars von Trier: Authenticity and Artifice*. New York: Columbia University Press.

Barnard, Linda. 2016. 'Reel Brief: Mini Reviews of Maggie's Plan, Khoya, Konelīne, and 45 Years, and 10 Cloverfield Lane on DVD'. *Toronto Star*, 9 June.

Barthes, Roland. 1981. *Camera Lucida: Reflections on Photography*. Translated by Richard Howard. New York: Hill and Wang.

Barthes, Roland. 1986. 'Diderot, Brecht, Eisenstein'. In *Narrative, Apparatus, Ideology: A Film Theory Reader*, edited by Philip Rosen, 172–8. New York: Columbia University Press.

Bataille, Georges. 1949. *The Cruel Practice of Art*. Translated by Supervert32C. http://supervert.com/elibrary/georges_bataille/cruel_practice_of_art. Accessed 2 August 2019.

Bataille, Georges. 1985. *Visions of Excess*. Edited by Allan Stoekl. Translated by Allan Stoekl. Minneapolis: University of Minnesota Press.

Bataille, Georges. [1957] 1986. *Erotism: Death and Sensuality*. Translated by Mary Dalwood. San Francisco, CA: City Lights.

Bibliography

Bataille, Georges. [1961] 1989. *The Tears of Eros*. Translated by Peter Connor. San Francisco, CA: City Lights.

Bataille, Georges. [1973] 1992. *Theory of Religion*. Translated by Robert Hurley. New York: Zone Books.

Bataille, Georges. [1949] 2012. *The Accursed Share: Vol. I*. Translated by Robert Hurley. Brooklyn, NY: Zone Books.

Bataille, Georges. 2012. *My Mother, Madam Edwarda, The Dead Man*. Translated by Austryn Wainhouse. London: Penguin Classics.

Bataille, Georges. [1943] 2014. *Inner Experience*. Translated by Stuart Kendall. Albany, NY: SUNY.

Baudry, Jean-Louis. [1974] 1986. 'Ideological Effects of the Basic Cinematographic Apparatus'. In *Narrative, Apparatus, Ideology: A Film Theory Reader*, edited by Philip Rosen, 286–98. New York: Columbia University Press.

Baudry, Jean-Louis. [1975] 1986. 'The Apparatus: Metapsychological Approaches to the Impression of Reality in the Cinema'. In *Narrative, Apparatus, Ideology: A Film Reader*, edited by Philip Rosen, 299–318. New York: Columbia.

Bazin, André. [1967] 2005. *What Is Cinema?* Translated by Hugh Gray. Berkeley: University of California Press.

Bédard, Philippe. 2017. 'The Protean Camera'. *Synoptique* 5 (2): 15–36.

Bell, Malacaster. 2014. 'Grizzly Man: Sentimentality and Our Relationships with Other Animals'. In *Understanding Love: Philosophy, Film, and Fiction*, edited by Susan Wolf and Christopher Grau, 15–36. Oxford: Oxford University Press.

Bennett, Jane. 2009. *Vibrant Matter: A Political Ecology of Things*. Durham, NC: Duke University Press.

Berclaz-Lewis, James. 2014. 'Berlin Review: Why the Shorter Version of "Nymphomaniac Volume I" Is Better Than Lars von Trier's Director's Cut'. *IndieWire*, 9 February.

Birks, Chelsea. 2015. 'Body Problems: New Extremism, Descartes and Jean-Luc Nancy'. *New Review of Film and Television Studies* 13 (2): 131–48.

Blanchard, Kathryn, and Kevin O'Brien. 2014. *An Introduction of Christian Environmentalism*. Waco, TX: Baylor University Press.

Boehler, Natalie. 2011. 'The Jungle as Border Zone: The Aesthetics of Nature in the Work of Apichatpong Weerasethakul'. *Australian Journal of South-East Asian Studies* 4 (2): 290–304.

Bonner, Michael. 2013. ' "The Blood in the Earth": An Interview with a Field in England Director Ben Wheatley'. *Uncut*, 3 July.

Bordwell, David, and Noël Carroll. 1996. *Post-Theory: Reconstructing Film Studies*. Madison: University of Wisconsin Press.

Botting, Fred. 1994. 'Reflections of the Real in Lacan, Bataille and Blanchot'. *SubStance* 23 (1): 24–40.

Bozak, Nadia. 2012. *The Cinematic Footprint: Lights, Camera, Natural Resources*. New Brunswick, NJ: Rutgers University Press.

Brassier, Ray. 2007. *Nihil Unbound: Enlightenment and Extinction*. London: Palgrave Macmillan.

Bratton, Susan. 1992. 'Loving Nature: Eros or Agape?' *Environmental Ethics* 14 (1): 3–25.

Brook, Timothy, Jérôme Bourgon and Gregory Blue. 2008. *Death by a Thousand Cuts*. Cambridge, MA: Harvard University Press.

Bryant, Levi. 2011. *The Democracy of Objects*. Ann Arbor: Open University Press.

Bryant, Levi, Nick Srnicek and Graham Harman. 2011. 'Towards a Speculative Philosophy'. In *The Speculative Turn: Continental Materialism and Realism*, edited by Levi Bryant, Nick Srnicek and Graham Harman, 1–18. Melbourne: Re-press.

Burt, Jonathan. 2006. 'Morbidity and Vitalism: Derrida, Bergson, Deleuze, and Animal Film Imagery'. *Configurations* 14 (1–2): 157–79.

Cahill, James. 2012. 'Forgetting Lessons: Jean Painlevé's Gay Science'. *Journal of Visual Culture* 21 (1): 2–36.

Cahill, James. 2013. 'Anthropomorphism and Its Vicissitudes: Reflections on Homme-Sick Cinema'. In *Screening Nature: Cinema Beyond the Human*, translated by Anat Pick and Guinevere Narraway, 73–90. New York: Berghahn.

Carman, Colin. 2012. 'Grizzly Love: The Queer Ecology of Timothy Treadwell'. *GLQ* 18 (4): 501–28.

Carnevale, Rob. 2012. 'Kill List: Ben Wheatley Interview'. *indieLondon*. http://www.indielondon.co.uk/Film-Review/kill-list-ben-wheatley-interview. Accessed 6 August 2019.

Carroll, Noël. 1985. 'The Specificity of Media in the Arts'. *Journal of Aesthetic Education* 19 (4): 5–20.

Carroll, Noël. 1988. 'Film/Mind Analogies: The Case of Hugo Munsterberg'. *Journal of Aesthetics and Art Criticism* 46 (4): 489–99.

Caruana, John, and Mark Cauchi. 2019. *Immanent Frames: Postsecular Cinema between Malick and von Trier*. New York: SUNY Press.

Chung, Una. 2012. 'Crossing Over Horror: Reincarnation and Transformation in Apichatpong Weerasethakul's Primitive'. *Women Studies Quarterly* 40 (1–2): 211–22.

Clark, Timothy. 2015. *Ecocriticism on the Edge: The Anthropocene as a Threshold Concept*. London: Bloomsbury.

Colebrook, Claire. 2010. 'Introduction'. In *The Deleuze Dictionary*, edited by Adrian Parr, 1–6. Edinburgh: Edinburgh University Press.

Connolly, Sean P. 2014. 'Georges Bataille, Gender, and Sacrificial Excess'. *The Comparatist* 38: 108–27.

Bibliography

Copjec, Joan. 2002. *Imagine There's No Woman: Ethics and Sublimation*. Cambridge, MA: MIT Press.

Cronin, Paul, ed. 2002. *Herzog on Herzog*. London: Faber and Faber.

Crutzen, Paul. 2002. 'Geology of Mankind'. *Nature* 415: 23.

Cubitt, Sean. 2005. *EcoMedia*. Amsterdam: Rodopi.

Deleuze, Gilles. [1985] 1989. *Cinema II: The Time Image*. Translated by Hugh Tomlinson and Robert Galeta. London: Abalone.

Deleuze, Gilles. [1986] 1988. *Foucault*. Translated by Sean Hand. Minneapolis: University of Minnesota Press.

Deleuze, Gilles. [1988] 1993. *The Fold: Leibniz and the Baroque*. Translated by Tom Conley. London: Athalone.

Derrida, Jacques. [1967] 1988. 'From Restricted to General Economy: A Hegelianism Without Reserve'. In *Bataille: A Critical Reader*, edited by Fred Botting and Scott Wilson, 102–38. Oxford: Blackwell.

Derrida, Jacques. [1976] 1997. *Of Grammatology*. Translated by Gayatri Spivak. Baltimore, MD: Johns Hopkins University Press.

Derrida, Jacques. 2008. *The Animal That Therefore I Am*. Translated by David Willis. New York: Fordham University Press.

Dienstag, Joshua. 2015. 'Evils of Representation: Werewolves, Pessimism, and Realism in Europa and Melancholia'. *Theory & Event* 18 (2).

Direk, Zeynap. 2007. 'Erotic Experience and Sexual Difference in Bataille'. In *Reading Bataille Now*, edited by Shannon Winnubst, 94–115. Bloomington: Indiana University Press.

Downing, Lisa, and Robert Gillet. 2011. 'Georges Bataille and the Avant-Garde of Queer Theory?: Transgression, Perversion and the Death Drive'. *Nottingham French Studies* 50 (3): 88–102.

Doyle, Briohny. 2013. 'Prognosis End-Time: Madness and Prophecy in Melancholia and Take Shelter'. *Altre Modernita* 9 (9): 19–37.

Dworkin, Andrea. 1981. *Pornography: Men Possessing Women*. New York: Putnam.

Elsaesser, Thomas. 2015. 'Black Suns and a Bright Planet: Lars von Trier's Melancholia as Thought Experiment'. *Theory & Event* 18 (2).

Evans, Christine. Forthcoming. *Slavoj Žižek and Film: A Cinematic Ontology*. London: Bloomsbury.

Faber, Alyda. 2003. 'Redeeming Sexual Violence? A Feminist Reading of Breaking the Waves'. *Literature and Theology* 17 (1): 59–75.

Faber, Michael. 2000. *Under the Skin*. San Diego: Harcourt.

Fay, Jennifer. 2008. 'Seeing/Loving Animals: André Bazin's Posthumanism'. *Journal of Visual Culture* 7 (1): 41–64.

Fay, Jennifer. 2014. 'Buster Keaton's Climate Change'. *Modernism/Modernity* 21 (1): 25–49.

Bibliography

Felperin, Leslie. 2014. 'Bigger, Longer, Uncut: A Critic's Take on the Director's Cut of *Nymphomaniac*'. *Hollywood Reporter*, 10 February.

ffrench, Patrick. 2007. 'Friendship, Assymetry, Sacrifice: Bataille and Blanchot'. *Parrhesia* 3: 32–42.

Figlerowicz, Marta. 2012. 'Comedy of Abandon: Lars von Trier's Melancholia'. *Film Quarterly* 65 (4): 21–6.

Foucault, Michel. [1963] 1988. 'A Preface to Transgression'. In *Bataille: A Critical Reader*, edited by Fred Botting and Scott Wilson, 24–30. Oxford: Blackwell.

Foucault, Michel. [1969] 1997. 'What Is an Author?' In *Language, Counter-Memory, Practice: Selected Essays and Interviews*, edited by Donald Bouchard. Ithaca, NY: Cornell University Press.

French, Sarah, and Zöe Shacklock. 2014. 'The Affective Sublime in Lars von Trier's Melancholia and Terrance Malick's The Tree of Life'. *New Review of Film and Television Studies* 12 (4): 339–56.

Galt, Rosalind. 2015. 'The Suffering Spectator? Perversion and Complicity in Antichrist and Nymphomaniac'. *Theory & Event* 18 (2).

Galt, Rosalind, and Karl Schoonover. 2010. *Global Art Cinema: New Theories and Histories*. Oxford: Oxford University Press.

Gelikman, Oleg. 2012. ' "Cold Pastoral": Werner Herzog's Version of Epson'. *MLN* 123 (5): 1141–162.

Gillette, Dan. 2012. 'Kill List Explained'. *CinemaDan.com*, 13 March.

Godfrey, Alex. 2013. 'Ben Wheatley: Master of the Macabre'. *The Guardian*, 22 June.

Groys, Boris. 2009. 'Comrades of Time'. *e-flux* 11. https://www.e-flux.com/journal/11/61345/comrades-of-time/. Accessed 15 November 2019.

Grusin, Richard. 2015. 'Introduction'. In *The Nonhuman Turn*, edited by Richard Grusin, viii–ix. Minneapolis: University of Minnesota Press.

Haraway, Donna. 2007. *When Species Meet*. Minneapolis: University of Minnesota Press.

Harman, Graham. 2002. *Tool-Being: Heidegger and the Metaphysics of Objects*. Chicago: Open Court.

Harman, Graham. 2011. 'On the Undermining of Objects: Grant, Bruno, and Radical Philosophy'. In *The Speculative Turn: Continental Materialism and Realism*, edited by Levi Bryant, Nick Srnicek and Graham Harman, 21–40. Melbourne: Re-press.

Harman, Graham. 2018. *Object-Oriented Ontology: A New Theory of Everything*. London: Penguin.

Harman, Graham, and Manuel DeLanda. 2017. *The Rise of Realism*. Cambridge: Polity.

Harmes, Marcus. 2013. 'The Seventeenth Century on Film: Patriarchy, Magistracy, and Witchcraft in British Horror Films, 1968–1971'. *Canadian Journal of Film Studies* 22 (2): 64–80.

Hediger, Ryan. 2012. 'Timothy Treadwell's Grizzly Love as Freak Show: The Uses of Animals, Science, and Film'. *ISLE* 19 (1): 82–100.

Henry, Elizabeth. 2010. 'The Screaming Silence: Constructions of Nature in Werner Herzog's Grizzly Man'. In *Framing the World: Explorations of Ecocriticism and Film*, edited by Paula Willoquet-Maricondi, 123–33. Charlottesville: University of Virginia Press.

Herbrechter, Stefan, and Ivan Callus. 2008. 'What Is a Posthumanist Reading?' *Angelaki* 13 (1): 95–111.

Hessel, Dieter, and Rosemary Ruether, eds. 2000. *Christianity and Ecology*. Cambridge, MA: Harvard University Press.

Higson, Andrew. 1989. 'The Concept of National Cinema'. *Screen* 30 (4): 36–47.

Hill, Leslie. 2011. *Bataille, Klossowsky, Blanchot: Writing at the Limit*. Oxford: Oxford University Press.

Hjort, Mette. 2011. 'The Problem with Provocation: On Lars von Trier, L'Enfant Terrible of Danish Art Film'. *Kinema* (Fall): 18–35.

Hoeij, Boyd van. 2014. 'Charlotte Gainsbourg on Being Lars von Trier's "Nymphomaniac": "I Was Disturbed, Embarassed, and a Little Humiliated"'. *IndieWire*, 25 March.

Hollier, Dennis. 1988. 'The Dualist Materialism of Georges Bataille'. In *Bataille: A Critical Reader*, edited by Fred Botting and Scott Wilson, 59–73. Oxford: Blackwell.

Holmes, Dave, Stuart J. Murray and Thomas Foth (eds.). 2018. *Radical Sex Between Men: Assembling Desiring-Machines*. London: Routledge.

Huffer, Lynne. 2015. 'The Nymph Shoots Back: Agamben, Nymphomaniac, and the Feel of the Agon'. *Theory & Event* 18 (2).

Hutchings, Peter. 2004. 'Uncanny Landscapes in British Film and Television'. *Visual Culture in Britain* 5 (2): 27–40.

Ingawanij, May Adadol. 2013. 'Animism and the Performative Realist Cinema of Apichatpong Weerasethakul'. In *Screening Nature: Cinema Beyond the Human*, edited by Anat Pick and Guinevere Narraway, 91–109. New York: Berghahn.

Ivakhiv, Adrian. 2008. 'Green Film Criticism and Its Futures'. *Interdisciplinary Studies in Literature and Environment* 15 (2): 1–28.

Ivakhiv, Adrian. 2014. *Ecologies of the Moving Image*. Waterloo, ON: Wilfrid Laurier University Press.

Jeong, Seung-hoon. 2009. 'André Bazin's Ontological Other: The Animal in Adventure Films'. *Senses of Cinema* 51.

Jeong, Seung-hoon. 2013. 'A Global Cinematic Zone of Animal and Technology'. *Angelaki* 18 (1): 139–57.

Johnson, Laurie Ruth. 2016. *Forgotten Dreams: Revisiting Romanticism in the Cinema of Werner Herzog*. Rochester: Camden House.

Kant, Immanuel. [1781] 2009. *The Critique of Pure Reason*. Translated by Paul Guyer and Allan W. Wood. Cambridge: Cambridge University Press.

Kara, Selmin. 2014. 'Beasts of the Digital Wild: Primordigital Cinema and the Question of Origins'. *Sequence* 1 (4).

Keenan, Dennis King. 2005. *The Question of Sacrifice*. Bloomington: Indiana University Press.

Kellog, Catherine. 2016. 'Love'. In *The Nancy Dictionary*, edited by Peter Gratton Marie-Eve Morin, 150–3. Edinburgh: Edinburgh University Press.

Kendall, Tina. 2011. 'Reframing Bataille: On Tacky Spectatorship in New Extremism'. In *The New Extremism in Cinema: From France to Europe*, edited by Tanya Horeck and Tina Kendall, 43–54. Edinburgh: Edinburgh University Press.

Kermode, Mark. 2016. 'Ben Wheatley: "Financing a Film as Crazy as This Takes Good Casting."' *The Guardian*, 6 March.

Knight, Chris. 2016. 'Koneline: Our Land Beautiful Serves Moral Ambiguity and Beautiful British Columbia Visuals'. *National Post*, 9 June.

Kollig, Danielle. 2013. 'Filming the World's End: Images of the Apocalypse in Epidemic and Melancholia'. *Amaltea* 5: 85–102.

Kracauer, Siegfried. 1960. *Theory of Film: The Redemption of Physical Reality*. Princeton, NJ: Princeton University Press.

Krishek, Sharon. 2008. 'Two Forms of Love: The Problem of Preferential Love in Kierkegaard's Works of Love'. *Journal of Religious Ethics* 36 (4): 595–617.

Kristeva, Julia. [1980] 1982. *Powers of Horror: An Essay on Abjection*. Translated by Leon Roudiez. New York: Columbia University Press.

Lacan, Jacques. [1954] 1988. *The Seminar of Jacques Lacan: Book I Freud's Papers on Technique 1953–1954*. Translated by John Forrester. Cambridge: Cambridge University Press.

Lacan, Jacques. [1957] 2017. *The Seminar of Jacques Lacan: Book V Formations of the Unconscious 1957–1958*. Edited by Jacques-Alain Miller. Translated by Russell Grigg. Hoboken, NJ: Wiley.

Ladino, Jennifer. 2008. 'For the Love of Nature: Documenting Life, Death, and Animality in Grizzly Man and March of the Penguins'. *ISLE* 16 (1): 53–90.

Lewis, Simon, and Mark Maslin. 2015. 'Defining the Anthropocene'. *Nature* 519: 171–80.

Libertson, Joseph. 1982. *Proximity: Levinas, Blanchot, Bataille and Communication*. The Hague: Martinus Nijhoff.

Lincoln, Ross. 2012. '"Kill List" Director Ben Wheatley Talks "End Deniers"'. *Pro. BoxOffice.Com*, 12 February.

Loren, Scott, and Jörg Metelmann. 2013. 'Lars von Trier and Woman's Films: Mysogyny or Feminism?' In *Irritation of Life: The Subversive Melodrama of Michael Haneke, David Lynch, and Lars von Trier*, 141–72. Marburg: Schüren Velag.

Lovatt, Philippa. 2013. '"Every Drop of My Blood Sings Our Song. There Can You Hear It?": Haptic Sound and Embodied Memory in the Films of Apichatpong Weerasethakul'. *New Soundtrack* 3 (1): 61–79.

Lowenstein, Adam. 2016. 'A Cinema of Disorientation: Space, Genre, Wheatley'. *Critical Quarterly* 5 (1): 5–15.

Lulka, David. 2009. 'Consuming Timothy Treadwell: Redefining Nonhuman Agency in Light of Herzog's Grizzly Man'. In *Animals and Agency: An Interdisciplinary Exploration*, edited by Sarah Macfarlane and Ryan Hediger, 67–88. Leiden: Brill.

Lunn, Oliver. 2014. 'Talking to Stacy Martin About Her Fake Sex with Shia LaBoeuf'. *Vice*, 26 February.

Macfarlane, Robert. 2015. 'The Eeriness of the English Countryside'. *The Guardian*, 10 April.

Marso, Lori. 2015. 'Must We Burn Lars von Trier? Simone de Beauvoir's Body Politics in Antichrist'. *Theory & Event* 18 (2).

Martin-Jones, David. 2016a. 'Introduction: Film-Philosophy and a World of Cinemas'. *Film-Philosophy* 20 (1): 6–23.

Martin-Jones, David. 2016b. 'Trolls, Tigers and Transmodern Ecological Encounters: Enrique Dussel and a Cine-ethics for the Anthropocene'. *Film-Philosophy* 20 (1): 63–103.

Martin-Jones, David. 2019. *Cinema against Doublethink*. London: Routledge.

Mattesich, Stefan. 2013. 'An Anguished Self-Subjection: Man and Animal in Werner Herzog's Grizzly Man'. *English Studies in Canada* 39 (1): 51–70.

McDaniel, Jay. 1989. *Of God and Pelicans: A Theology of Reverence for Life*. Louisville, KY: John Knox.

McMahon, Laura. 2012. 'Unwinding the Anthropological Machine: Animality, Film, and Arnaud des Pallières'. *Paragraph* 35 (3): 373–88.

Meillassoux, Quentin. 2008. *After Finitude: An Essay on the Necessity of Contingency*. Translated by Ray Brassier. London: Continuum.

Milton, Kay. 2002. *Loving Nature: Towards an Ecology of Emotion*. London: Routledge.

Morton, Timothy. 2007. *Ecology without Nature: Rethinking Environmental Aesthetics*. Cambridge: Cambridge University Press.

Morton, Timothy. 2014. *Hyperobjects: Philosophy and Ecology after the End of the World*. Minneapolis: University of Minnesota Press.

Nancy, Jean-Luc. [1986] 1991. *The Inoperative Community*. Translated by Peter Connor, Lisa Garbus, Michael Holland and Simona Sawhney. Minneapolis: University of Minnesota Press.

Nancy, Jean-Luc. [1992] 2008. *Corpus*. Translated by Richard Rand. New York: Fordham University Press.

Nancy, Jean-Luc. [2005] 2008. *Dis-Enclosure: The Deconstruction of Christianity*. Translated by Bettina Bergo, Gabriel Malenfant and Michael B. Smith. New York: Fordham University Press.

Nancy, Jean-Luc. [2009] 2011. *God, Justice, Love, Beauty: Four Little Dialogues*. Translated by Sarah Clift. New York: Fordham University Press.

Nancy, Jean-Luc. 2005. *The Ground of the Image*. Translated by Jeff Fort. New York: Fordham.

Nancy, Jean-Luc. 2015. 'Inside Out'. *The Philosophical Salon*, 4 April.

Noys, Benjamin. 2000. *Georges Bataille: A Critical Introduction*. London: Pluto.

Noys, Benjamin. 2007. 'Antiphusis: Werner Herzog's Grizzly Man'. *Film-Philosophy* 11 (3): 38–51.

O'Gorman, Michel. 2014. 'Speculative Realism in Chains: A Love Story'. *Angelaki* 18 (1): 31–43.

Osterweil, Ara. 2014. 'Under the Skin: The Perils of Becoming Female'. *Film Quarterly* 67 (4): 44–51.

O'Sullivan, Simon. 2010. 'The Fold'. In *The Deleuze Dictionary*, edited by Adrian Parr, 107–8. Edinburgh: Edinburgh University Press.

Peterson, Christopher. 2015. 'The Gravity of Melancholia: A Critique of Speculative Realism'. *Theory & Event* 18 (2).

Pettman, Dominic. 2009. 'Grizzly Man: Werner Herzog's Anthropological Machine'. *Theory & Event* 12 (2).

Pick, Anat. 2011. *Creaturely Poetics: Animality and Vulnerability in Literature and Film*. New York: Columbia University Press.

Pick, Anat. 2013. 'Three Worlds: Dwelling and Worldhood on Screen'. In *Screening Nature: Cinema Beyond the Human*, edited by Anat Pick and Guinevere Narraway, 21–36. New York: Berghahn.

Pick, Anat, and Guinevere Narraway. 2013. 'Introduction: Intersecting Ecology and Film'. In *Screening Nature: Cinema Beyond the Human*, edited by Anat Pick and Guinevere Narraway, 1–20. New York: Berghahn.

Prager, Brad. 2007. *The Cinema of Werner Herzog: Aesthetic Ecstacy and Truth*. New York: Wallflower.

Rio, Elena del. 2016. *The Grace of Destruction: A Vital Ethology of Extreme Cinemas*. London: Bloomsbury.

Robertson, Eric. 2017. 'Wasted Sex, Wasteful Bodies: Queer Ecology and the Future of Energy Use'. *English Language Notes* 55 (1–2): 33–40.

Roffe, Jonathan. 2010. 'Exteriority/Interiority'. In *The Deleuze Dictionary*, edited by Adrian Parr, 97–8. Edinburgh: Edinburgh University Press.

Rorty, Richard, ed. 1967. *The Linguistic Turn: Essays in Philosophical Method*. Chicago: University of Chicago Press.

Rosen, Philip. 2001. *Change Mummified: Cinema, Historicity, Theory*. Minneapolis: University of Minnesota Press.

Schantz, Ned. 2013. 'Melodramatic Reenactment and the Ghosts of Grizzly Man'. *Criticism* 55 (4): 593–613.

Schutten, Julie. 2008. 'Chewing on the Grizzly Man: Getting to the Meat of the Matter'. *Environmental Communication* 2 (2): 193–211.

Shaviro, Steven. 1990. *Passion & Excess: Blanchot, Bataille and Literary Theory*. Gainesville: University Press of Florida.

Shaviro, Steven. 2014. *The Universe of Things: On Speculative Realism*. Minneapolis: University of Minnesota Press.

Shaviro, Steven. 2017. 'Come, Come Georges: Steven Shaviro on Georges Bataille's Story of the Eye and Ma Mère'. *ArtForum*, 1 May.

Sinnerbrink, Robert. 2014. 'Anatomy of Melancholia'. *Angelaki* 19 (4): 111–26.

Sinnerbrink, Robert. 2016. 'Planet Melancholia: Romanticism, Mood, and Cinematic Ethics'. *Filozofski Vestnik* 37 (2): 95–115.

Stoekl, Alan. 1985. 'Introduction'. In *Visions of Excess*, by Georges Bataille, translated by Alan Stoekl, ix–xxv. Minneapolis: Minnesota University Press.

Taylor, Kate. 2016. 'Into the Forest and Koneline are Two Women-Driven Stories of Survival'. *Globe and Mail*, 3 June.

Teh, David. 2011. 'Itinerant Cinema: The Social Surrealism of Apichatpong Weerasethakul'. *Third Text* 25 (5): 595–609.

Tobias, Scott. 2012. 'Cult Horror, Plus some Hatred on the Homefront'. *NPR.org*, 2 February.

Trahair, Lisa. 2007. *The Comedy of Philosophy: Sense and Nonsense in Early Cinematic Slapstick*. Albany, NY: SUNY.

Vint, Sheryl. 2015. 'Skin Deep: Alienation in Under the Skin'. *Extrapolation* 56 (1): 1–16.

Watkin, Christopher. 2011. *Difficult Atheism: Post-theological Thinking in Alain Badiou, Jean-Luc Nancy and Quentin Meillassoux*. Edinburgh: Edinburgh University Press.

Williams, Linda. 1989. *Hardcore: Power, Pleasure, and the Frenzy of the Visible*. Berkeley: University of California Press.

Wilson, Scott, and Fred Botting. 1988. 'Introduction'. In *Bataille: A Critical Reader*, edited by Fred Botting and Scott Wilson, 1–23. Oxford: Blackwell.

Winnubst, Shannon. 2006. *Queering Freedom*. Bloomington: Indiana University Press.

Winnubst, Shannon. 2007. 'Bataille's Queer Pleasures: The Universe as Spider or Spit'. In *Reading Bataille Now*, edited by Shannon Winnubst, 77–93. Bloomington: Indiana University Press.

Wolfe, Cary. 2009. *What Is Posthumanism?* Minneapolis: University of Minnesota Press.

Zalasiewicz, Jan, Colin N. Waters, Mark Williams, Anthony D. Barnosky, Alejandro Cearreta, Paul Crutzen, Erle Ellis, Michael A. Ellis, Ian J. Fairchild, Jacques Grinevald, Peter K. Haff, Irka Hajdas, Reinhold Leinfelder, John McNeill, Eric O. Odada, Clément Poirier, Daniel Richter, Will Steffen, Colin Summerhayes, James P. M. Syvitski, Davor Vidas, Michael Wagreich, Scott L Wing, Alexander P. Wolfe, An Zhisheng, Naomi Oreskes. 2015. 'When Did the Anthropocene Begin? A Mid-Twentieth Century Boundary Level is Stratigraphically Optimal'. *Quarternary International* 383: 196–203.

Žižek, Slavoj. 2009a. 'From Che Vuoi? To Fantasy'. *Lacan.com*, 7 April.

Žižek, Slavoj. 2009b. *The Plague of Fantasies*. 2nd edn. London: Verso.

Zolkos, Magdalena. 2011. 'Violent Affects: Nature and the Feminine in Lars von Trier's *Antichrist*'. *Parrhesia* 13: 177–89.

Filmography

Primary sources

A Field in England, directed by Ben Wheatley, 2013, UK: Picturehouse Entertainment, 2013, DVD.

Grizzly Man, directed by Werner Herzog, 2005, USA: Revolver Entertainment, 2005, DVD.

Jauja, directed by Lisandro Alonso, 2014, Argentina: Soda Pictures, 2015, DVD.

Kill List, directed by Ben Wheatley, 2011. UK: Studiocanal, 2011, DVD.

Konelīne: Our Land Beautiful, directed by Nettie Wild, 2016, Canada: Canada Wild Productions, 2016, Blu-Ray.

Melancholia, directed by Lars von Trier, 2011, Denmark: Artificial Eye, 2012, DVD.

Nymphomaniac Vol. I and Vol. II, directed by Lars von Trier, 2014, Denmark: Mongrel Media, 2014, DVD.

Syndromes and a Century, directed by Apichatpong Weerasethakul, 2006, Thailand: BFI, 2008, DVD.

Tectonics, directed by Peter Bo Rappmund, 2012, USA: Peter Bo Rappmund, 2012, Blu-Ray.

Tropical Malady, directed by Apichatpong Weerasethakul, 2004, Thailand: Second Run, 2008, DVD.

Under the Skin, directed by Jonathan Glazer, 2013, UK: StudioCanal, 2014, DVD.

Uncle Boonmee Who Can Recall His Past Lives, directed by Apichatpong Weerasethakul, 2010, Thailand: Strand Releasing, 2011, DVD.

Secondary sources

2001: A Space Odyssey, directed by Stanley Kubrick, 1968.

Avatar, directed by James Cameron, 2009.

Avengers: Endgame, directed by Joe Russo and Anthony Russo, 2019.

Beasts of the Southern Wild, directed by Benh Zeitlin, 2012.

196   *Filmography*

The Big Sky, directed by Howard Hawks, 1952.

The Big Country, directed by William Wyler, 1958.

Blissfully Yours, directed by Apichatpong Weerasethakul, 2002.

The Blood on Satan's Claw, directed by Piers Haggard, 1971.

BNSF, directed by James Benning, 2013.

California Trilogy, directed by James Benning, 1999–2000.

Cowspiracy, directed by Kip Anderson and Keegan Kuhn, 2014.

Cry of the Banshee, directed by Gordon Hessler, 1970.

Dancer in the Dark, directed by Lars von Trier, 2000.

Down Terrace, directed by Ben Wheatley, 2009.

Earthlings, directed by Shaun Monson, 2005.

FIX: Story of an Addicted City, directed by Nettie Wild, 2002.

Gravity, directed by Alfonso Cuarón, 2013.

High-Rise, directed by Ben Wheatley, 2015.

The Hills of Disorder, directed by Andrea Tonacci, 2005.

How the West Was Won, directed by John Ford, Henry Hathaway, and George
    Marshall, 1962.

An Inconvenient Truth, directed by Davis Guggenheim, 2006.

Kanehsatake: 270 Years of Resistance, directed by Alanis Obomsawin, 1992.

La libertad, directed by Lisandro Alonso, 2001.

Liverpool, directed by Lisandro Alonso, 2008.

Los muertos, directed by Lisandro Alonso, 2004.

Nightfall, directed by James Benning, 2012.

Opus, directed by Mariano Donoso, 2005.

The Orphanage, directed by J. A. Bayona, 2007.

A Place called Chiapas, directed by Nettie Wild, 1998.

A Rustling of Leaves: Inside the Philippine Revolution, directed by Nettie
    Wild, 1988.

Sightseers, directed by Ben Wheatley, 2012.

Ten Skies, directed by James Benning, 2004.

Tree of Life, directed by Terrence Malick, 2011.

The Wicker Man, directed by Robin Hardy, 1973.

Witchfinder General, directed by Michael Reeves, 1968.

Index

Abbott, Matthew 142
The Accursed Share 164
Acéphale 13
aesthetics 4, 8, 36, 39, 52, 54, 57, 60–1, 79, 81, 94–5, 159, 162–6, 175, 177
After Finitude: An Essay on the Necessity of Contingency (Quentin Meillassoux) 2
agape 140
age of ecological crisis ix
Aksoy, Mete Ulas 115
Alonso, Lisandro 36, 82–3
  frames and out-of-focus shots 83
  Jauja 70, 78, 81–2, 84, 86
  La libertad 83, 92
  Liverpool 83, 92
  Los muertos 83, 92
  use of wandering camera 92
alterity 16–17, 36, 38–9, 55–7, 107, 114–16, 119, 121, 124, 130, 142, 147, 156, 166–7, 176, 179–80
Andermann, Jens 82
The Animal That Therefore I Am 12
Anthropocene xi, 3–4, 7, 9, 21, 37, 96, 175, 180
Anthropocene paradox 3–4
anthropocentrism ix, 3, 8–9, 12–13, 17, 20, 24, 51, 57, 64, 70, 73–4, 81, 89, 91–2, 106, 130, 163–4, 166, 175, 178–9
anti-authoritarian rebellion 42
antirealist philosophies 73–4
apparatus theory 8, 11, 22, 24, 69–71, 77, 95, 98n.27
Attenborough, David 146
autopoiesis 17, 87, 107, 142, 176
Avatar (James Cameron) 180
Avengers: Endgame (Anthony Russo and Joe Russo) 180

Barnard, Linda 159
Barthes, Roland xi, xiii, 90
Bataille, Georges xiii, 10–11, 18–19, 21, 37–40, 84, 96, 115, 121, 175

The Accursed Share 105–6, 116
aesthetics 52
association between sex and nature 114, 116–24
central values of 'expenditure, risk, loss, sexuality, death' 12–15
on communication 9
concept of inner experience 13–14, 16, 18, 20
death 56, 127, 129–30
dualist materialism 47
early life 12–13
eros 165
erotic, definition 141
eroticism 55–6, 119, 145–7
Erotism 5–6, 105–6
film-philosophies 18, 23–4
ideas about gender 108
Inner Experience 105
ipseity, notion of 16, 56, 103–4, 106–7, 111, 117, 119, 130, 141
relationship between knowledge and nonknowledge 126
sacred, notions of 24, 35–6, 47, 69, 127
on sacrifice 39–40
sex acts in 108
sexuality and death 5, 116–19
The Tears of Eros 6
theory of subjectivity 15–16, 18, 103–9
transgression logic 12–21, 23, 96, 105, 115, 129–30, 137, 146, 150, 176–7, 179
understanding of objectivity 35
Bataillean film-philosophy 2, 58, 69, 84, 87, 154, 161–2, 175
Bataillean negation 115
Baudry, Jean-Louis 69, 77, 89, 103
apparatus theory 8, 11, 22, 24, 69–71, 77, 95, 98n.27
cinematic apparatus 86–7
subjective illusion of objectivity 88

Index

Bazin, André 8, 69, 75, 77
  objectivity of cinema 75–6
  realism 75–6
  What Is Cinema? 155
Bell, Malacaster 155–6
Bennett, Jane 9, 138, ix
  distinction between living and
    non-living things 80
Benning, James 78
Berclaz-Lewis, James 121–2
The Big Country (William Wyler) 93
The Big Sky (Howard Hawks) 93
Blanchot, Maurice 18
blindness 126–7, 129
The Blood on Satan's Claw (Piers
  Haggard) 42, 52
Bogost, Ian 138
Bordwell, David 72
Botting, Fred 13, 19
Brassier, Ray 9, 72
Bratton, Susan 140–1
British folk horror 40–2
Bryant, Levi 10, 73
Buddhism 53–4, 60, 64, 177

Cabinet de la Licorne xii
Callus, Ivan 153
Carroll, Noël 72
Christian environmentalism 140, 142
Christian eschatology 47
Christian ethics 140
Christian rationalism 40, 42
Christian salvation 47
Chung, Una 53
cinematic apparatus 70, 78, 86–7
cinematic realism 75–7.
  see also speculative realism
  mode of perception 77
cinematic subjectivity 24
Clark, Timothy 4
climate change and associated
    problems 4
  views of reality 1
communication 9, 17
Comolli, Jean-Louis 77
Connolly, Sean 108
Conquest of the Desert (1870–84) 81–2
contemporary art 1
Cooper, Susan 41

Copernican revolution 2
correlationism 2, 9, 72
Cowspiracy 143
critical theory 1, 8, 12
Crutzen, Paul 3
Cry of the Banshee (Gordon
  Hessler) 42
Cubitt, Sean 8–9
Culture ix–x, xii, 4, 12, 36, 38, 41–2, 54,
  56–7, 60, 108, 134n.40, 146, 150,
  162, 164–5

Dancer in the Dark (von Trier) 126
d'Anthenaise, Claude x
death xii–xiii, 5–7, 12–14, 38, 56, 161
  discontinuity and 124–30
  sexuality and 5, 116–19
  sexual reproduction and 116–17
Deleuze, Gilles x, 18–19
  concept of the fold 131n.14
  time-image 18–19
Deleuzian ethical project 21
Dennis, Oscar 159–60, 165
Derrida, Jacques 11, 107
Down Terrace 36
Dussel, Enrique 71

Earthlings 143
ecocriticism 8
ecological crisis ix, xi, 21–2, 137, 180
ecological metaphysics 74
English countryside, representation
    of 41
environmental degradation 4
environmentalist documentaries 143
eroticism 5–6, 55–7

Faber, Michael 117
Fabre, Jon xi
A Field in England 15, 41–2, 48–53,
  99n.43
  black-and-white cinematography 49
  collapse of civilization in 48
  disorientation and nonhuman
    scale in 51
  editing and framing of 49–50
  irrational, circular logic of 51
  sacrifice in 52
  significance of field in 49

Index

film ecocriticism 17, 20
film-philosophy ix, x.
   see also Bataillean film-philosophy
FIX: Story of an Addicted City 159
Foucault, Michel 12, 14–15, 72, 150
Freudian/Lacanian ideas 12

Galileo's theory of heliocentrism 89
Galt, Rosalind 22
Garner, Alan 41
genre cinemas 23
global warming 1, 140, 143, 177
God concept 7, 14–15, 24, 37–8, 40, 47–9,
   51–2, 55, 65, 137, 141, 146, 165–6
Grant, Ian Hamilton 72
Gravity 71
Grizzly Man (Werner Herzog) 25, 137,
   143–57, 180
   auteurist perspective 145
   cross-species interactions 147–8, 157
   final scene 157
   Herzog's position in 150–7
   love in 143–4
   photographic/cinematic images in 155
   representation of nature 144
   sentimentality in 155–7
   Treadwell/Herzog debate 144–5, 147,
   150–4, 157
   Treadwell's engagements with wild
   nature 146–50
Grusin, Richard 10
The Nonhuman Turn 8

Haraway, Donna 12
Harman, Graham ix, 9–10, 72–4, 138–9
Harmes, Marcus 42
Heath, Stephen 77
Hegel, G. W. F. 13, 55, 115
Heidegger, Martin 72
Herbrechter, Stefan 153
Higson, Andrew 41
hippie culture 42
Hollier, Denis 13
Hollywood 23
Holocene 4
How the West Was Won (Ford, Hathaway
   and Marshall) 93
humanity's relationship ix
Husserl, Edmund 72

Hutchings, Peter 41
hyperobjects 1–2, 175, 180
*Hyperobjects: Philosophy and Ecology after
   the End of the World* 1

impossible imperative 22
An Inconvenient Truth (Al Gore) 143
indeterminacy 42, 55, 110, 118, 159
Ingawanij, Adadol 60
inner experience 13–14, 16, 18, 20
Inner Experience 13
interiority 110–11, 120, 127
International Union of Geological
   Sciences 4
invagination 25, 107–8, 111, 133n.35, 179
ipseity 16, 25, 56, 103–4, 106–7, 111, 117,
   119, 130, 141
Ivakhiv, Adrian 143

James, MR 41
Jauja 15, 24, 70, 78, 81–2, 84, 86, 95, 178
   attitude towards nature 81
   cinematography 84, 92–3
   colonial ideology and natural world 81
   critique of anthropocentrism 81
   critique of colonialism 82
   ecological reality 94
   frames and out-of-focus shots 84, 91
   narrative logic 84–6, 94
   subjectivity and cinematic
   apparatus 86–95
   wilderness in 93
Jeong, Seung-hoon 53
Johnson, Laurie Ruth 145

Kanehsatake: 270 Years of Resistance
   (Alanis Obamsawin) 160
Kant, Immanuel 1, 3, 71
   The Critique of Pure Reason 2–3
   metaphysics 2–3
Kara, Selmin
   Beasts of the Southern Wild 71
   The Tree of Life 71
Keenan, Dennis King 38
Kiarostami, Abbas 36
Kierkegaard 140–2, 149
   non-preferential love 139
   Works of Love 139
Kill List 36–7, 41–8, 52

cult symbol 43–4
  disorder and violence in 43
  doubled events and images 46
  escalation of violence 46
  hammer torture scene 45–6
  sacrifice in 43–5
Knight, Chris 159
Koneline: Our Land Beautiful (Nettie Wild)
    25, 137, 143–4, 157–65, 180
  aesthetics in 162–6
  awards 158
  characters and events 159–60
  helicopter shots 158–9, 162
  hunting sequences 160–1
  industrial sequences 162
Kracauer, Siegfried 8, 69, 75, 77
  Theory of Film 75
Kristeva, Julia 38

Lacan, Jacques 19–20, 120
  relation between subjectivity and Real 20
Latour, Bruno 138
Lee, Christopher 42
Libertson, Joseph 13, 17, 106–7, 142
limit experiences 5, 10
limit image 6–7, 19
linguistic turn 10–12
Lovatt, Philippa 58
love 138–9, 142, 167n.6
  Christian notions of 139–40
  in *Grizzly Man* 143–4
  for nature 140, 142
  non-preferential 139–41
  preferential 139
Lowenstein, Adam 40
Lynch, David 46

Macfarlane, Robert 41
Madame Edwarda 108
Martin-Jones, David 71, 74
Maskell, Neil 43
mass extinction x
Meillassoux, Quentin 2, 73, 176
  After Finitude 72
Melancholia xii–xiii, 4–5, 9, 71
  CGI shots 5
  final moments of 7
  interplay between subjective and
    objective 5

Justine's wedding 5
  lingchi photograph 6–7
  presence of extra hole (Hole
    19) xiii, xiv, 6
  relationship between sisters 5
  tensions between external reality and
    phenomenal experience 5
Merleau-Ponty, Maurice 72
  theory of flesh 107
metaphysics 2–3, 9, 16, 38, 73–5,
    103, 175
Milton, Kay 142–3
Mohawk struggle 160
Morton, Timothy ix, 1–2, 21,
    126, 175
  ambient poetics 125
  Ecology Without Nature 58
  Musee de la chasse et la nature xi–xii
  My Mother 108

Nancy, Jean-Luc 25, 38, 107, 111, 120–1,
    142, 167n.6, 176, 180
  descriptions of love 139
  excessive logic of subjectivity 109
  gendered binaries 108
  notion of invagination 25, 107–8, 111,
    133n.35, 179
  photographic images 129
Narboni, Jean 77
Narraway, Guinevere 8, 74
nature, representation of ix, 54,
    81, 104, 112, 114–15, 140,
    142, 144
  association between sex and nature
    114, 116–24
  Bataillean view xii
new materialism ix, 8–9, 138
Nietzsche, Friedrich 13
nonhuman reality ix, 11, 18
nonhuman turn 8, 10–12
Noys, Benjamin 126
Nymphomaniac (Vol I & II) (Lars von
    Trier) 24, 104, 109, 111–16,
    125–9, 179
  blindness 129
  director's cut 124–5
  final shot 127
  importance of nature in 104,
    112, 114–15

Index

narrative structure 115
opening sequence of 127
religious themes 125
sexuality in 116, 121–4
use of CGI 121

objectivity of cinema 24, 35, 69–70,
  75–6, 175–6
ocean acidification 4
O'Gorman, Michel 138, 155, 180
oil prices x
Oka Crisis 160, 172n.77
'openness from closure' 18
Opus (Mariano Donoso) 83
Osterweil, Ara 110
outfox correlationism 10

Paganism 40–2, 47
Pagan violence 40
perception, modes of 1–2, 4–5, 7, 24, 70–8,
  89, 96, 127, 142, 151, 153, 155
pessimistic realism 9
Peterson, Christopher 5, 71, 74
Pettman, Dominic 149
phenomenology 2, 75, 77, 96, 98n.27, 130
Pick, Anat 8, 17–18, 74
A Place Called Chiapas 159
Planet Earth 146
Plato 1, 139
polyphony 123
posthumanism ix, x, xiv, 12, 17, 23, 138
poststructuralism x, 71, 138–9
pro-pipeline protests x
psychoanalysis 8, 12, 89, 98n.27, 130

Rappmund, Peter Bo 78.
  see also Tectonics
reason 1–3, 5, 11–13, 16–17, 20, 22–3, 35,
  39–40, 48–9, 60, 72, 84, 86, 114–15,
  119, 123–4, 137, 142, 150, 153, 157–8,
  160, 176, 180
Roffe, Jonathan 18, 21
Room of Diana xi–xii
Royko, Von 162

sacrifice 37–40
  as an ethical act 39–40
  in Bataille 39–40
  as 'beyond' of experience 39

link between art and 39–40
as waste 39
Western/Christian conception of 47
Western thought 38
in Wheatley 38, 40
Sartre, Jean-Paul 72
Schantz, Ned 144
Schoonover, Karl 22
Schutten, Julie 145–6
Screening Nature 74–5
self-constitution 17, 107
self-destruction 35, 116
self-enclosure 17, 56
Serras da desordem (Andrea Tonacci) 83
sexual desire 35, 108
sexual imagery 15
sexuality 5, 12–13, 116–19, 121–4
sexualized paganism 42
sexual obscenity 125
sexual reproduction 116–17
Shaviro, Steven ix, 2–3, 10, 71, 73, 162–4
  *The Universe of Things: On Speculative
  Realism* 3, 104
Smiley, Michael 43
social constructivism 10
speculative realism ix, 2–3, 8–11, 22–3,
  69–77, 95, 138, 140
  application to film studies 71–7
  desire for objects in 138–9
  objectivity in relation to 24
  problems with 74
speculative realist aesthetic 71
The Speculative Turn 73
Srnicek, Nick 10, 73
Stoekl, Allan 12
Story of the Eye 15, 108
subjectivity 17–18, 22, 24, 69–70, 72, 74,
  76–8, 141, 175–6, 179
  cinematic apparatus and 86–95
  excessive logic of 103–9
Syndromes and a Century 15

Tahltan language 159, 165
Tahltan Nation 159–61
Tarr, Béla 36
Taylor, Kate 159
Tectonics 24, 70, 78–81, 84, 86, 91, 95, 178
  ecological awareness 89
  perspective, movement and time 90–1

Teh, David 53, 63
Thai Buddhism 60, 177
Thai culture 60
things-for-us 10
things-in-themselves 10
Thunberg, Greta x
Trahair, Lisa 154
transgression 12–21, 23, 36, 63, 96, 105, 115, 129–30, 137, 150, 179
2001: A Space Odyssey 109

uncanniness 46
Uncle Boonmee Who Can Recall His Past Lives (Palme d'Or) 24, 36
Under the Skin (Jonathan Glazer) 15, 24, 104, 109–12, 179
   contradiction between recognition and estrangement 120
   division between inside and outside 120
   ending of 128
   evocation of death 130
   interiority in 110–11
   sexual act in 118–19
   sexuality in 116–19, 121

Watkin, Christopher 37
waves 78–9
Weerasethakul, Apichatpong 24, 35–6, 52–5, 58, 176–7
   animist aesthetics 60–1
   Blissfully Yours 54–5
   conception of sacred 59
   desublimating of sacred 59–64
   erotic encounters 55–8
   erotic encounters between humans and animals in 59–62
   erotic sensuality related to jungle 54

materiality of natural world 60–1
narrative ambiguities of films 53–4
nature/culture division 54
relations between self and other in 54
religious themes of 54
rural and urban spaces 62
sex 54
Syndromes and a Century 36, 54, 62–4
transmigration of souls 55
Tropical Malady 36, 54–9
two-act structures of films 54
Uncle Boonmee 36, 54, 60–2
use of Buddhist themes and imagery 54
Weil, Simone 17
Western Enlightenment humanism 17
Western philosophy ix, 1–2
Wheatley, Ben 35–6, 54, 176–7
   British cinema and culture 40–1
   eeriness in films 41
   evocation of sacred 36
   A Field in England 36–7, 41–2, 48–53
   Kill List 36–7, 41–8
   nihilism 53, 63
   sacrifice-of-sacrifice 40
   Sightseers 37
   themes of death and sacrifice 37–8, 40
Whitehead, Alfred North 105, 162
Wicker Man (Robin Hardy) 37, 41–3, 48
Wilson, Scott 13
Witchfinder General (Michael Reeves) 37, 42, 48, 50
Wolfe, Cary ix, 17–18, 107, 126
   What Is Posthumanism? 176
Woodward, Edward 42

Zapatista Indigenous uprising 159
Žižek, Slavoj 12

Printed in the USA
CPSIA information can be obtained
at www.ICGtesting.com
LVHW022006260424
778553LV00001B/131